State of India's Livelihoods Report 2011

Livelihoods India Advisory Group

Anshu Bhartia
Maneesha Chadha
Arindom Datta
Sankar Datta
Prema Gera
Ajit Kanitkar
Brij Mohan
Vipin Sharma
Madhukar Shukla
Vanita Suneja
Ajay Tankha

Editors

Sankar Datta
Orlanda Ruthven
Vipin Sharma

SOIL Coordinating Team

Aarti Dayal
Puja Gour

State of India's Livelihoods Report 2011

Edited by

Sankar Datta

Orlanda Ruthven

Vipin Sharma

⑤SAGE www.sagepublications.com
Los Angeles • London • New Delhi • Singapore • Washington DC

Jointly published in 2012 by

SAGE Publications India Pvt Ltd
B1/I-1 Mohan Cooperative Industrial Area
Mathura Road, New Delhi 110 044, India
www.sagepub.in

SAGE Publications Inc
2455 Teller Road
Thousand Oaks, California 91320, USA

SAGE Publications Ltd
1 Oliver's Yard, 55 City Road
London EC1Y 1SP, United Kingdom

SAGE Publications Asia-Pacific Pte Ltd
33 Pekin Street
#02-01 Far East Square
Singapore 048763

ACCESS Development Services
28, Hauz Khas Village
New Delhi 110 016
www.accessdev.org

Published by Vivek Mehra for SAGE Publications India Pvt Ltd, typeset in 10/13 pt Minion by Star Compugraphics Private Limited, Delhi and printed at Rajkamal Electric Press, Kundli, Haryana.

Library of Congress Cataloging-in-Publication Data Available

ISBN: 978-81-321-0708-8 (PB)

The SAGE Team: Rudra Narayan, Swati Sengupta, Rajib Chatterjee and Umesh Kashyap

Cover photograph: Anna Garriott

Contents

Thank you for choosing a SAGE product! If you have any comment, observation or feedback, I would like to personally hear from you. Please write to me at <u>contactceo@sagepub.in</u>

—Vivek Mehra, Managing Director and CEO,
SAGE Publications India Pvt Ltd, New Delhi

Bulk Sales

SAGE India offers special discounts for purchase of books in bulk. We also make available special imprints and excerpts from our books on demand.

For orders and enquiries, write to us at

Marketing Department
SAGE Publications India Pvt Ltd
B1/I-1, Mohan Cooperative Industrial Area
Mathura Road, Post Bag 7
New Delhi 110044, India
E-mail us at <u>marketing@sagepub.in</u>

Get to know more about SAGE, be invited to SAGE events, get on our mailing list. Write today to <u>marketing@sagepub.in</u>

This book is also available as an e-book.

List of Tables

List of Figures

List of Boxes

List of Abbreviations

3PL	third-party logistics provider
ADB	Asian Development Bank
AEPS	Aadhaar-enabled payment system
AICTE	All India Council for Technical Education
ANM	auxiliary nurse midwife
APL	above poverty line
APMC	Agricultural Produce Marketing Committee
ARC	Administrative Reforms Commission
ARWSP	Accelerated Rural Water Supply Programme
ASHA	Accredited Social Health Activist
ASI	Annual Survey of Industries
BC	Business Correspondent
BIRD	Bankers Institute of Rural Development
BMI	Body Mass Index
BoP	Bottom of the Pyramid
BPL	below poverty line
BRGF	Backward Regions Grant Fund
CACP	Commission on Agricultural Costs and Prices
CAG	Comptroller and Auditor General
CAGR	compounded annual growth rate
CCT	conditional cash transfers
CED	Centre for Entrepreneurship Development
CED	chronic energy deficiency
CEFS	Centre for Environment and Food Security
CHIAK	Comprehensive Health Insurance Agency of Kerala
CHIS	Comprehensive Health Insurance Scheme
CII	Confederation of Indian Industry
COP	Conference of Parties
CPI	Consumer Price Index
CPI-AL	CPI Agricultural Labourer
CPI-IW	CPI Industrial Worker
CPI-RL	CPI Rural Labourer
CRPs	Community Resource Persons
CSO	Central Statistical Organisation
CSP	Centrally Sponsored Plan
CSR	Corporate Social Responsibility
CSS	centrally sponsored scheme
DPC	district planning committee
DWCRA	Development of Women and Children in Rural Areas
EAG	Empowered Action Group
EAS	Employment Assurance Scheme
EGMM	Employment Generation and Marketing Mission

EIA	Environment Impact Assessment
FAO	Food and Agriculture Organization
FCI	Food Corporation of India
FDI	Foreign Direct Investment
FICCI	Federation of Indian Chambers of Commerce and Industry
FISME	Federation of Indian Micro and Small and Medium Enterprises
FPS	Fair Price Shop
FRA	Forest Rights Act 2006
FTAs	foreign tourist arrivals
FY	Financial Year
GDP	Gross Domestic Product
GHI	Global Hunger Index
GLPC	Gujarat Livelihood Promotion Company
GNIDA	Greater Noida Industrial Development Authority
HH	household
HI	Hunger Index
HR	Human Resources
HRD	Human Resource Development
IAY	Indira Awaas Yojana
ICDS	Integrated Child Development Services
ICRs	Implementation Completion Reports
IFPRI	International Food Policy Research Institute
IGNOAPS	Indira Gandhi National Old Age Pension Scheme
IHDS	India Human Development Survey
ILO	International Labour Organization
IMaCS	ICRA Management Consulting Services
IPCC	Intergovernmental Panel on Climatic Change
IRDP	Integrated Rural Development Programme
IT	information technology
ITC	Industrial Training Centre
ITES	IT-enabled services
ITI	Industrial Training Institute
JFM	joint forest management
JMP	Joint Monitoring Programme
JRY	Jawahar Rozgar Yojana
KYC	know your customer
KYR	know your resident
LFPR	labour force participation rate
LWE	Left-Wing Extremism
MBCY	Mukhyamantri Balika Cycle Yojana
MDG	Millennium Development Goal
MDM	Mid Day Meal
MES	Modular Employable Skills
MEtS	Ma Foi Randstad Employment Trends Survey
MGNREGA	Mahatma Gandhi National Rural Employment Guarantee Act
MGNREGS	Mahatma Gandhi National Rural Employment Guarantee Scheme
MICE	meetings, incentives, conferencing and exhibitions
MIS	Management Information System
MKSP	Mahila Kisan Shashaktikaran Pariyojana

MKSS	Mazdoor Kisan Shakti Sanghatan
MoEF	Ministry of Environment and Forests
MoRD	Ministry of Rural Development
MPCE	monthly per capita expenditure
MSMEs	Micro, Small and Medium Enterprises
MSP	minimum support price
MSSRF	M.S. Swaminathan Research Foundation
MTA	mid-term appraisal
NABARD	National Bank for Agriculture and Rural Development
NAC	National Advisory Council
NASSCOM	National Association of Software and Services Companies
NCEUS	National Commission for Enterprises in the Unorganized Sector
NCR	National Capital Region
NCVT	National Council of Vocational Training
NER	North Eastern Regions
NFHS	National Family Health Survey
NGO	non-governmental organization
NPCI	National Payment Corporation of India
NPSO	National Policy on Skill Development
NREGA	National Rural Employment Guarantee Act
NREGP	National Rural Employment Guarantee Programme
NREGS	National Rural Employment Guarantee Scheme
NREP	National Rural Employment Programme
NRHM	National Rural Health Mission
NRLM	National Rural Livelihoods Mission
NSAP	National Social Assistance Programme
NSDC	National Skill Development Corporation
NSDF	National Skill Development Fund
NSIC	National Small Industries Corporation
NSS	National Sample Survey
NSSO	National Sample Survey Organization
OBC	Other Backward Classes
OECD	Organization for Economic Cooperation and Development
OEMs	original equipment manufacturers
OOP	out-of-pocket
OTFDs	other traditional forest dwellers
P&RD	Panchayat and Rural Development
PCMCE	per capita monthly consumption expenditure
PCNSDP	per capita net state domestic product
PDS	Public Distribution System
PESA	Panchayats Extension to Scheduled Areas
PIA	Project Implementation Agency
PMGSY	Pradhan Mantri Gram Sadak Yojana
PMLA	Prevention of Money Laundering Act
POPRC	Persistent Organic Pollutants Review Committee
PPP	public private partnership
PRDE	participation, representation, dignity and empowerment
PRI	Panchayati Raj Institution
PVTGs	Particularly Vulnerable Tribal Groups

RADP	Rainfed Areas Development Programme
RDA	recommended dietary allowance
RIDF	Rural Infrastructure Development Fund
RKVY	Rashtriya Krishi Vikas Yojana
RLEGP	Rural Landless Employment Guarantee Programmes
RNFE	rural non-farm enterprises
RSBY	Rashtriya Swasthya Bima Yojana
RSETI	Rural Self-Employment Training Institute
RTE	Right to Education
SC	Scheduled Castes
SERP	Society for Elimination of Rural Poverty
SEZ	Special Economic Zone
SGRY	Sampoorna Grameen Rozgar Yojana
SGSY	Swaranjayanti Gram Swarozgar Yojana
SHG	self-help group
SIA	Social Impact Assessment
SIDBI	Small Industries Development Bank of India
SN	Supplementary Nutrition
SOIL	State of India's Livelihoods
SPIP	State Perspective and Implementation Plan
SS	subsidiary status
SSA	Sarva Shiksha Abhiyan
ST	Scheduled Tribes
TF	Task Force
TLU	TeamLease University
TPDS	Targeted Public Distribution System
TRYSEM	Training of Rural Youth for Self-Employment
UBSP	Urban Basic Services for Poor
UID	unique identification
UIDAI	Unique Identification Authority of India
UNME	Urban Non-Manual Employee
UNSNA	United Nations System of National Accounts
UPS	usual principal status
VE	vocational education
VTP	Vocational Training Provider
WFPR	work force participation rate
WIEGO	Women in Informal Employment: Globalizing and Organizing
WPI	Wholesale Price Index
WPR	Work participation rate
WTO	World Trade Organization

Preface

ACCESS has been bringing out the *State of India's Livelihoods (SOIL) Report* since 2008. The endeavour, right from the beginning, was to bring together a document which helps in stocktaking of all the efforts and initiatives, policies and programmes, current trends and emerging potential for greater sustainable livelihoods options for the poor. Given the complexity of a large number of factors that impact and influence the livelihoods of the poor, it has not been an easy task and the SOIL format has been tweaked from year to year towards generating greater relevance and higher value from the Report for the sector. In its fourth year, the SOIL Report is seemingly settling down in terms of its content and orientation. Over the last four years, the Report has become established as a good reference document that is found useful both by policy-makers as well as practitioners.

While the first two volumes traced broad trends, factors and conditions that influenced the livelihoods of the poor, cutting across sectors, in the third volume, we attempted to focus on a sub-sector, specifically on agriculture-based livelihoods. In an effort to gauge the success of the first three volumes of SOIL in tracking the impact on livelihoods of the poor, this year ACCESS commissioned two independent reviews of the first three volumes of SOIL for an in-depth critical analysis of the reports. The reviews looked at quality, content, structure and value and relevance of the report to the sector, on one hand, and made suggestions for its improvement, on the other. The analysis from the two reviews was kept in mind while planning for an improved fourth volume of the report. Accordingly, the orientation of the Report has been restored to align to an Annual Report format with an effort to make it broad and more comprehensive.

Further, in a significant departure from the earlier process where single authors wrote different chapters, for 2011, a group of pre-eminent authors were brought together as a core group for the SOIL from the inception stage. It definitely proved advantageous to the writing process to have the expertise and viewpoints of multiple authors to give a comprehensive look at a topic as diverse and complex as livelihoods of the poor. Each member brought specific knowledge of a subject matter to the table and the group benefitted from the frequent brainstorming with their fellow collaborators.

The 2011 SOIL Report revisits the original 4P framework focusing on the Poor, the Policy environment, Potential and Promoters. The chapters are also interrelated, each taking off from where the last one left, making for a more comprehensive and complete reading on the status of livelihoods of the poor. *State of India's Livelihoods Report 2011* is divided into six chapters, authored by some well-known names in the sector like Sankar Datta, Orlanda Ruthven, Professor Ashok Sircar, Suryamani Roul and Professor Madhukar Shukla.

In this year's report, Chapter 1 presents an 'Overview' of the status of livelihoods during 2010–11 while looking at the key debates and conflicts such as different definitions of poor, impact of rising wages on inflation and the conflicting demand on land. It also presents an overview of the policy environment for livelihoods promotion. In Chapter 2, 'Livelihoods of the Poor', the authors examine the impact of changes in the economy and the macroeconomic policies on employment, food security and health of various sections of the poor, focusing on migrants, and other vulnerable occupational groups such as domestic workers, pastoral communities, scavengers and forest-dependent communities. It also brings the employment of women as well as the youth into picture. The pervious year has also witnessed some new policy initiatives to support the livelihoods of the poor. Chapter 3, 'Reflections on Livelihoods Policies', takes stock of the ongoing and emerging policy initiatives of Government of India that are in various stages of formulation and adoption. In India, state is the largest livelihood promoter and Chapter 4, 'State as the Largest Livelihoods Promoter', analyses two major flagship livelihoods programmes—MGNREGS and NRLM—of the government at different stages of evolution, apart from reviewing the various skill development initiatives in India. Chapter 5, 'Private Industry and Services—What Is "India Inc" Delivering in Employment to the Poor?' tries to capture the role of corporates in creating and promoting livelihoods. While the private sector influences livelihoods in many ways, being a foremost purchaser and processor of primary sector goods from India's farmers, and helps to generate livelihoods in trade and logistics when its goods and services are channeled to the 'bottom of the pyramid', this chapter addresses the topic of jobs for India's poor in private sector industry, services and their supply chains. Chapter 6, 'Potential and Possibilities', suggests a qualitative shift in the manner in which services and subsidies will be provided to the poor. It discusses the key livelihood initiatives which are likely to be included in the 12th Five Year Plan and provides an overall direction of resource deployment and policy framework while also discussing the newly introduced Unique ID (Aadhar) Project and the proposed Direct Cash Transfer scheme and their implications for the poor as well as livelihood professionals.

I am deeply appreciative of the authors whose involvement with the report went beyond writing their own chapters. Each of the authors took time off from their extremely busy schedules to attend the various consultations and write-shop as well as critically review and provide inputs on chapters of all other authors to bring the Report to its final shape. Special thanks are due to Orlanda, who volunteered to carry out the structural and content editing of the report and helped improve it immensely. Thanks are also due to Lucid Solutions and its Director, Shreemoyee Patro, for carrying out the language edit of the Report and providing valuable editorial comments during the authors' write-shop.

The direction and guidance of the Advisory Group comprising of Ajay Tankha, Ajit Kanitkar, Anshu Bhartia, Arindom Datta, Brij Mohan, Madhukar Shukla, Maneesha Chadha, Prema Gera, Sankar Datta and Vanita Suneja has been instrumental in shaping the *SOIL 2011 Report*. I am indeed grateful for the continued support to the Report by Ford Foundation, Citi Foundation and UNDP India. I really appreciate their deep engagement with the process of report writing and high ambition for its value to the sector. I would also like to thank Oxfam India for coming on board for the first time and supporting the *SOIL 2011 Report*.

I am thankful to the Livelihood School for partnering with us on the effort. I would especially like to thank Sankar, Dean, The Livelihood School for his spirited support and valuable inputs and his constant guidance to keep the Report on track.

Lastly, I would like to acknowledge the super effort put in by my Livelihoods India team, at ACCESS, in providing all the support to the process of bringing out the *SOIL 2011 Report* in time. The team has done a tremendous job under the overall supervision of Suryamani Roul. My special thanks go to Puja, who tirelessly coordinated with all the authors and the publishers and ran a very effective process. She was ably supported by Aarti. I would also like to thank my Programme Support team for handling the logistics and making the necessary arrangements.

ACCESS is extremely happy that its efforts have contributed towards bringing out this knowledge product. It is the support and feedback from the sector that has encouraged us to bring out yet another volume of SOIL. I sincerely hope that it will be a useful resource book for the entire gamut of stakeholders involved in livelihoods promotion of the poor and contribute in improving better understanding and appreciation of the issues and challenges that need to be addressed to make a significant impact on the livelihoods of the poor.

Vipin Sharma
CEO
ACCESS Development Services

Acknowledgements

A lot of work, energy and enthusiasm were expended by various individuals in making this report a reality. Publishing an edited book by several contributors is a team effort of many committed individuals; this book is no exception to that general belief and understanding. Our first 'thank you', therefore, goes to the contributors: Sankar Datta, Orlanda Ruthven, Radhika Desai, Ashok Sircar, Suryamani Roul and Madhukar Shukla for committing themselves to the effort wholeheartedly and taking out time from their extremely busy schedules to deliver on time. Much appreciation is extended to Orlanda for the content editing of a rather diverse report. Special thanks goes out to Lucid Solutions and its Director, Shreemoyee Patro, for her editorial guidance and language edit of the report. The *SOIL 2011 Report* has benefited immeasurably from the unwavering direction provided by Sankar Datta, Dean, The Livelihood School. Finally, the process of collating an edited book, with many contributions coming in from many authors was made possible because of the background support provided by the Livelihoods India Team at ACCESS.

State of India's Livelihoods 2011: A Time of Volatility*

Chapter 1

A major proportion of India's population faced a number of ups and downs in terms of livelihoods in 2010–11. After a major downturn, the economy started recovering in the first half of the year, but has started to slow down again. The job market which was picking up is starting to stagnate. Inflation, especially food inflation, has touched double digits, though it had been controlled in the beginning of the year.

International economic and political factors have also played a role in India's economic downturn. The Indian economy was less affected by the economic slowdown in 2008, and interestingly enough, some segments of India's economy even benefited to an extent.[1] Political stability and good monsoons also helped slightly in reducing the impact of the slowdown. Due to changes in crude oil prices on the one hand and deregulation of oil prices on the other, the oil prices increased by nearly 23 per cent between June 2010 and June 2011. This coupled with correction in food prices the world over, pushed inflation rates to new heights. This not only affected the consumption level, but also called for stringent monetary policy intervention which has significant implications on the overall economic growth, and thereby affects livelihood opportunities.

In spite of food price inflation, the net return to farmers from agriculture has continued to come down. While there has been a perceptible increase in the wage rates, especially for farm labour, its real impact is yet to be revealed. On the one hand we have witnessed an increase in pro-poor policies aiming to improve the inclusiveness of growth to the *aam aadmi* level. On the other hand, we have also witnessed an increase in conflicts and sociopolitical unrests, and several charges of corruption, which reflect a serious failure in governance. The space for civil society action has decreased, while private sector engagement in delivery of public goods and services has increased significantly. Though this increased role of the private sector has generated some positive impacts, it has also created conflicting demands on various limited resources, especially land for agriculture, industry and environmental sustainability. It is being argued that the gap between the haves and have-nots has widened in the last decade.

Though both Gross Domestic Product (GDP) and employment have grown in the last decade, this has not been reflected in terms of employment generation. The recent National Sample Survey Organization (NSSO) 66th Round data shows that while the workforce increased by 60 million between 1999–2000 and 2004–05, it increased by only 2 million between 2004–05 and 2009–10 (Anant and Mehta 2011). Though the decline in paid work was visible in both rural and urban India, it was more severe in rural labour markets. The survey also showed that in recent years the real

---

* This chapter was written with research support from Resmi Bhaskaran.

[1] For example, the relatively small production capacity of Indian garment sector units gained competitive advantage against bulk Chinese manufactures.

income of the people has gone up. But the rise in the inflation rate, especially the food inflation rate invalidates the positive effects of wage increase. In this context, where India has been applauded for a consistent growth of over 8 per cent in GDP since economic reforms were undertaken in 1991, the status of livelihoods of the people, especially the poor, has not kept pace. Not only is relative poverty increasing, but the opportunities for the poor to better themselves in the labour market appear to have been decreasing since the mid-2000s.

The overview of the State of India's Livelihoods (SOIL) Report 2011 is divided into four parts: the first presents the status of livelihoods during 2010–11, the second zooms in on some key debates and conflicts, the third takes a brief look at the policy framework and the fourth lays out the structure of the rest of this report. This report places before its readers the different trends, and various challenges, some resolved, and some still under debate.

PART I: LIVELIHOOD SCENARIO: PERIOD OF VOLATILITY

1.1. Economy on the recovery path?

The 11th Five Year Plan period (2007–12) will come to an end next year. It had estimated a growth rate of 9 per cent. Though it began with a near 10 per cent growth rate, with the economic meltdown across the globe, the growth rate declined to 7.3 per cent in 2008–09. The last two years reflected recovery and the economy again aimed for a growth rate of 9 per cent. But, the economists are worried that in the present scenario the growth rate may hardly cross 8 per cent (see Box 1.1).

The impressive growth in the export segment during 2010–11, at 37.5 per cent, showed that the economy is recovering. In fact many labour intensive sectors such as gems and jewellery (growth rate y-o-y 15.3 per cent), ready-made garments (4.3 per cent), cotton yarn fabrics (42.9 per cent) and carpet, jute and leather industries reported considerable growth. It is also important to note that for the first time, India's exports crossed US$ 200 billion which was the set target for 2009–10. But whether it will be able to meet the target of US$ 450 billion which has been set for 2011–12 is doubtful. In fact, one positive impact of the economic crisis in 2008 was that many Indian manufactures explored new markets through which Latin American and African countries became significant contributors to the export basket.

Imports on the other hand grew at a slower pace of 21.5 per cent despite the increasing pressure on crude oil prices. Imports for 2010–11 aggregated to US$ 350.3 billion, leaving a trade deficit of

---

Box 1.1: *India a country of 1.2 billion—population profile Census 2011 (provisional figures)*

According to the provisional tables of Census 2011, India's population is 1,210.19 million. The decadal population growth has declined to 17.64 per cent from 21.54 per cent in 2001. In absolute terms, 2001–11 is the first decade since 1911–21 to add a smaller number to the population than the preceding decade.

This decade also witnessed significant improvement in literacy which has increased from 64.83 per cent in 2001 to 74.04 per cent. Growth in female literacy, from 53.67 per cent in 2001 to 65.46 per cent, led to this jump.

Male literacy moved from 75.26 per cent in 2001 to 82.14 per cent in 2011.

The sex ratio is still a cause for worry. In fact the overall sex ratio reported improvement from 932.91 in 2001 to 940.27 in 2011, thanks to the better natural longevity of women and improvements in health care over the years. But, the sex ratio of children in the age group of 0–6 is alarming as it has declined from 927.31 in 2001 to 914.23 in 2011, and is the worst since Independence.

Source: Government of India (2011b).

Table 1.1: Growth rate of Gross National Product (at factor cost) between 2006–07 and 2010–11

Year	GNP (at factor cost)
2006–07	9.8
2007–08	9.3
2008–09	7.3
2009–10	8.6
2010–11	8.3

Source: Government of India (2011a).

US$ 104.4 billion. The country's merchandise trade has almost touched US$ 600 billion—half of India's GDP of US$ 1.2 trillion.

Though attention towards agriculture and a good monsoon have helped improve agricultural performance marginally, it still has miles to go. But there is also concern over industrial growth and increasing inflation, which, as the Honourable Finance Minister told the country, 'might lead to significant impact on growth' (*Business Today* 2011). The small and micro-enterprises which are already experiencing inadequacy of credit from the formal financial institutions are further vulnerable to the credit rationing policies of the government.

1.2. Farm sector

In spite of a reduction in the number of people dependent on agriculture, more than 42 per cent of the people's livelihoods revolve around agriculture even today (Reserve Bank of India 2010).

A mid-term appraisal of the 11th Five Year Plan noted that during the 1994–2006 period, the increase in per worker GDP[2] in the agriculture sector was only 2.24 per cent per annum, as compared to 4.35 per cent per annum growth in aggregate GDP per worker. Interestingly, the agricultural productivity (per acre) in many places has declined since the Green Revolution. Continuing high labour dependency on agriculture invalidates any improvement in

the per worker productivity. In other words, if some labour from the agriculture sector was shifted to other sectors with higher per worker productivity, the total productivity of labour may go up. It indicates the prevalence of disguised unemployment in agriculture. The service sector and industry are skill intensive rather than labour intensive. These structural imbalances increase inequality, and also worsen the growth elasticity of poverty reduction. In other words, the high growth rate has not had the desired effect on poverty reduction.

1.2.1. Agricultural crisis

Growth in the agriculture sector is critical for the overall growth of the Indian economy. Agriculture has grown at an annual average rate of 4 per cent, when the economy was growing at 9 per cent per annum during the 11th Five Year Plan period. The share of agriculture in GDP declined from 30.3 per cent in 1991–92 to 14.2 per cent in 2010–11.

Growth of this sector is critical in two ways as it affects the food security of the country that has to feed 1.2 billion people, and provides employment to nearly 50 per cent of the workforce. Food production in India has increased consistently, and it ranks high in the production of wheat, rice, milk, vegetables and fruits.

The Indian agriculture sector poses a serious dilemma for the nation: whether to ensure availability of food to 1.2 billion mouths or to ensure adequate returns to the 500 million pairs of hands that produce them. Due to inflationary pressure and increased possibilities of labour mobility as a result of the government's intervention through the National Rural Employment Guarantee Programme (NREGP), the agricultural wage rates have started increasing. On the one hand, the withdrawal of subsidies, increasing wage rates and inflation was increasing the cost of cultivation for the farmers (Aiyer and Swaminathan 2011), and on the other hand, every effort was being made to contain the increase in food price

---

[2] GDP per worker can be related to per worker productivity with regard to GDP.

in an attempt to make food available, to a large population, at an affordable price. This in turn was squeezing the margins available to the farmers (see Box 1.2).[3]

Agricultural productivity in India has been stagnant since after the Green Revolution. This near-stagnant productivity also restricted gross returns from farming, making agriculture an unattractive livelihood opportunity. This problem was further aggravated by a decline in public investments in agriculture, for technology and infrastructure development, as well as degradation of land and water resources.

Had the rural non-farm enterprises (RNFE) kept pace with the increase in workforce, it could have reduced dependency on farming, and could have added off season and additional income to the farming households. But due to the slow, almost stagnant, growth of this sector, people could not move away from low-margin agriculture unless they moved from the rural hinterland to urban centres to earn their livelihood.

To encourage private investments in RNFE, it is essential to boost public investment in education—especially in skill development—roads, health care, information technology (IT) and electricity.

1.2.2. Reflection on climatic change

The climatic change has had enormous implications for livelihoods in India. Various studies indicated that our agriculture, biodiversity, coastal zones, water, natural ecosystems and health are impacted by the change in climate. A recent report of the Intergovernmental Panel on Climatic Change (IPCC) warns of climate change impacts, such as, a rise in sea levels, increase in cyclonic intensity, reduced crop yield in rain-fed crops, stress on livestock, reduction in milk productivity, increased flooding and spread of malaria (Government of India 2011a). Our field observations also show that farmers have started preferring shorter duration varieties of food crops to manage the risks of uncertainty of rainfall. The

---

Box 1.2: *Agricultural wages—finally some reflection of inclusive growth*

Data of Labour Bureau of India, Shimla shows that there is an impressive hike in the actual agricultural wages in India between January 2008 and December 2010. For the first time during the neoliberal period, the growth in GDP is reflected in the actual agricultural wage, indicating inclusiveness.

Andhra Pradesh reported 106.5 per cent growth in actual agricultural wage. It was 84.4 per cent in Punjab, 74.4 per cent in Haryana and among the poor states it was 62.8 per cent in Orissa, 58.3 per cent in Bihar, 56.3 per cent in Madhya Pradesh and so on.

Kerala has still the highest agricultural wage in the country at ₹ 319.13 per day. Lowest per day wage at ₹ 84.43 was in Madhya Pradesh.

Rise in agricultural growth has been reported in all states (except Gujarat), regardless of their growth in state GDPs. Gujarat which reported 9 per cent growth

in agricultural production had only 24.1 per cent rise in wages during these 35 months. This is because Gujarat experienced a labour shortage and attracted migrant labour from its neighbouring state Rajasthan at ₹ 145.69 per day. Agricultural wages in other migrant labour supply states like Bihar and Orissa were higher than Gujarat's.

When we look at the reasons for a wage hike, besides growth in GPD, we find that a good monsoon also contributed to the high growth in agricultural wage.

Punjab and Haryana faced a shortage of migrant labour from Orissa and Bihar which was reported as a reason for a hike in the labour wages in these places. Though it is a welcome change from the perspective of agricultural growth, it has a multiplier impact on the entire economy.

Source: Aiyer (2011).

---

[3] See Discussion in Datta and Sharma (2010).

phenomenon of repeat sowing is becoming a frequent requirement, leading to high costs, lower quality seeds and increased labour cost, thereby increasing cost of cultivation in face of the non-increasing farm-gate prices discussed earlier.

Based on Cancun negotiations in December 2010, India has decided to increase energy efficiency, through proactive policies, by 20 per cent by 2016.[4] Similarly, the government has pursued aggressive strategies for forestry and formulated a major programme that aims to address the adaptation challenges that affect 300 million vulnerable people in the coastal regions of India. Economic Survey (2011) showed that India's expenditure towards adaptation-oriented climatic change schemes has increased from 1.45 per cent of GDP in 2000–01 to 2.82 per cent in 2009–10 (Government of India 2011a).

1.3. Growth of the unorganized sector and casual work

A feature of growth since liberalization has been a persistent decline in the growth rate of organized sector employment, while employment growth in the unorganized sector has kept pace with the population growth. While organized sector employment grew at an annual average of 1.2 per cent in the years before 1991, since then it has grown only 0.3 per cent annually. The National Commission for Enterprises in the Unorganized Sector (NCEUS), 2008[5] tells us that 93 per cent of workers in India are unorganized, and as per NSSO 66th Round (2009–10), the proportion of casual workers in the workforce at 33 per cent, in both, the organized and the unorganized sector, is higher than ever.

As the growth of employment in the organized sector has not been able to keep pace with the growth in population, the number of people engaged in unorganized firms and in casual work has been going up. Due to this excess supply of labour in the informal sector, the real wage rate of workers in this sector has neither gone up and nor has it kept pace with the inflation. It has been difficult to estimate the real wage of the workers in the unorganized (or informal) sector, which is known for keeping few records, not reporting these regularly to the authorities, and frequently paying piece rate wages.

The shift towards unorganized and casual work happens in a variety of ways which need to be distinguished: workers shift from organized to unorganized firms as formal sector manufacturing contracts are outsourced; workers shift from organized (regular, permanent) to unorganized (casual) status in 'organized' firms as the firms reduce their labour costs (this is often accompanied by payroll being outsourced by the employer to a contractor); finally, workers shift from an outside workplace to their home, often leading to an increase in the number of women and children involved.

A majority of the workforce lacks skills to be absorbed by the service and industrial sectors. As a result, their income level did not improve even with the increase in per capita income of the country over that period. The conditions of the informal and unorganized sector illustrated by NCEUS shows that they are the most vulnerable lot in the economy. According to NCEUS, around 77 per cent of the informal sector workers earn ₹24 which is far below US$ 1.25 per day. So the poor quality and low intensity of much of casual employment creates challenges to its value.

---

[4] This will be achieved by reducing emissions intensity of the GDP by 20–25 per cent of the 2005 level by 2020.

[5] NCEUS (2008). Using the terms as they are used by NCEUS, all enterprises which have 10 workers or less and are not incorporated but are instead functioning as proprietorships or partnerships are 'unorganized'. All workers working in such enterprises (except those receiving full permanent entitlements), as well as those working in the organized sector but without full employment and social security benefits, are termed 'unorganized' or 'informal' workers (the two terms are used interchangeably).

Figure 1.1:   Pattern of GNP and employment[6] growth rate (2003–04 to 2009–10)

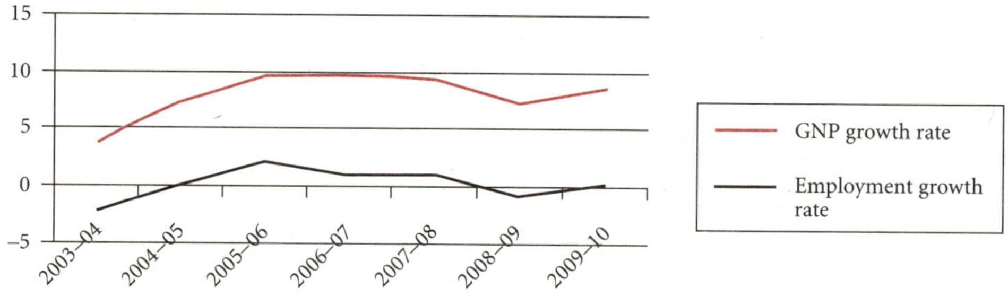

Sources: NSSO (2009) and Reserve Bank of India (2010).

1.4. Urbanization—Inevitable shift in spatial development

Urbanization is closely associated with globalization, mass production and consumption. As Gandhiji argued, producing for the market necessarily leads one to search for consumers, which in turn, leads to consumption beyond need. New markets need to be constantly explored and resources from the rural areas are drawn to urban centres. Production is increasingly global and city-centric.

As a result more and more people move to urban centres for livelihood, and so, the pressure on urban infrastructures and habitats has increased tremendously in the last one decade. Experts estimated that by 2030 nearly 50 per cent Indians will be in urban areas. Also, the share of the urban sector in the GDP, which was 62 per cent in 2010, is expected to increase to 70–75 per cent by 2030. This increased focus on the urban centres demanded increased policy attention. Rapid urbanization led to a rise in slum population, shelterlessness, and street population, and expansion of informal sector in the suburban areas.

Spatial growth of cities has also posed another set of development complexities, such as, expansion to the nearby rural and agricultural areas for habitat and livelihood. For example, the National Capital Region (NCR) has expanded into 24 districts in four states—Delhi, Uttar Pradesh, Haryana and Rajasthan. Though this has reduced the cultivable land area in this region, it

has also opened up a new set of livelihood opportunities for the rural population in and around the NCR. The number of people, who move circularly from rural to urban centres on a daily basis for employment, has also increased in the last few years.

1.5. People on the move: Migration

Migration is increasingly a key livelihood strategy for households across the country. Seasonal rural–urban migration has been an integral part of the rural life in northern India for a long time. Improvements in transportation facilities provided quick travel options and development in telecommunication infrastructure provided information about the employment opportunities at the destination, thereby causing a steep rise in the spread of people's movement in the last few years. It is estimated that nearly 30 per cent of Indians are moving internally[7] (Census 2001 cited in Bhaskaran 2011).

---

[6] It refers to the employment generated in the formal sector (both public and private). We have given this to indicate that the growth rate of employment in formal sector is far below the GDP growth rate and if it is argued that employment is generated in informal sector, it is largely a wage labour without any social security or without ensuring any decent employment conditions. So the issue of quality of employment generated also becomes a point to be discussed.

[7] They are moving largely for employment and better wage. Marriage-led migration is also a critical component in case of females in India.

Recent studies show that men migrate mostly for employment, and for women marriage leading to migration is a major factor. Similarly, men migrate across states while women largely move within the boundaries of a state (Census 2001 cited in Bhaskaran 2011).

Dominance of rural–rural migration is slowly paving way for rural–urban migration, indicating an element of 'step migration' in India. 'Step migration' is a process where people first move to some rural or semi-urban areas and gain some skills. From there they move to the urban or industrial centres for better income. As a result of their exposure to urban service sector and industrial sector, the awareness of the need for education and skill enhancement is very high. In the initial days of migration, due to the absence of skills, their earning capacity is low. Another important feature of migration is that the role of a labour contractor is replaced with social network. So some experts argued that the negotiation power of the labour is slightly better as he/she is informed about the nature of the work and scope of opportunities at the destination.

While migration offers better income to a large segment in the urban and non-agricultural sectors, it has adversely affected the supply of labour to the rural and agricultural segment. Young population in the rural agricultural sector prefers employment in only non-agriculture sectors and urban areas. From the context of urbanization, this is a challenge. But from the context of labour supply in urban areas, these constant flows of migrants stabilize the wage level to some extent. Though it is an accepted livelihood strategy across the country, there have been hardly any policy interventions to regulate and ensure protection for migrants.[8]

---

[8] Rashtriya Swasthya Bima Yojana (RSBY) to migrant workers, proposal of providing pension support to migrant labours in Kerala by the Left Democratic Front in their election manifesto in 2011 and the notoriously unimplemented Inter-state Migrant Labour Act, are exceptions.

1.6. Marginalized segments: Women and excluded social groups

In the labour markets, the negotiation power is very weak for certain segments. Females and socially excluded communities like dalits and tribals are marginalized in the labour market negotiations. Their low capacity as workers, low quality of labour, and limited negotiation skills affect their scope of mainstreaming. This argument is related to the lower segments of the labour markets. Many studies have cited that in the upper segments, social group-based marginalization is very prevalent even under affirmative policies. Whatever be the reason, marginalization of various social groups is a serious issue for debate. Gender-based discrimination in the labour market also calls for serious attention as it clearly reflects in the wage levels. Moreover, as we mentioned above, expansion of informal sector has also lead to the feminization of work. But their return from production process has been constantly undermined, and hence, underpaid or unpaid. Marginalization of female workers in the labour market is discussed in detail in Chapter 3.

Segmentation of the labour market based on social class, and thereby, marginalizing them in the mainstream production process is also very prevalent in India. Along with the poor labour quality due to poor health and poor educational/skill level, their level in the social hierarchy has also limited their access to services that would enhance their capabilities.

In order to address this marginalization, the government has implemented affirmative policies to enhance their involvement in the labour market by reserving jobs, providing subsidized credit, training, market support facilities and so on. However, the success of many such intervention programmes is very limited due to the lack of will. Social class focused livelihood intervention from non-governmental organizations (NGOs) are also limited.

1.7. Deteriorating health: A new challenge for livelihoods

Health is a key determinant of the quality of labour available for generating livelihoods. With an increased population and pressure on resources, the quality of life has deteriorated, in urban as well as rural areas. Prevailing nutritional standards, increased industrial emissions, use of chemicals, etc., are also damaging the health of the people.

Poor health conditions have a double effect on the livelihoods of people as they not only reduce the number of working days and quality of the labour, but also reduce the income and increase the expenditure on health care. As it can be seen from the government budget, the state allocation of resources for health has been reduced to less than one per cent of the GDP during the 11th Five Year Plan. This is pushing people to procure services from the private health sector which is often more expensive.

In recent years there have been quite a few efforts to develop health-insurance products which can help the poor mitigate this risk. But such efforts have not yet been able to address issues of delivery of health services and erratic medical treatment.

The health of a worker and his family is affected by the working environment and hazardous elements she/he is exposed to. The debate on the ban of endosulfan, a pesticide widely used by farmers in India and banned elsewhere, has received international attention. This shows how vulnerable these poor workers and their families are, due to the use of endosulfan which is otherwise known as a good helper to the farmers in fighting against insects (*The Hindu* 2011) (see Box 1.3).

1.8. Penetration of organized business into new space

The organized private sector is closely engaged with the poor in several ways. First, as a purchaser and processor of outputs from rural producers for their value chains to market; second, when they encompass

---

Box 1.3: *Endosulfan—farmers' friend to fight against insects, but leaves a major mark on the trans-generation killer*

Endosulfan, the dangers of which first came to light in Kerala's cashew plantations in the 1980s, is a pesticide which is widely used by Indian farmers though it is banned elsewhere. Studies conducted in Kerala clearly showed its impact leading to a prevalence of congenital malformations, low IQ, learning disability, early menarche in girls and delayed puberty in boys, apart from the severe ecological hazards.

The public debate around it has now reached the Stockhom Convention. Two states, Kerala and Karnataka, banned its use. Since 2008, it has got international attention. Stockholm Convention held in Geneva and various other international bodies came together to ban endosulfan. At the sixth meeting of Persistent Organic Pollutants Review Committee (POPRC) to the Stockholm Convention, in October 2010, Geneva; India, the largest producer of endosulfan, opposed global ban on the manufacture, use, import and export of endosulfan against the stand of the majority of the member countries. But, the Conference of Parties (COP) of Stockholm Convention held in April 2011, adopted a risk management evaluation and recommended a ban to endosulfan despite the strong opposition from the Indian government.

The Indian government's argument against the ban is that the ill effects have only been reported in one state and are not true. Also, unless it has been replaced with another pesticide, it will affect the farm production. In fact, similar health issues have been reported in Haryana, Uttar Pradesh and Tamil Nadu, but have not yet been studied from the perspective of the use of endosulfan.

The case of endosulfan demonstrates the vulnerability of farmers as most of them are not aware about the usage pattern of most of the pesticides and also its impact on the soil, ecology and their own health to a trans-generational level.

Source: *The Hindu* (2011).

the poor as distributors, traders and consumers of their goods 'at the bottom of the pyramid'; third, as employers of workers in industry and services. However, increasingly, the private sector is perceived to be more efficient in delivery of services, which has traditionally been the domain of the government. Models of service delivery using revenue sharing have been developed and various state governments are inviting private sector players to take over delivery. In Rajasthan, the government shared the school infrastructure with Bharti Foundation to deliver quality education.

As the engagement in delivery of services by private sector entities grows, and these activities generate revenue from their market operations, which cannot be clearly distinguished from the cost of services delivered, even the donor funding available for 'livelihood support' is coming down. Even the tax laws have started reflecting livelihood-support services as not being charitable in nature. This is squeezing the space available for non-profits to perform these service-delivery functions.

Skills development is an emerging key area of partnership between the public and private sector. As is self-evident, development of a capable workforce is of key interest to the business sector, increasingly constrained by manpower shortages. While corporates have tried to tackle skilling on their own, with mixed results, the National Skills Development Corporation (NSDC), itself a public private partnership (PPP), is mandated to support skills-building companies, many of them pioneered by those with corporate backgrounds.

PART II: DEVELOPMENT DILEMMAS: CONFLICTING INTERESTS AND OUTCOMES

1.9. Who is poor?

There have been a variety of agreements and disagreements on both quantitative and qualitative measures of poverty. This debate has become acute in recent years due to the enhanced focus on the social sector interventions by the government. The Planning Commission, the National Advisory Council (NAC), the Economic Advisory Council to the Prime Minister and different government ministries, all have used different definitions to identify the poor. These definitions, apart from spurring academic debates have also created a new politics of who should or should not be included under different schemes (see Box 1.4).

In the recent past one commission and three high-level committees such as the NCEUS (2006), the NC Saxena Committee (2009),[9] the Tendulkar Committee (2010)[10] and the Expert Group (Hashim Committee 2010)[11] were constituted to deliberate on the poor and poverty (see the chapter on Policy for details). Moreover, depending on the context and spatial coverage of the scheme, the definition of poor differs in various central and state government schemes.

Depending on the variables and methodology, the number of poor (poverty level) differs in each study report of poverty. According to a 2005 World Bank estimate, 42 per cent of India falls below the international poverty line of US$ 1.25 a day. However, according to the criterion used by the Planning Commission, 27.5 per cent of the population was living below the poverty line in 2004–05. But, none of them denoted any significant decline in the number of below poverty line (BPL) households in India. More importantly, if we convert the poverty ratio into an absolute number, it might come to about 330 to 600 million

[9] Government of India. 2009. Expert Group Report to Review the Methodology for Conducting BPL Census in Rural Areas, Chaired by N.C. Saxena, set up by Ministry of Rural Development, Government of India.

[10] Government of India. 2009. Report of the Expert Group to Review the Methodology for Estimation of Poverty Chaired by Suresh Tendulkar, Planning Commission.

[11] Government of India. 2010. Expert Group (S.R. Hashim Committee) on the Methodology for Identification of BPL Families in Urban Areas set up by Ministry of Urban Affairs, Government of India.

Box 1.4: *Trickle down theory and concerns of Professor Amartya Sen*

GDP growth has increased from 4.4 per cent in the 8th Plan to around 7 per cent in the 11th Plan—a remarkable growth in a span of 15 years. However, it is not similarly reflected in the Human Development Indicators. India ranks 65th in the global hunger index, child malnutrition rate is 46 per cent, and 66 per cent of the children enrolled in schools reached only the middle school.

As Amartya Sen (*The Hindu*, 14 February 2011) put it, '… the amazing growth that India achieved in GDP during the last few years has not reflected in the same manner in its socio-economic development indicators'. Professor Sen cited that the expected trickle down effect has not taken place. It is really

a worrisome situation. If trickle down is not taking place in the perceived manner then the macroeconomic development policies increase the vulnerability of the poor which demands increased investment in social development programmes. This will further widen the fiscal deficit of the governments, leading to political crisis. The Planning Commission Expert Report (2008) titled, 'Development Challenges of Extremist Affected Areas', cited development deprivation and increased vulnerability of the poor as the key reason for the expansion of extremist political thinking such as Maoism in many parts of the country.

Source: Sen (2011).

---

poor[12] in India. This gap between who gets included or excluded from the list of the poor is not only more than the population of many nations, but also more than all the poor in several African[13] countries put together.

The Tendulkar Committee Report, which is accepted by the Planning Commission, has redefined the poverty level. According to this report, poor are those who earn below ₹15 in rural and ₹20 in urban areas, per day, though this was widely criticized. According to this report nearly 37 per cent of Indians fall below the poverty line. This has been used to define the entitlement of the poor to access support under the proposed Food Security Act. However, whatever be the poverty ratio, the level of nutritious food intake in India has declined to a level lower than that of the 1964 famine period. The percentage of malnourished children in the country is still 46 per cent (Sen 2011).

---

[12] Based on 1.219 billion population.

[13] A study by the Oxford Poverty and Human Development Initiative using a Multi-dimensional Poverty Index (MPI) found that there were 421 million poor living under the MPI in eight north India states of Bihar, Chhattisgarh, Jharkhand, Madhya Pradesh, Orissa, Rajasthan, Uttar Pradesh and West Bengal. This number is higher than the 410 million poor livig in the 26 poorest African nations.

1.10. Wages versus prices

Wages, whether agricultural or industrial, have gone up in India in the last few years. Rural wage doubled from ₹112 in 2004–05 to ₹232 in 2009–10 per day (NSSO 2011). Other rural wages such as the daily wage for casual *labour*, for other than public work, has increased to ₹102 for men and Mahatma Gandhi National Rural Employment Guarantee Act (MGNREGA) offers ₹91 for men and ₹87 for women (see Chapter 3 for more discussion). This wage rise is linked to factors like:

1. The marginal rise in minimum support price (MSP) of cereals and pulses.
2. An assurance of minimum wage for works under MGNREGA.
3. Increased labour migration from agriculture to non-agriculture sectors and urban centres.

A rise in agricultural wage has created a complex situation. It might help to sustain the livelihoods of some labourers, one of the weakest parts of the economic pyramid, but the overall cost of production has shot up as labour cost is high, thereby leading to a rise in food prices, and pushing the farmers out of agriculture. If a large number of farmers leave the agriculture sector, then it poses a challenge to our food security. This is not going to be a pleasant choice.

India, a country of more than 400 million poor people, faces a major challenge of making food available to all, at an affordable price. Any increase in food prices, whether caused by an increase in wages, or other causes such as increasing petroleum prices or global correction of agricultural prices, creates a serious stress on the exchequer while exerting multilayered pressure on all parts of the economy including on the common man. Upward-moving food price inflation also affects the economic growth which in turn would be reflected in the employment generation capacity (Chapter 2 discusses it in detail).

High food price inflation was driven more by persistent rise in the price of nutritional food items such as cereals. Vegetable price also skyrocketed in 2010–11. The sudden eruption of onion prices in the last week of December 2010 also affected overall consumption level of the people (see Section 3.4.3, Onion Crisis: A Case of Policy Failure in Chapter 3). However, response of the government towards food inflation was less effective. On many occasions, the slow response led to further aggravation of the situation. In the latest Economic Survey, the government has cited the importance and success of Public Distribution System (PDS) in Kerala in curbing food inflation during 2010–11, but initiatives to revamp the PDS require more policy attention and political will. Finally, the approval to increase Foreign Direct Investment (FDI) in retail is argued to be an opportunity in the context of rising food inflation and fair price for agricultural produce, but, it also poses a challenge to the livelihood of numerous small retailers.

Inflation management strategy of the government is largely focused on the monetary policy intervention. It has hardly reflected in easing inflation levels, even after constant interventions. On the other hand, credit intake of many sectors, especially real estate, declined, which reflects badly on the construction industry, a major employment provider (see Chapter 2 for further discussion). The farm sector credit supply also declined substantially.[14] Implications of all these factors will be felt in the coming days, argue economists.

1.11. Conflicting demands on land

In the last few years, in a growing economy, the increased population pressure and multiple demands on land created very complex situations. Expansion of the industrial and service sector also requires land which is usually being used to its full extent to feed the increasing population. This often creates not only a conflict between the industry and agriculture but also with the ecological sustainability of the economy. Debates on use of the land between two or more conflicting activities is getting increasing attention as usually the demand for land is imposed on the land-owning communities on an urgent basis. Besides, the project plans of government or private investors hardly consider the development cost. The development cost includes all the aspects of land use, such as livelihood, habitat, culture as well as decent and healthy living.

The dependency on farm sector for livelihood is still very high. The constant criticism of agricultural land acquisition is:

1. It is done without the consensus of the farming community (see Box 1.5 on land acquisition).
2. Agencies acquire more area than the actual requirement.
3. It mostly targets the cultivable land and areas that are rich in biodiversity.

Various land acquisition disputes in Uttar Pradesh, Kerala, Madhya Pradesh,

---

[14] This argument is evolved from the various analytical media reports and the major concern on the monetary-focused policy changes in the last few months that it would adversely affect economic growth. Padmanabhan (2011) and Ahya (2011).

Box 1.5:   *Greater Noida land acquisition cases and its aftermath*

Cancellation of land acquisition by Greater Noida Industrial Development Authority (GNIDA) by the court and the people's agitation against it is becoming a news item. In May 2011, the Allahabad Court cancelled three land acquisition projects citing the flaws in the acquisition process by GNIDA. The state had invoked the clause of urgency under Section 17(1) of the Land Acquisition Act, 1894.

But GNIDA failed to prove the urgency factor in the court which cancelled the acquisition citing that the invocation of Section 17(1) was arbitrary, illegal and discriminatory.

In another case, in July 2011, the Supreme Court had cancelled land acquisition by GNIDA citing inappropriate use of land in the acquired area. GNIDA had acquired this land in 2007 for industrial purposes invoking urgency criteria. But, it was allotted to real estate and builders for housing. Builders have sold their property units to nearly 6,500 buyers without informing them that the land was in dispute. At present, the court has to hear the appeals of both the farmers who had to sell off or leave the land when GNIDA acquired it, and also, of the people who invested in the residential units and had started paying their EMIs.

It is quite a complex situation and also indicates how both the farmers and the other common people are vulnerable to the bureaucracy and private capital.

Source: Sarkar (2011) and *Business Standard* (2011).

Orissa and Maharashtra received public and judicial attention in 2010–11. The NAC has reinstated the need to address the grievances of those who were displaced with or without land ownership under the Resettlement and Rehabilitation Policy. NAC suggested that even the landless in the acquired region have to be given a minimum of 120 days of wage in a year, for a period of 20 years, at the time of land acquisition (*Business Standard* 2011). Finally, most of these projects with a heavy capital investment have been criticized quite often, as they have a limited capacity to generate livelihoods, and are unable to absorb semi-skilled/unskilled workers.

PART III: THE POLICY ENVIRONMENT FOR LIVELIHOOD PROMOTION

1.12. Inclusive growth at centre stage

Faster and more inclusive growth was the core objective of the 11th Five Year Plan. To achieve broad based growth, the 11th Five Year Plan developed programmes under inclusive framework for a large number of the vulnerable population, particularly the Scheduled Castes (SC), Scheduled Tribes (ST), the Other Backward Classes (OBC), women and the minorities. It also focused on development of backward regions, north-east regions and the informal sector. All these interventions were aimed at enhancing access to health, education and other essential services and programmes for livelihood support. However, critics of the 11th Five Year Plan argue that even if it has evolved around an inclusive agenda, it was less successful in incorporating the key principles of inclusion, such as a combination of institutions and processes leading to improved access, participation, representation, dignity and empowerment. Besides, the slow growth at the bottom of the pyramid against the impressive national growth rate is a major policy concern.

The 12th Five Year Plan agenda evolved as a response to the criticisms of the 11th Five Year Plan, such as, the declining pace of inclusiveness, and an implementation gap in policy and programmes. Since the issues of accountability and transparency have been constantly debated in the last few years, the 12th Five Year Plan envisages major improvement in the governance structure. Agriculture is expected to receive core policy attention during the 12th Five Year Plan. Inclusive programmes aimed at the vulnerable and marginalized groups and regions would be increasingly targeted and a shift is expected towards a cash transfer mode. Though, leakage under cash-transfer would be low, many fear that the exclusion rate might be higher.

1.13. From welfare to entitlement and ways to deliver it

This period has also witnessed a change in the orientation of the state: it is focused more on the entitlements of the people than on dispensing welfare. This is reflected in the various laws promulgated, such as, Particularly Vulnerable Tribal Groups (PVTGs) in 2006–07, ST and the Other Forest Dwellers (Recognition of Forest Rights) Act in 2006 or the Panchayat Extension to Scheduled Areas (PESA). Even the NREGA entitles every rural citizen to an assured livelihood. Rights-based programmes and schemes like Social Security Act 2006, Right to Education Act 2010, Food Security Bill and Integrated Child Development Services (ICDS) scheme, were core of the entitlement initiatives during the 11th Five Year Plan.

This orientation has changed the livelihood situation substantially. As was observed by the former Chief Statistician of India and Advisor to the Planning Commission, Pranab Sen, 'the bargaining power of rural Indians has increased from 2009, coinciding with the universal coverage of National Rural Employment Guarantee Scheme (NREGS) that has created a floor for wages'.[15]

These entitlement-oriented programmes are committed to deliver services to all people—the *aam aadmi*—entitled to them. However, as identifying the defined target population and ensuring that the services

have reached them is a big challenge for the state, it is making significant improvement in an effort to keep track of the necessary information using IT. The newly established banking infrastructure and Aadhaar (the government's effort to provide a unique identification [UID] number to all citizens) afford a platform for entitlement delivery. It is also developing systems for Conditional Cash Transfer (CCT) of entitlement directly to the no-frill bank accounts of the ultimately entitled persons, subject to their meeting some pre-specified performance conditions.[16]

A critical element of this entitlement debate was that it has stressed the need for social auditing in public spending. Though social audits revealed the flaws related to the fund in MGNREGA implementation, it has provided an opportunity to cross verify the process of programme implementation and created awareness about citizens' rights. Strengthening the rights-based policies and expanding entitlement-based schemes with tight public auditing would be the core of the 12th Five Year Plan. It is also expected to contribute more into the transparency and governance structures of the programmes and schemes. However, a criticism of the entitlement-led approach is that it limits itself to those qualifying under a certain category and meeting rigid requirements; for example, entitlement based on BPL ignores a large majority that is on the fringes of BPL and that can fall under BPL with even a minor rise in food prices or due to minor health issues. Critics further argue that imposing conditions would lead to elimination and thereby reduce the actual number of beneficiaries.

---

[15] *The Economic Times*, Hyderabad, 16 July 2011.

[16] For example, the Ladli Scheme of Delhi government (scholarships for girl students), under which students have to meet a minimum attendance at school on achievement of which the funds will be directly transferred to the specified bank account. Similarly, to access the Janani Suraksha Scheme, a pregnant woman has to complete specified number of hospital consultations and the child should be born at the hospital.

1.14. Skilling up India: Focus on market, focus on jobs and not self-employment

As a nation of young people, India has no dearth of labour. But, how many of them are employable, beyond the petty self-employment and unorganized work which has traditionally made their careers? Quality of labour is determined by the skill sets she/he has acquired or developed. Our mainstream education—still not accessed by one out of four persons in the country—provides only the basic literacy and academic skills, paying little or no attention to the skills required in the market. The demand for new skills is growing fast, especially in new economy-related sectors, and many required skills are in short supply.

Looking at this as an opportunity and a need, the government is collaborating with the private sector to build the skills of the able-bodied population. The market orientation of the current initiatives is a significant shift, with a far greater effort being made to identify the skills requirement of the market, and then to develop them. The major thrust towards employability indicates a new intolerance to the traditional dominance of the informal sector in employment. For the industry to grow and for poverty to become 'history', our youth must be channelled into organized employment.

PART IV: STRUCTURE OF THE SOIL REPORT

Capturing livelihood debates in India during 2010–11 has been a process of capturing the significant initiatives both by the government and private sector in enhancing and securing the livelihoods of millions in this dynamic state of the economy. In addition, SOIL Report 2011 reviews the major debates, policy initiative, implications of key macroeconomic policies with a futuristic perspective.

SOIL 2011 has been done in the background of the recent statistics on the employment status in India, especially the NSS 66th Round. Chapter 2, 'Livelihoods of the Poor', explores the impact of some changes in the economy and the government's macroeconomic policies of growth and welfare on employment, health and food security on different sections of the poor. It briefly reviews the earnings and expenditures of the households. It explores the implications of hunger on the poor in the face of the global slowdown and inflation, especially of food inflation. Health is a key determinant of poverty status of households in the post-liberalization period. Another key determinant of vulnerability of the lower strata of the society is health. Therefore, the chapter deliberates on the role of health and the initiatives of the government to support health-risk mitigation such as Rashtriya Swasthya Bima Yojana (RSBY). While dealing with these broader issues with statistical evidences it also brings in discussion on invisible workers in the economy—female workers, from the perspective of emerging demographic dividend it brings the employment of 'youth' and key health social security scheme for BPL households and other vulnerable groups.

This period has also witnessed a more alert and sensitive policy environment. Chapter 3, 'Reflections on Livelihood Policies', captures the emerging policy initiatives of Government of India that are in various stages of formulation and adoption, as reflected in forms of Acts, Policy Declarations, Schemes, Missions, Plans and the like. The chapter also looks into the five year plans; budgets; allocation priorities; various new initiatives like skill development mission, Micro, Small and Medium Enterprises (MSMEs), CCT, Food Security as entitlements, policy issues on a few schemes like Mahatma Gandhi National Rural Employment Guarantee Scheme (MGNREGS), Mahila Kisan Shashaktikaran Pariyojana (MKSP) and Mukhyamantri Balika Cycle Yojona (MBCY), all of which aim to improve and augment livelihoods of the poor in particular. The discussion also narrates when the government attempts to promote livelihoods with policies, its failures and also the adverse impact of policies affecting the livelihood of many. The chapter also discusses certain cases like land acquisition in case of Vedanta–POSCO, and sudden rise in onion prices. When we analyze the policy implications of livelihoods, it is essential to understand the formulation of Livelihoods Schemes Coverage Index as a measure of actual depth and width of reach of all livelihoods schemes considered together. The discussions culminate with a general caution that despite various affirmative action initiatives and large outlay of resources, the state's capacity to deliver social good is in greater question today than ever before. The hope lies though in the strength of an ever maturing electorate and proactive civil society.

Followed by the macro-analysis of livelihood policies, it is essential to know how state and other key players such as cor-porates promote livelihoods. In India, state is still the largest livelihood promoter and Chapter 4, 'State as the Largest Livelihoods Promoter', illustrates it by broadly analyzing two flagship livelihood promotions programmes of Government of India, that is, MGNREGS and National Rural Livelihoods Mission (NRLM). This analysis has been done in the backdrop that the government's efforts in schemes have played their role, though results have been mixed. The chapter critically evaluates the MGNREG programme from the perspective of wage controversies, changes in the demand and supply pattern of rural labour which in turn enhanced their negotiation powers, the high transparency of the resource-utilization data and the social audits conducted at local level to capture the flaws. It also argues that though MGNREGS has been instrumental in improving the capacity of few states and some panchayats in delivering such programmes at present, it needs to be expanded to larger territories. It also suggests the functional strategies to improve the implementation of MGNREGS. NRLM is the restructured version of Swaranjayanti Gram Swarozgar Yojana (SGSY) programmes aiming to invest in self-managed institutions of the poor and aggregate those institutions beyond the community level yields impressive returns for poverty reduction. The programme recognizes that the poor people have the potential to come out of poverty with proper *handholding, training and capacity building and credit linkage.* The chapter illustrates its features, delivery system, key implementation challenges critically. The success of the livelihood programme is attributed to it capacity to enhance skill by way of vocational training. The last part of the chapter reviews the various skill-development initiatives launched by Government of India. In conclusion it raises concern on the declining role of civil society organizations in implementation of NRLM.

The private sector in India also affects the livelihoods of a large number of people: through marketing of their produce (like agro-industries), supplying necessary raw material to them (like agro-input industries), by creating employment opportunities for them and through their Corporate Social Responsibility (CSR) efforts. In this period covered by this report it can be seen that the private sector has become quite active in delivery of public goods in partnership with the State. Even the CSR initiatives have started growing with the government making a contribution of 2 per cent of the profits of all joint-venture companies for CSR. With emphasis being laid on skill building by the government, many corporate entities have started playing an important role in that space as well. Chapter 5, 'Private Industry and Services—What Is "India Inc" Delivering in Employment to the Poor?' tries to capture the role of corporate in creating and promoting livelihoods. The employment potential of various private sector industries and services are discussed in detail with a futuristic perspective to cite the emerging skill gap. It is argued that if the skill gap would not address, it would affect the sustainable growth of these sectors. The subsequent sections in the chapter cover the prevailing hiring practices and quality of jobs offered to both skilled and semi-skilled workers citing the promotion of informal sector by the private sector to overrule the governance and regulatory compliances. The discussion clearly indicates that in order to compete in the globalized job market the labourer has to improve certain skills and capabilities beyond the soft skills on one hand. On the other hand, the private sector also needs to realize that the age-old hiring practices involving traditional style of wage negotiations may not work in the new context as the information base of the labourers have multi-folded.

The livelihood scenario in the country within last year or two has seen many significant changes. While the government has reiterated its commitment to the inclusive growth, the emerging trends suggest a qualitative shift in the manner in which services and subsidies will be provided to the poor. There is also a perceptible movement from merely providing services to enhancing the opportunities for the poor to improve their livelihood options. The last chapter, 'Potential and Possibilities', looks at some of the key emerging and ongoing developments in government policies and practices. The discussion covers the four key livelihood initiatives (skilling and employment, market inclusion, decentralization and revival of agri-rural economy) which are likely to be included in the 12th Five Year Plan, and which will provide the overall direction of resource deployment and policy framework, newly introduced UID (Aadhar) Project and the proposed Direct Cash Transfer scheme, and its implications for the poor as well as livelihood professionals.

References

Ahya, Chetan. 2011. India facing downsize risk to growth. *The Economic Times*, 13 July.

Aiyer, Anklesaria. 2011. Agri-cultural wages have sky-rocketed: Poors have benefited from GDP growth. *The Economic Times*, 7 July.

Anant, T.C.A., and Rajiv Mehta. 2011. Has employment fallen in India. *Mint*, 30 June.

Bhaskaran, Resmi P. 2011. From country to the city: The changing dynamics of migration in contemporary India, in C. Bandhopadhay (ed.), *India: The country and the state in historical perspective*. Kolkata: Vikas Publications.

Business Standard. 2011. Court quashes land acquisition in two more Greater Noida villages. *Business Standard*, New Delhi, 20 July.

Business Today. 2011. Tight monetary policy may impact growth: Pranab. Press Trust of India New release, *Business Today*, 17 June.

Datta, Sankar, and Vipin Sharma. 2010. *State of India's livelihoods reports 2010: The 4P report 2010*. New Delhi: SAGE Publications.

Government of India. 2011a. *Economic survey—2011*. New Delhi: Ministry of Finance.

———. 2011b. Provisional population tables. *India Census 2011*. New Delhi: Registrar General and Census Commissioner, Ministry of Home Affairs.

NCEUS (National Commission for Enterprises in the Unorganized Sector). 2008. *Report on the conditions of work and promotion of livelihoods in the unorganised sector*. New Delhi: Government of India.

NSSO. 2009. Employment pattern—60th and 61st rounds of NSSO. New Delhi: Central Statistical Organisation.

———. 2011. Key indicators of employment and unemployment in India, 2009–10. Press note from NSSO, 24 June. New Delhi: Ministry of Statistics and Programme Implementation, Government of India.

Padmanabhan, Anil. 2011. Governance action and RBI. *Livemint*, 31 July.

Reserve Bank of India. 2010. *Handbook of Indian economy 2009–10*. Mumbai: Reserve Bank of India.

Sarkar, Renju. 2011. Allahabad High Court land order creates panic. *Business Standard*, New Delhi, 22 May.

Sen, Amartya. 2011. Growth and other concerns. *The Hindu*, 14 February.

The Hindu. 2011. Supreme Court to hear seeking ban on Monday. *The Hindu*, Chennai, 1 May.

Livelihoods of the Poor

It is now commonly accepted that contrary to expectations the growth experienced by the economy since liberalization has neither altered the structure of the economy, nor increased the growth rate of employment. The growth in the economy has been capital intensive and skill intensive; the few 'good' jobs generated required a high level of education and/or skill, while the vast majority of people have been absorbed into low-quality jobs in the informal sector.

The working poor and the poor are deeply affected by the Indian state's move to liberalization–globalization. The poor experience the slowdown in growth, uneven growth across sectors, changes in the availability of jobs, credit, agricultural inputs, and displacement from land due to large-scale power and infrastructure projects; the loss of workers' rights in the Special Economic Zones (SEZs); and the benefits from the government's health, employment, education and food security initiatives. In the preceding three years, due to the slowdown in the global economy, the poor have experienced the consequences of living in a global economy even more acutely.

This chapter will explore the impact of some of the changes in the economy, and the government's macroeconomic policies for growth and welfare for employment, health and food security of the poor. Then a brief overview of the framework of livelihoods anchors the ensuing sections. This is followed by two sections devoted to discussion on employment. First is a general section which looks at employment growth, status and sectoral and wage shifts (Section 2.2); then a section which addresses two groups in particular—women and youth—and shifts in their labour-market participation (Section 2.3). The subsequent sections focus on the impact of global slowdown (Section 2.4), food inflation and hunger on the poor (Section 2.5) and a final section on health (Section 2.6), before conclusions.

2.1. Understanding livelihoods

Livelihood status of a poor household is the outcome of judicious use of capacities—in the face of exposure to risks; of material resources—monetary and non-monetary; of expenditures—for health, education and social security and so on; and strategy adopted to ensure the sustenance of household members. Income of poor households is dependent on the terms on which they can trade their labour and assets in the market, and on returns from the marginal means of production, such as, land, livestock (or small animals) and technology. It will also depend on what can be derived from common property resources, including fish and forest produce. Labour may be exchanged as wage labour (regular or casual), contractual labour, salaried employment or self-employment. Poor also earn some income from government transfers and social protection programmes such as old age and disability pension. Expenditures include those that are necessary for daily reproduction of life, to ensure a minimum standard of living; for improving the lives of the present as well as the next generation (e.g., education); for sociocultural activities (e.g., marriage); for savings and investments to mitigate risks and vulnerabilities, and secure future sustenance.

Livelihoods of the poor are significantly mediated by the specific location of the individual, the household and the community/group in the maze of caste, religious and ethnic stratification. Exclusion and discrimination as a result of hierarchies of caste, gender and other markers of differentiation, such as, disability and HIV infection, additionally disadvantage one's position in the labour market, independent of other endowments. The chart below clearly shows the inequality in outcomes based on social and economic groups among Indian children (UNICEF 2011, p. 16).

2.2. Overall employment trends

Earnings in the labour market provide a fair, though not exhaustive picture of the livelihood status of a family. 'Labour markets are the main channel through which economic growth is distributed across regions and people' (World Bank 2010, p. 2), and an increase in earnings by itself explains about 66 per cent of the variation in the household per capita expenditure in India (ibid., p. 2, Figure 1). This section begins with a brief overview of the recent employment trends before discussing the current status.

The total workforce in the country during 2004–05 is estimated to have been 455.7 million, based on the NSS 61st Round Employment-Unemployment Survey and census population projections for different states. Of these 86.21 per cent worked in the informal sector.[1] This estimate applied to 33.4 million of the 45 million workers in the manufacturing sector (Unni 2006, cited in World Bank 2010, p. 8). This concentration

Figure 2.1: Disparity in levels of under-five mortality (per thousand) by socioeconomic characteristics

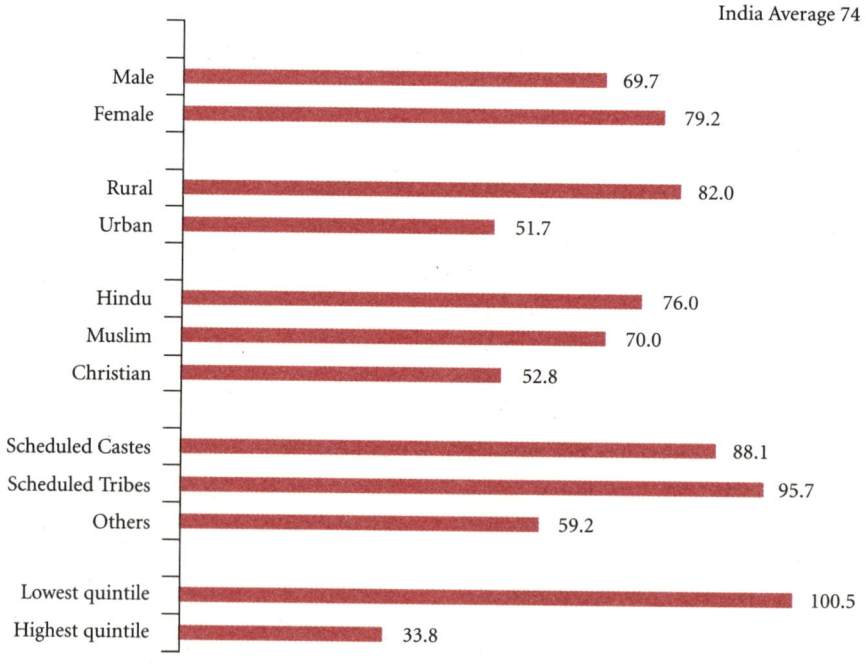

Source: UNICEF (2011, p. 16).

---

[1] Raveendran (2010). The NCEUS definition of informal economy (see Chapter 1, n9) is used here

of employment in the unorganized sector indicates a dualism in the manufacturing sector: concentration of value-addition and employment in very large firms (more than 500 workers with relatively high wages) and the very small firms (less than 20 workers with relatively low wages), leaving a conspicuously 'missing middle'. A similar dualism is observed in the tertiary sectors. Trade, hotels and restaurants, construction and community services which generate the bulk of the employment in services have low productivity, low wages, and are largely informal (World Bank 2010), while the highly productive and highly waged IT-enabled services (ITES) and finance employ only 6 million workers (out of a labour force of 400 million).[2]

2.2.1. Employment growth by status

The annual employment growth in 1993–2004 was 1.9 per cent, a decline from 2.1 per cent in the previous decade (1983–93). When we look at the latter half of the decade, the annual growth was higher, at 2.3 per cent (between 1999–2000 and 2004–05). However, most of this growth was in the subsidiary (part-time) employment and in self-employment in the rural areas. Self-employment is in fact often an indicator of underemployment or distress employment,

as remuneration from self-employment is in many instances lower than from casual labour. Growth of employment for principal (full-time) workers actually slowed down, and unemployment increased. There was almost no employment growth in the manufacturing and formal sectors. The increase in employment in the formal service sector (ITES) and financial sectors are the main source of growth—has no visible impact because they employ relatively few workers.

The result of India's growth through the 1990s to 2005 was that the share of the organized sector as an employer declined substantially (Ghose 2010). Surplus labour was being absorbed into the unorganized sector, which was able to sustain jobs due to a healthy growth, but this was at the cost of job quality and security. An increasing proportion of overall jobs were either in the unorganized sector (so informal by definition), or casual jobs within the organized sector, adding to the number of workers in 'vulnerable employment'.[3]

The recent release of NSSO 66th Round (July 2009–June 2010) data shows a sharp deceleration in the total numbers employed, from an annual rate of around 2.7 per cent in the previous five-year period to only 0.8 per cent in the last five years[4] (see Figure 2.2[5]).

The biggest factor in the decline in growth relates to women's self-employment, but male employment growth shows a sharp

---

to estimate the percentage of workers in informal (or unorganized) economy. However, by official definition employment in the government or establishments employing more than 10 workers is 'organized'; all workers who do not fall in this are in the 'unorganized'. The official government estimates put the percentage of unorganized workers at 93 per cent while other estimates based on NSSO (1999–2000) give figures for informal sector between 86–89 per cent. This description of informal sector is given on p. 47 of the World Bank (2010) report on employment cited earlier in the text.

[2] The World Bank report from which these numbers are drawn states that their report is based on fresh research by a team of Indian economists and World Bank staff. Their researchers used the thick rounds of NSSO surveys from 1983 to 2004–05, reports from the Annual Survey of Industries, information from Labour Bureau of Government of India and Informal Sector Modules of NSSO (see p. 2 for further details).

[3] The ILO defines workers in vulnerable employment as the sum of own-account workers and contributing family workers. They are less likely to have formal work arrangements, and are therefore more likely to lack decent working conditions, adequate social security and 'voice' through effective representation by trade unions and similar organizations. Vulnerable employment is often characterized by inadequate earnings, low productivity and difficult conditions of work that undermine workers' fundamental rights.

[4] This discussion draws heavily from C.P. Chandrasekar and Jayati Ghosh's article, 'Latest Employment Trends in NSSO' in *Business Line*, 12 July 2011.

[5] All charts in this section are from C.P. Chandrasekar and Jayati Ghosh's article, 'Latest Employment Trends in NSSO' in *Business Line*, 12 July 2011.

deceleration as well. There is a deceleration in employment growth for both, urban as well as rural areas, although it is sharper in the rural areas, and applies to the agriculture and non-agriculture sector. The rate of increase for non-agricultural employment halved, for all workers taken together.

Once again the drop is the maximum for female workers but as Figure 2.3 shows, there has been a decrease in the growth of non-agricultural employment even among male workers.

Self-employment has decreased for both men and women, and the decline is

Figure 2.2: Rates of growth of total employment

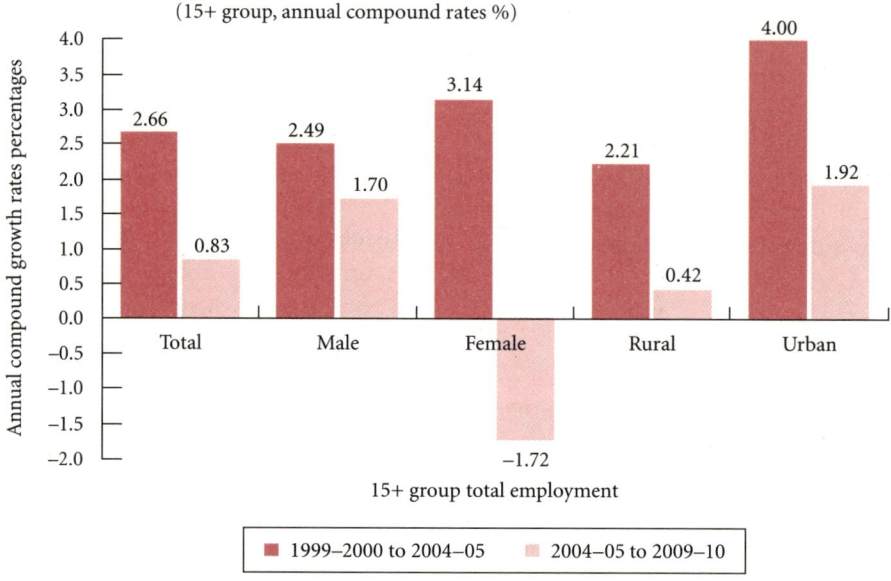

Source: Chandrasekar and Ghosh (2011, Chart 1).

Figure 2.3: Rates of growth of non-agricultural employment

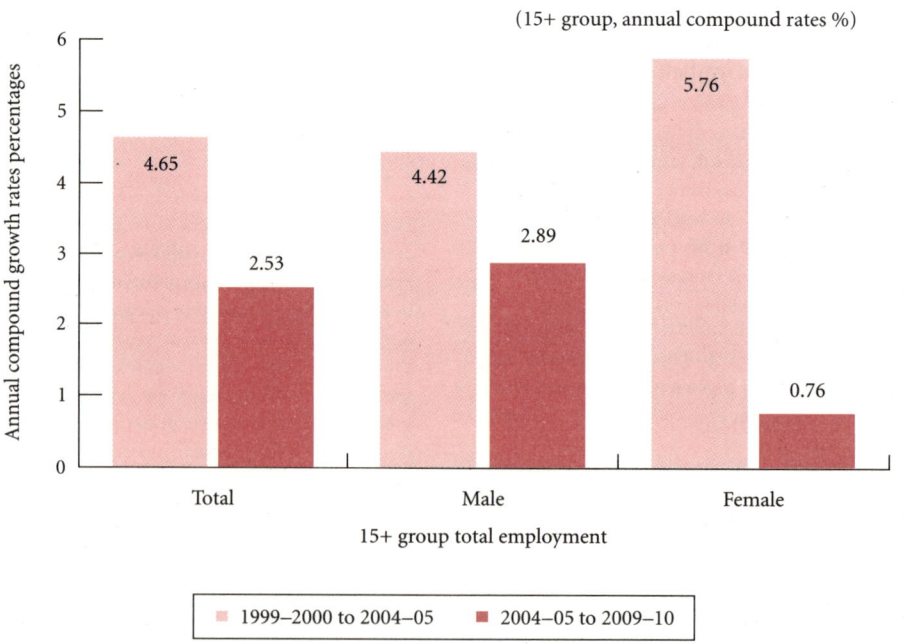

Source: Chandrasekar and Ghosh (2011, Chart 2).

significantly more for urban men. Regular employment has increased marginally for both categories. Casual employment for both male and female workers has increased to a greater extent. Specifically for the age cohort 25 to 59 years for all of India, there were around 18.2 million more casual workers, compared to 6.4 million additional regular workers and 4 million more self-employed.

Overall, self-employment continued to be the most common form of employment; 51 per cent of the labour force was self-employed (as compared to 52.4 per cent in 2004–05). Of the rest one-third (33.5 per cent) work as casual labour (increased from 31.1 per cent in 2004–05) and 15.6 per cent work in regular wage/salaried jobs (decreased from 16.5 in 2004–05). These numbers though hide the rural–urban disparities.

In urban areas an almost equal number of the employed are in regular/salaried employment and in self-employment (41.1 per cent and 41.4 per cent respectively). Less than one-fifth (17.5 per cent) were employed in casual labour; whereas, in rural areas a large percentage is employed in casual labour (38.6 per cent). Also, more than half (54.2 per cent) of the rural workers are self-employed and only 7.3 per cent are regular wage/salaried employees. This clearly shows the fragility of the majority of rural livelihoods.

Finally, the unemployment rate has decreased (from 8.82 per cent in 2004–05 to 6.6 per cent in 2009–10). But the jury is still out on its meaning as this decrease has occurred in a period of low aggregate job creation and a decline of 2.8 per cent in workforce participation.

To summarize, the labour market trends on worker status, casual employment , the most vulnerable form of employment, has shot up 2.5 per cent as a share of total in the last two years, while self-employment has declined by the same amount, bringing it down to around 2004–05 levels.

Meanwhile, regular employment has maintained the same proportion. The differences in employment patterns of the rural and urban areas have become even more pronounced. Overall, India's economic growth is having spectacularly little effect on the status of the workers across the three employment categories of self-employed, casual and regular. Figure 2.4 shows this for all workers since 2004.

2.2.2. Sectoral shifts

The most recent data sources on distribution of workers by sector are the NSSO's 66th Round and also the new annual survey by the Ministry of Labour and Employment (2010). The latter gives the following distribution for total employed population (rural and urban together).

Figure 2.5 shows that in 2010, 45.5 per cent of all employed persons were primarily engaged in agriculture, 8.9 per cent worked in manufacturing, a further 8.8 per cent in trade, 8.4 per cent in community services (including health and education) and 7.5 per cent in construction. NSSO 66th Round shows that 63 per cent of rural male workers were engaged in agriculture and the remainder were distributed evenly across the secondary (19 per cent) and tertiary (18 per cent) sectors.[6] In urban areas, the tertiary sector provided employment to 59 per cent male workers and 53 per cent female workers, while the secondary sector employed 35 per cent of male and 33 per cent of female workers.

NSSO data permits us to review trends in sectoral employment over 22 years (1988–2010), disaggregated for rural, urban, males and females. This gives a better insight into employment prospects, since we can view the shifts from one kind of employment to another.

---

[6] The primary sector includes agriculture, animal husbandry, fishing, mining, forestry and so on. The secondary sector includes manufacturing, construction and utilities while the tertiary sector includes trade, transport, hotels, social and business services and public administration.

Figure 2.4: Trends in worker status, all India, 2004–05 to 2009–10

Source: NSSO Rounds 61, 64 and 66.

Figure 2.5: Distribution of total employed population by sector

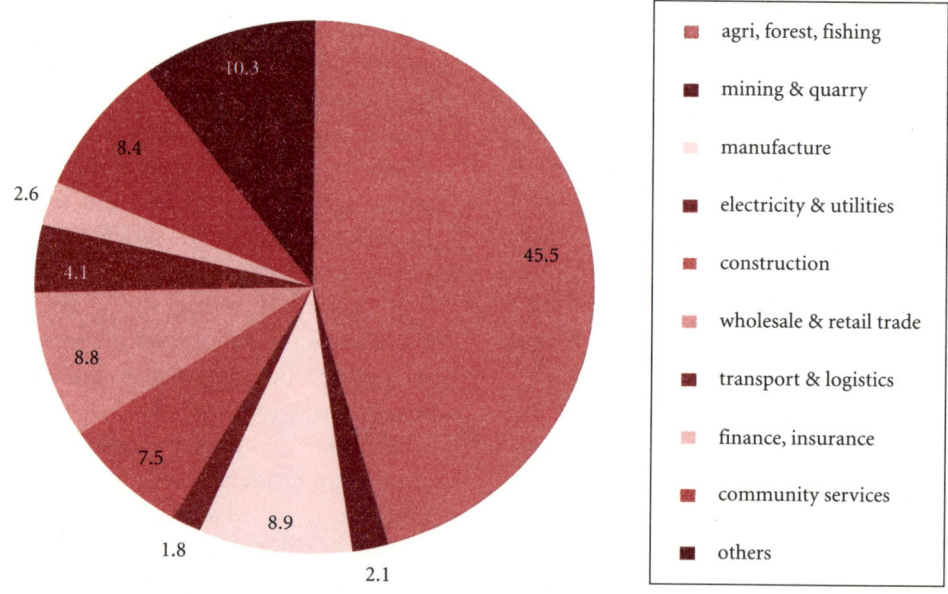

Source: Ministry of Labour and Employment, Annual Employment Survey 2010.

The following four graphs show trends in employment, disaggregated for male and female workers and rural and urban areas. Agriculture being the predominant rural sector, it has been excluded from the first two rural graphs because it makes it hard to view trends in other sectors, and warrants a special discussion.

Employment in agriculture among rural men has decreased steadily from 739 to 628 in a thousand, between 1988 and 2010 (the downward trend has sharpened in the last two years). However, the picture is more complex for rural women. Employment in agriculture for rural women peaked at 847 in a thousand in 1994 and had dropped to 814 in 2004–05 (Rustagi 2010); a decrease of about 3 per cent over the decade. Though, within the past five years, there has been a slight increase in the rate of decrease of employment for women workers in agriculture to about 4 per cent; in 2004–05 it stands at 793 in a thousand. However, when compared to rural men this trend for rural women continues to be relatively muted.

What are the implications of this gender imbalance in the shift from agriculture? It suggests that rural men are accessing off-farm employment more successfully than women. It would also suggest a growth in the number of women-managed farms: as men from marginal farmer households leave cultivation, it is the women who are left with the main responsibility. This may improve the food availability for household

members, especially children, since women are more likely to focus on producing food crops (Banerjee 2010). But households with only women cultivators are likely to suffer from reduced access to farm credit and the mismatch between women farmers' needs and the male-centred targeting of inputs and extension services.

Let us now turn to non-agricultural employment for rural workers.

From Figures 2.6 and 2.7, we can see:

- Manufacturing took a slowly increasing share of rural male workers from 1993 till 2005, when this trend tailed off. Overall, manufacturing is now hiring a smaller proportion of rural men than in 1988. While in 1988, 76 in 1,000 rural men worked in manufacturing, in 2010, this figure was 70, and the sharpest decline has been in the last two years.
- Neither has manufacturing succeeded in absorbing a rising share of rural female

Figure 2.6: Employment by sector per 1,000 rural employed males, 1988–2010 (excluding agriculture)

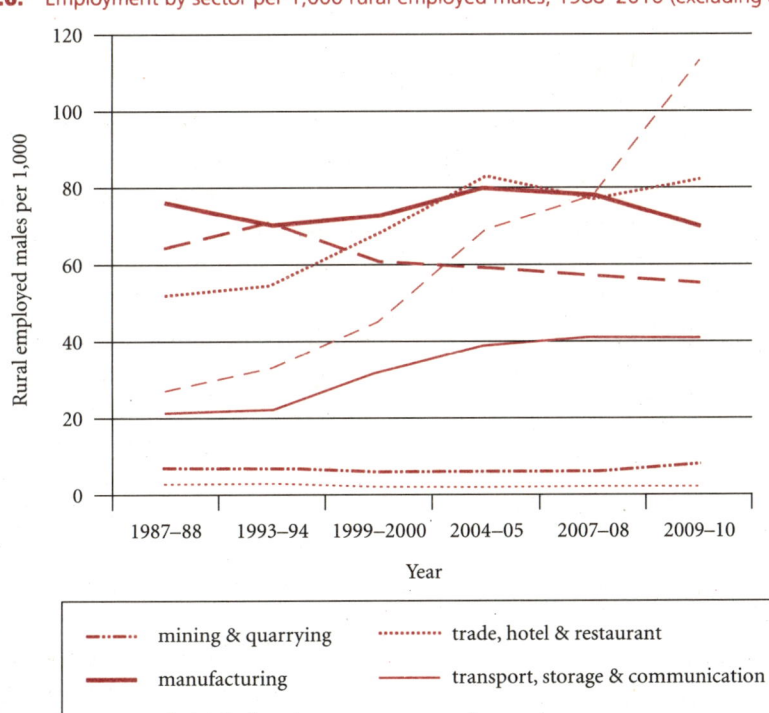

Source: NSSO 2007–08 (Round 64) and 2009–10 (Round 66).

Figure 2.7:   Employment by sector per 1,000 rural employed females, 1988–2010 (excluding agriculture)

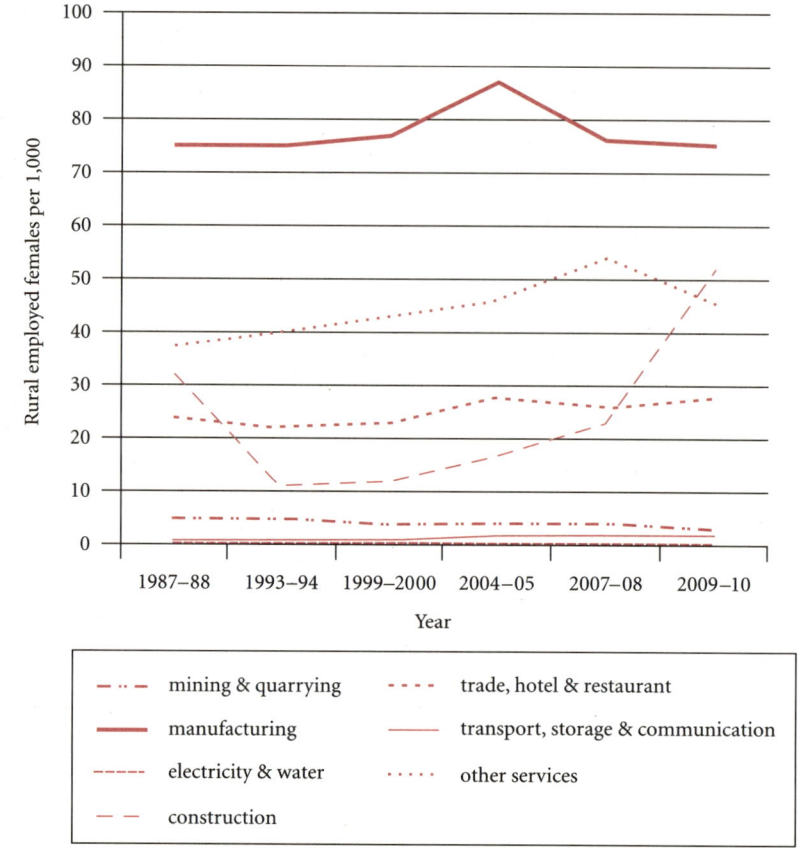

Source: NSSO 2007–08 (Round 64) and 2009–10 (Round 66).

workers, though levels are the same as in 1988 (75 in 1,000). A surprising peak in 2004–05 was short-lived.

- The sectors which saw a sharp increase in the number of rural men employed are construction (rising continuously and shooting up by nearly 50 per cent in the last rwo years), trade, hotels and restaurants (rising since 1988 and again, after a dip in 2007–08) and transport, storage and communications (peaked in 2004–05 and has been holding steady since then).
- The participation of rural women in construction has increased exponentially; it more than doubled in the last two years (now at 52 in 1,000).
- Rural women have not increased their participation in any other off-farm sector, except trade, and hotels and restaurants which show a slow but uncertain upward trend.

Now for the urban data on employment trends, 1988 to 2010 (this time agriculture has been kept in since it is not the dominant sector).

From Figures 2.8 and 2.9, we gather:

- All trends, both upward and downward are much milder and more muted for urban than for rural workers. There are no equivalents to the rapid growth of share by construction and other services in rural areas. Given the growth trends, the distribution across sectors in urban areas has remained surprisingly constant.
- Having said that, there has been some increase in the number of urban men involved in trade, and hotels and restaurants (215/1,000 in 1988 to 270/1,000 in 2010), but this has been falling since 2000. There has been some increase in the

Figure 2.8: Employment by sector per 1,000 urban employed males, 1988–2010

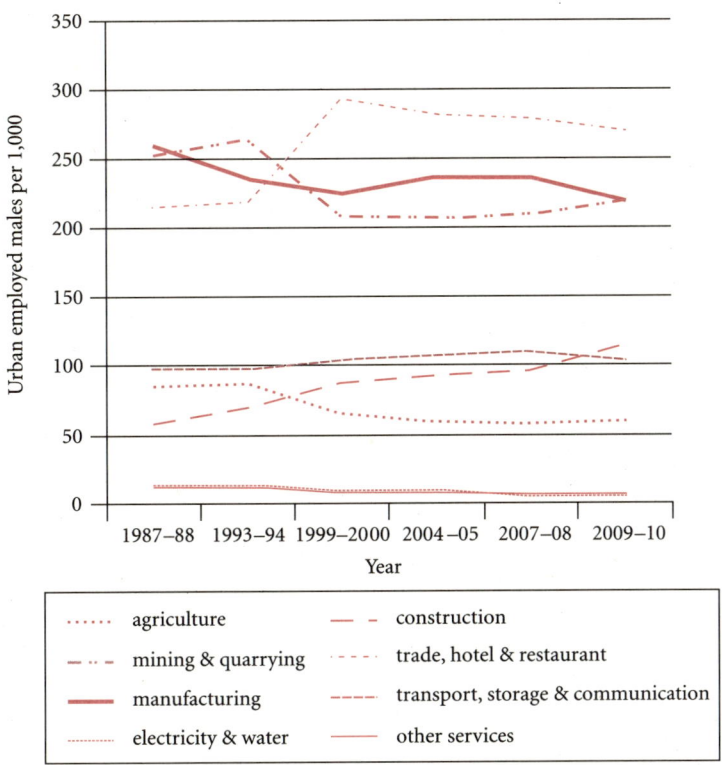

Source: NSSO 2007–08 (Round 64) and 2009–10 (Round 66).

Figure 2.9: Employment by sector per 1,000 urban employed females, 1988–2010

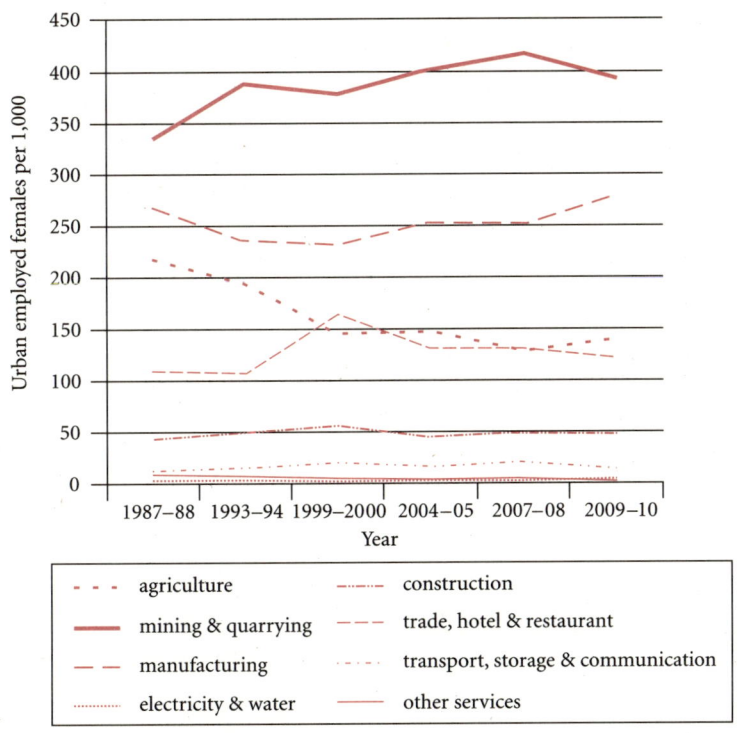

Source: NSSO 2007–08 (Round 64) and 2009–10 (Round 66).

number of urban women involved in 'other services' from 336/1,000 in 1988 to 383/1,000 in 2010 but this has also decreased in the last two years.[7] One of the fastest growing sub-sectors in 'other services' is probably domestic work where jobs are of notoriously poor quality.

- Participation of urban male workers in manufacturing has clearly declined (falling from 260/1,000 in 1988 to 218/1,000 in 2010).
- Participation of urban female workers in manufacturing may be on the rise but at 279 in 2010, still only stands at a little above the 1988 levels of 269 of 1,000.
- This increase is unlikely to indicate a rise in particularly good quality jobs, since a large proportion of women's work in urban manufacturing tends to be home-based, offering flexibility but very low wages.

2.2.3. Work participation in the 'invisible' domestic sphere

A range of productive and reproductive activities that are integral to livelihoods occur in the domestic sphere. Women are the primary workers engaged in these activities but men too are involved although in much fewer numbers. The productive value of unpaid work that women do is often 'invisible' as work, even to women themselves—they consider it as a natural extension of their traditional household and childcare responsibilities.

The definition of work and workers in the NSSO is such that it includes only a part of women's productive and reproductive work as 'work', and only those women in such works as 'workers'. Self-employed women who are helpers in the family enterprises and do not earn any regular wages fall in this definition of work and are counted as workers in categories 92 and 93. However, even these women, unless they are subsidiary workers, are not counted as being in the labour force—as those working or willing to work.

According to the United Nations System of National Accounts (UNSNA), production of any good for consumption is included in the definition of economic activity and hence those engaged in such activities are considered as workers.[8] See Table 2.1 for the list of tasks.

Table 2.1: 'Domestic' tasks included in NSSO Category 92 and 93, and UNSNA

Principal Activity Status 92 and 93 and engaged in specific economic activities but not included in subsidiary status workers category	Maintenance of kitchen gardens, orchards, etc.	Work in household poultry, dairy, etc.	Free collection of fish, small games, wild fruits, vegetables, etc., for household consumption	Free collection of firewood, cow dung, cattle feed, etc., for household consumption
UNSNA activities not classified as economic activities in India and also not included in the subsidiary status workers category	De-husking of paddy for household consumption	Grinding of foodgrains for household consumption	Preparation of *gur* for household consumption	Sewing, tailoring, weaving, for household use
	Preservation of meat and fish for household use	Making baskets and mats for household use	Preparation of cow dung cake for use as fuel in household	

Source: Raveendran (2010).

---

[7] 'Other services' requires some further explanation since it may be growing in importance for urban women workers. It includes education and health workers, public administration, real estate, financial intermediation and urban services. The most significant for urban women are health and education, and for urban men, public administration and real estate (NSSO 2011).

[8] Thus, processing of primary products like de-husking of paddy, grinding of foodgrains, preparation of *gur* and preservation of meat, fish, etc., for household consumption are treated as economic activities as per the UNSNA. Similarly, making of baskets and mats, preparation of cow dung cake, sewing, tailoring, weaving, etc., for household use are also included in the

If persons with usual principal status activity status codes 92 and 93, and engaged in various UNSNA activities, but not included in the category of subsidiary status workers were included in the workforce, the total workforce in the country in 2004–05 would increase to 554.99 million[9] and the share of women in the workforce would increase to 44.2 per cent.

2.2.4. Wages

Employment data in conjunction with wages earned add substantially to the picture of livelihoods. First, let us look at the long-term trends. Although real wages grew between 1993–94 and 2004–05, the rate of growth was lower than in the previous decade.

Real-wage growth was slower for most workers between 2000–04 and showed a decline for unskilled workers. Increasing wage disparity has been another conspicuous feature of employment in India since the period of liberalization. From the 1990s till 2005, at least, wage increases which have taken place have benefitted the wage earners in the top two deciles and the bottom decile the most (see Figure 2.10 [World Bank 2010, p. 20, Figure 1.1]). For example, in the 1990s, while real-wage growth for persons among managerial and executive rank was 10 per cent per annum, it was only 3 per cent for the workers in the middle 40 per cent group.

Figure 2.10: Average real daily wages and wage growth

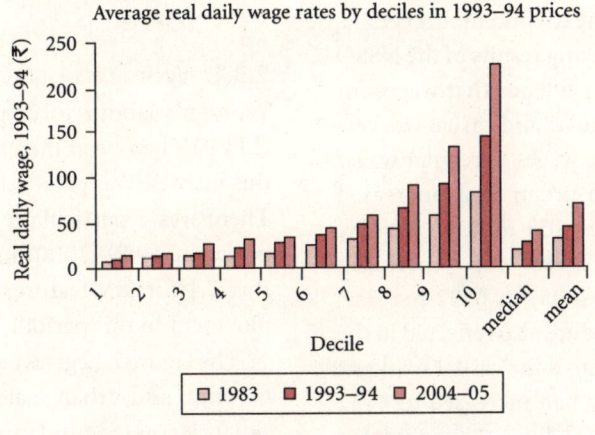

Average real daily wage rates by deciles in 1993–94 prices

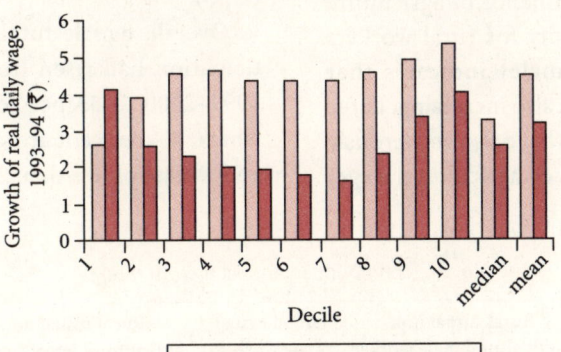

Annual growth of rural daily wages rates at 1993–94 prices

Source: World Bank (2010, p. 37).

---

definition of economic activity. In addition, there are activities like tutoring one's own or others' children free of charge and bringing water from outside household premises which form part of the extended UNSNA but are generally not regarded as economic activities in most countries including India.

[9] This number would also include men engaged in these activities and not included in NSSO.

The wage growth rate for casual labourers was positive only for rural areas; for urban male casual labour the growth rate was negative (−0.46 per cent). Also, for rural casual labourers (who constitute the bottom deciles of workers) though wage growth rate was positive it showed a marked deceleration (0.72 per cent) in the period 2004–05 (see Table 2.2 [World Bank 2010, p. 20, Table 1.3]).

Even after 2004–05, we see little increase in wages for workers in low-quality casual jobs. In 2004–05, the overall average wage for casual workers was ₹51. In 2007–08, this figure was ₹63. So these three years of high and—in theory—inclusive economic growth, delivered only ₹12 per day extra for the country's 31 per cent of casually employed workers.

However, moving to contemporary data, one of the most striking results of the NSSO 66th Round is the evidence that wages for all categories of regular and casual workers have increased. The wages of regular wage/salaried workers in urban areas increased from ₹183 (in 2004–05) to ₹365 per day while in the rural areas, wages increased from ₹112 (in 2004–05) to ₹232 per day. The increased wages are also reflected in the earnings of daily wages for casual workers; in urban areas they had increased to ₹132 per day and for rural areas they increased to ₹102. The predominance of agriculture as the principal activity for rural workers (both, male and female) indicates that agricultural wages are also increasing. Large farmers in some states have also vociferously complained of increased agricultural wages

(as a result of shortage of labour due to competition from the NREGS). Increases in consumption and expenditure in NSSO 66th Round are also evidence of an increase in agricultural wages (see Section 2.5 for a more detailed discussion).

Figure 2.11 looks at nominal wages for casual workers, disaggregated by gender and urban/rural, between 2007–08 and 2009–10. The figure shows that the increase has been equally significant in all four categories, over the two-year period. The extent of this wage rise in real terms (in a period of inflation) and its distribution across states are issues still being hotly debated.

2.3. Participation of women and youth in the labour force

2.3.1. Women's participation

Women's labour force participation rate (LFPR)[10] had been increasing till 2004–05; this increase was greater than that for men. There was a particularly marked increase between 1999–2000 and 2004–05. See Box 2.1 for key features of women's employment in this period.

The Figure 2.12 gives percentage increases for rural and urban male and female subsidiary status (SS) and usual principal status (UPS).

Overall, female rural labour force participation had risen from 30 per cent in 1999–2000 to 33 per cent in 2004–05, of which, 8.4 per cent are subsidiary workers; an increase of less than 2 per cent from the

Table 2.2: Annual real-wage growth (compounded annual growth rate)

	Rural casual non-agricultural male worker	Urban casual male worker	Rural casual non-agricultural female worker	Urban casual female worker
1983 to 1987–88	3.0	2.8	2.0	3.2
1987–88 to 1993–94	1.2	0.7	1.7	1.3
1993–94 to 1999–2000	3.2	3.0	4.6	4.9
1999–2000 to 2004–05	2.8	−0.8	2.5	−0.6
1983 to 1993–94	2.6	2.1	2.2	2.7
1993–94 to 2004–05	3.3	1.3	4.0	2.6

Source: World Bank (2010, p. 37).

Figure 2.11:   Changes in nominal wages for casual workers 2007–08 and 2009–10 (₹ per day)

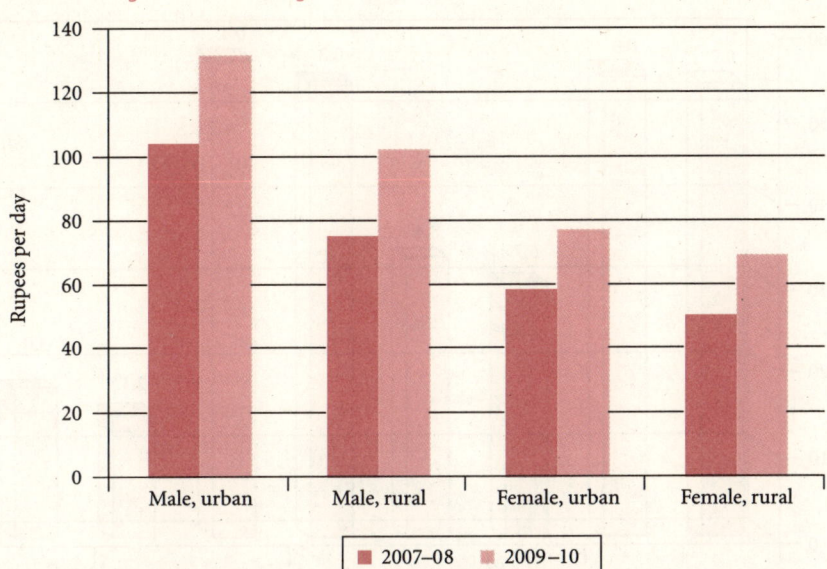

Source: NSSO Round 64 and Round 66.

Box 2.1:   *Key features of women's employment[11] during the peak period of their labour force participation 1999–2000 to 2004–05*

- Approximately 9 out of 10 (90.8 per cent) of all women workers were working in agriculture, manufacturing, trade or education. And except for education more than 90 per cent of these women were working in the informal sector of the other categories.
- Private household and extraterritorial organizations (74.3 per cent), education (41.9 per cent) and agriculture (41.5 per cent) were the industries with the highest share of women workers.
- Wearing apparel (33 per cent), computer and related activities (25.4 per cent) and private households (24.3 per cent) were the industries with the highest growth rate of women's employment.
- In the manufacturing sector, the women's share in overall urban manufacturing had increased by 8.5 per cent and women gained employment in modern industries like leather goods, garments and auto parts. But these jobs were home based

manufacturing and women's average daily earnings in most states (where growth rate of women's employment in urban manufacturing had been relatively fast) were even lower that the National Rural Employment Guarantee Act (NREGA) daily wage rate of ₹100.
- The traditional sectors in which 78.5 per cent women workers worked—wood products, tobacco products, private households and agriculture—were the ones for which the average value added per worker (productivity) was the lowest.
- While 50 per cent women core workers (UPSS category) in urban areas were in the services, the fastest growth was at the bottom level—in the private households.
- Women workers, who constituted 32.2 per cent of the total workforce, contributed a mere 19.8 per cent to the gross domestic product (GDP).

Source: Raveendran (2010).

---

[10] Labour force participation rate (LFPR) is defined as those who are currently working and/or available for work (NSSO 2011).

[11] Raveendran (2010). Similar data (and analysis) is unavailable as yet for the recent 66th NSSO Rounds of 2009–10.

Figure 2.12:   Labour force participation rate (per cent)

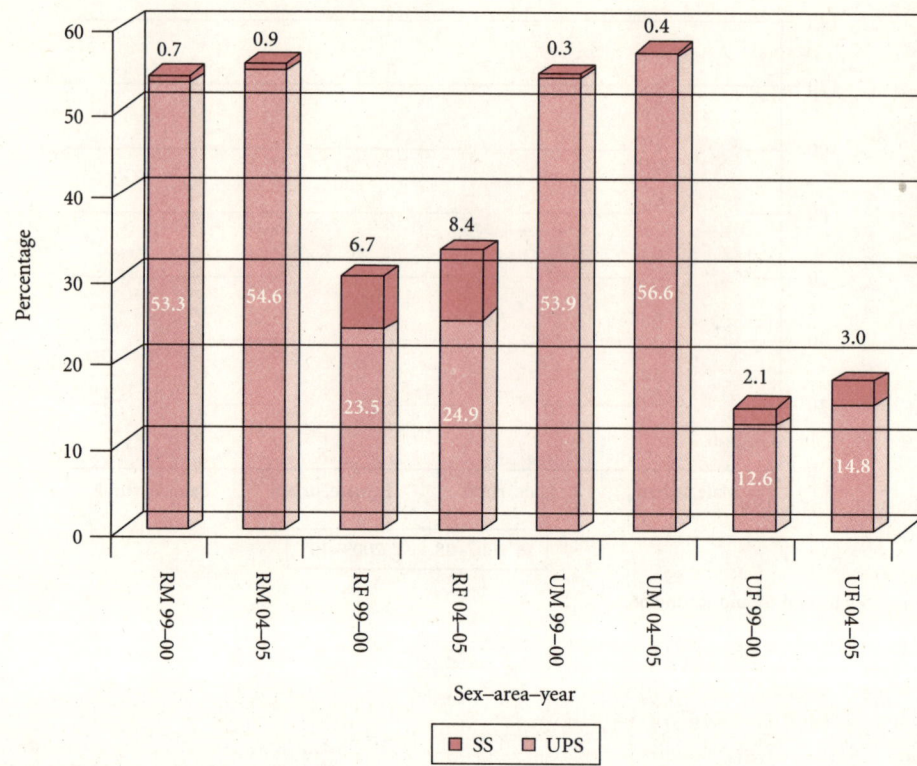

Source: Rustagi (2010).

6.7 per cent subsidiary workers in 1999–2000. This clearly indicates that though small, there was an increase in the principal category of rural women workers. Although, most of this increment was accounted for by the growth in subsidiary activities[12] in the usual status category. In the urban areas, growth of both, the principal and subsidiary activities among women played a role, and this was interpreted as a positive sign because it indicated an increase in the 'core workers'. In the urban areas, the increase in the principal status labour force for women was greater than in the rural areas (Rustagi 2010). It increased from 13 per cent in 1999–2000 to 15 per cent in 2004–05, while the subsidiary status labour force of urban women moved from 2 per cent to 3 per cent over the same period.

However, the 2010 NSSO data shows a sharp decline in the percentage of women in the labour force compared to 2004–05. In fact, women's LFP, whether it is estimated by taking only those with principal productive activities, or those with subsidiary productive activities too, is between 2 and 7 per cent, lower than it was in 2004–05. When we look at the trends across 1999–2000 to 2009–10 in rural areas, we see a decline in the LFPR of women workers of about 3 to 4 per cent below the level at the start of the decade, and a return to the level of 2000 in urban areas, after a mid decade spike (see Table 2.3). The gains of 2004–05 seem to have been washed away by 2009–10.

---

[12] In its broadest definition of 'labour force' (i.e., usual status over the year preceding the survey), the NSSO notes two types of productive activities: first, that which is 'principal', that is, the activity on which 'the major time [was] spent during the 365 days preceding the survey'; second, that which is 'subsidiary', that is, pursued by the person 'for a shorter time … which is not less than 30 days' alongside the principal activity. Crucially, however, a person is classified as participating in the labour force even if they have only a subsidiary activity and even if their principal activity would exclude them from it, that is, they are a student, a housewife and so on (NSSO 2011, A6, 1.13.3).

Table 2.3: Trends in women's labour force participation, 1999–2010

Year	Status	Area	LFPR
1999–2000	Principal	Rural	23.5
		Urban	12.6
	Usual	Rural	30.2
		Urban	14.7
2004–05	Principal	Rural	24.9
		Urban	14.8
	Usual	Rural	33.3
		Urban	17.8
2009–10	Principal	Rural	20.8
		Urban	12.8
	Usual	Rural	26.5
		Urban	14.6

Source: NSSO various rounds.

Taking the same decade 1999–2000 to 2009–10, Figure 2.13 maps the various principal activities (productive and 'non productive') of urban women, to better understand these shifts in labour force participation.

The figure shows that the shifts in the urban female workforce can be related to an increased participation in education, from 9.1 per cent of all urban women in 1999–2000, to 15.3 per cent in 2009–10.

We also see that there was a proportionate rise in self-employment between 1999–2000 and 2004–05, but most of this was eroded by 2009–10. See Box 2.2 for nature of women's self-employment in this period.

Hence, one of the key reasons for the decline in women's LFP is the increased number of girls continuing education beyond 15 years of age. This is discussed in more detail in the next section on labour force participation of youth.

Another key explanation is linked to the fact that women's labour is treated as a flexible resource by the family, and traditionally women's lack of labour force participation is associated with a high household status. Women are withdrawn from participation in paid work if household earnings have increased through alternate means. Also, as women have an alternative use for their time for household tasks their decision to participate in the labour market is influenced by their expectation of available employment opportunities and wage rates. Thus there are two likely explanations for women withdrawing from the labour force. First,

Figure 2.13: *Distribution of urban females*

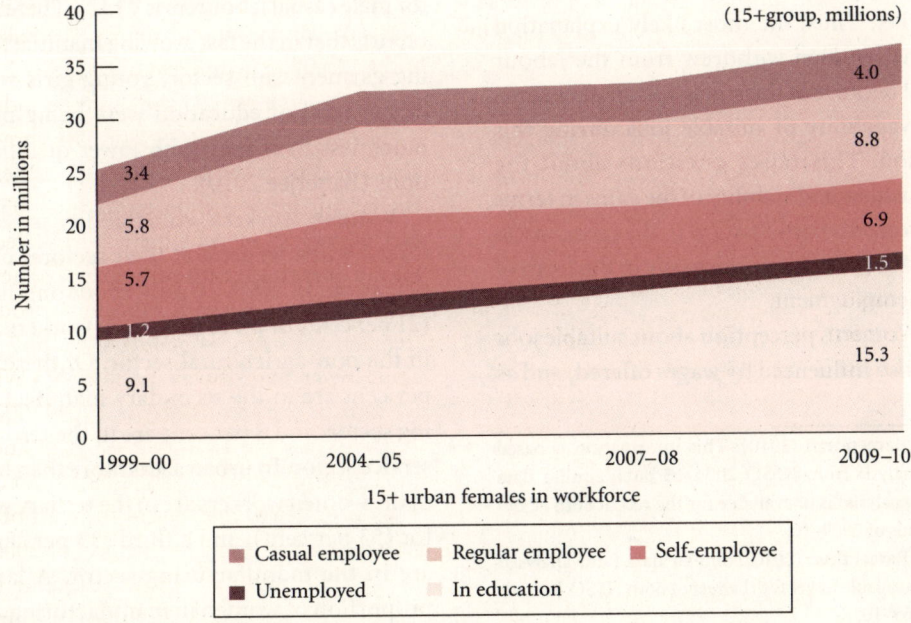

Source: Chandrasekar and Ghosh (2011, Chart 5).

Box 2.2: *Key features of women's self-employment[13] during 1999–2000 to 2004–05[14]*

- In rural areas, 74 per cent of the self-employed women worked as mere helpers in the household enterprises (for urban areas the number is only 27 per cent). Of these, agriculture, forestry and logging accounted for 90 per cent of the total female helpers in household enterprises.
- Women were also economically active as self-employed helpers in cattle breeding, rearing of goats and sheep and raising of silk worms (about 7 per cent).

- A substantial number of 'female helpers' (28 per cent) pursued different activities in paid work as subsidiary workers, for a shorter time period over the year.
- Sectorally, manufacturing accounted for about 32 per cent and retail for 14 per cent of the self-employed helpers.

Source: Raveendran (2010); based on analysis from NSSO 2004–05 data.

---

poor households in a bid to push for higher status voluntarily withdrew women from the labour force because they had sufficient income. Second, women did not find suitable jobs and decided to retreat into homes, that is, the 'dropout effect' (Mazumdar and Sarkar 2008).

It seems highly unlikely that poor households had sufficient incomes so that they could afford to voluntarily withdraw women from the labour market in 2009–10 (timing of NSSO survey)—a period of severe drought, and high food inflation. NREGS reports also show high levels of women's participation whenever work was available; this is contrary to the hypothesis of women's voluntary withdrawal from the labour market. Thus, the most likely explanation is that women withdrew from the labour pool because of their perception of chronic unavailability of suitable jobs during this period. This raises questions about the robustness and viability of the gains in terms of women's participation in the economy in 2004–05 which was primarily in the form of self-employment.

Women's perception about suitable jobs are also influenced by wages offered, and as women casual workers continue to be the least paid of all workers these jobs may not be attractive enough. Women casual workers' wage in 2009–10 was a mere ₹69 in spite of having increased as per NSSO 2009–10 data; this is well below the prescribed minimum wages. And the female to male wage ratio for casual workers in rural areas is 68 per cent. For the MGNREGS public works the wage rates for females were higher (₹87), although still below the prescribed minimum wages. In urban areas while the wage rate for casual women labourers is higher (₹77), but at 58 per cent, the female to male wage ratio in urban areas shows even more disparity than in rural areas (wage rate for male casual labourers is ₹132). There are reports that in the fast growing manufacturing garment sub-sector, young girls with higher level of education were being paid much less than men with lower qualifications (Banerjee 2010).

Women workers' vulnerability is reinforced when we look at their sectoral participation. In 2009–10 only about one-fifth (21 per cent) of the total women workers are in the non-agricultural sector. Of these 13 per cent are in the secondary manufacturing sector, and 8 per cent are in the tertiary service sector. In urban areas more than half of the women workers are in the tertiary sector (53 per cent), and a third (33 per cent) are in the manufacturing sector. A large proportion of women in manufacturing are

---

[13] Raveendran (2010). This information is based on analysis from NSSO 2004–05 data; similar data (and analysis) is unavailable for the recent 66th NSSO Rounds of 2009–10.

[14] Raveendran (2010). Similar data (and analysis) is unavailable as yet for the recent 66th NSSO Rounds of 2009–10.

home-based workers. Even in industries in which women work in significant numbers, less than 10 per cent are in the formal sector of that industry. Two of the three industries with the fastest growth rates for women workers—private households and wearing apparel—are ghettoes of women labour in the informal economy. More than three quarters (78.2 per cent) work in the least productive sectors of the economy, and only a few work in modern industries with significantly high productivity; their numbers there are too low to make a difference (Raveendran 2010).

In sum, paid women workers in the economy get low pay, work in low productivity sectors, suffer poor working conditions, have little job security or social protection, and have no potential for improvement in skills or incomes. Little wonder then that some women workers have moved into sex-work to improve incomes. See Box 2.3.

2.3.2. Youth[17] participation

Indian economy is expected to benefit from the 'demographic dividend'—the increased proportion of young people in the working age population. The share of youth population increased from 16.7 per cent in 1961

Box 2.3: *Entry in sex work: 'Kaam se pet nahin bharta'[15]*

A pan-India survey of sex workers[16] with a sample of 3,000 female and 1,355 male and trans-persons in sex work drawn from 14 states and one union territory was conducted over a period of two years (2009 and 2010). Their findings show that more than half of those surveyed had 'experience of alternative work compared with those with experience of sex work alone; 1,488 females had worked in other labour markets before entering sex work, while 1,158 females entered sex work directly'.

For many females, sex work was not their first category of paid work. Even 'for females who started engaging in sex work in their mid to lateteens, it emerged as an activity much later in their working life'. In the sample, the largest category of prior work was of domestic workers, followed by daily wage earners and those in petty services in formal/informal establishments.

Young girls and women have left their jobs in the informal markets for a variety of economic reasons including 'low pay, insufficient salary, no profit in business, no regular work, seasonal work, not getting money even after work, could not run home

with that income—"*is kaam se pet nahin bharta*"'. The ways in which the economic reasons reinforce each other in the process of decision-making for leaving informal work and entering into sex work are as follows:

- **Working conditions:** Hard physical work and low pay, hard work from morning to evening, had to spend a lot of time earning money as in the case of *bidi/agarbatti*-rolling, had to travel long distances as in the case of wood-cutting or water-fetching, poor income plus not good for health, less rate for crafts combined with eye and body strain in making them.
- **Personal or family-based reasons:** Poor income combined with parents not sending to work after puberty, father/husband taking away all the money.
- **Migration:** Shifted to dancing in Uttar Pradesh and Bihar for more money, migrated along with parents/husband in search of better livelihoods.
- **Harassment:** Poor income coupled with physical/sexual abuse, was asked to make sex for keeping my job.

---

[15] Poor income in informal sector drives majority of sex workers into flesh trade: Survey. Available at http://infochangeindia.org/livelihoods/books-reports/poor-income-in-informal-sector-drives-majority-of-sex-workers-into-flesh-trade-survey.html

[16] The survey was conducted by Rohini Sahni and V. Kalyan Shankar with the assistance of several organizations.

[17] The age group included in the category of youth is between 15 and 24 years of age.

to 20 per cent in 2001, and to 20.5 per cent in 2007–08.[18] Though, for the dividend to accrue, the youth have to seek work and find employment. Jobs have to be generated commensurate to the pace of entry of young (and old) people in the labour market. If not, then, the 'demographic dividend' may turn into a 'demographic nightmare', as the unemployed young become a social and economic burden on the household and the country.

Let us first look at the patterns of youth employment and unemployment in India.[19] A little more than half of the youth workers in 2007–08 were employed in the agriculture sector (54.4 per cent). The other sectors which employ youth in a significant proportion were manufacturing (15 per cent), wholesale (10.8 per cent), construction (7.2 per cent) and community services (5.1 per cent). The share of computer-related services, a major component of the highly publicized information technology (IT) sector brimming with youth, to total employment is less than half a per cent (0.18) and the percentage of young workers in it is almost half of those in the 25 to 34 age group.

Urban and rural youth and male and female youth employment patterns show significant differences on several fronts. Rural youth in 2007–08, were employed in far greater proportion (38.6 per cent versus 21 per cent urban youth) as casual labour, with the least proportion in regular salaried work (7.6 per cent versus 43.5 per cent urban youth). More than half the rural youth were self-employed (53.8 per cent versus 35.5 urban youth).

When we examine unemployment patterns we find that youth have the highest unemployment rate (usual status measure) and in this demographic the age cohort 20 to 24 years has a higher unemployment level (see Figure 2.14) (Mitra 2008).

The work force participation rate (WFPR) and the LFPR declined for the below 30 age group over the 1983 to 2007–08 period. This can be seen in rural and urban areas as well as among males and females (ibid.). In 2004–05, a total of 107.3 million youth were in the workforce and of these 8.6 million were unemployed. Disturbingly, this is about 8 per cent of the youth workforce and 64.1 per cent of the total unemployed

Figure 2.14:   Unemployment rate in India by age group, 1983 to 2007–08

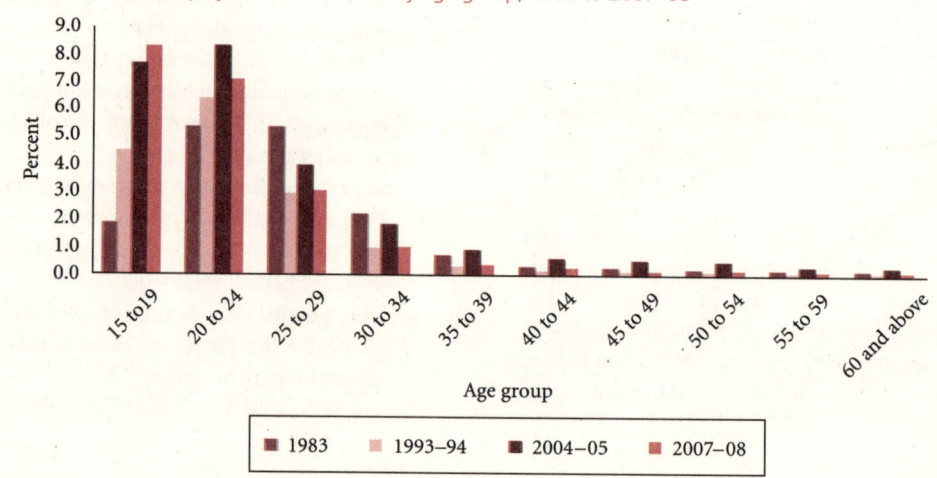

Source: Mahendra and Venkatnarayana (2011, p. 9).
Note: Usual status.

[18] The entire discussion draws heavily from Dev and Venkatnarayana (2011). It covers the period from 1983 to 2004–05 unless mentioned otherwise.

[19] Ibid., pp. 15–16, Table 4.4.

(13.4 million of all age groups). The unemployment rate of literates is significantly higher (9.9 per cent) than that of illiterates (2.2 per cent) and it is the astoundingly high among young graduates (35.5 per cent). See Box 2.4 for key features of youth employment.

The work participation rate[20] of employed youth (as a percentage of the total population) has been reducing for the past two decades, and there has been a greater decline for the male youth (11.4 percentage points).[21] Indeed, between 2004–05 and 2009–10, the labour force aged 24 and under actually contracted by one-fifth, from 89 million to 74 million (NSSO 2011, quoted in Anant and Mehta 2011).

As with the decline in female labour force participation, a large part of the decrease can be attributed to youth staying in school for a longer period, as well as children who would have been working in an earlier time, now go to school. One-third of the youth population was enrolled in educational institutions in 2007–08, the highest ever. The latest NSSO data shows the continuation of this trend. There has been around 50 per cent increase in those enrolled in education, among rural youth compared to 2004–05. In absolute numbers it means, that, nearly 20 million more young people (above 15 years of age) are pursuing education as their principal activity (see Figure 2.15). The biggest increases are in the younger cohort (15 to 19 years) who are probably staying in school for secondary and higher secondary education. But surprisingly, there are also substantial increases in the older cohort (20 to 24 years). This suggests that they are enrolled in different forms of tertiary education in the hope of improving job prospects. Rural and urban youth together constituted an increase of nearly 30 million in the number of young people availing educational opportunities in the hope of accessing better jobs.[22]

What are the implications of such a sharp increase in the number of school-and college-goers? These are nicely summed up in the *Economic & Political Weekly* leader article on the topic:

Box 2.4: *Key features of youth employment*

- Only 4.9 per cent of young workers had post-secondary level education in 2007–08.
- The share of young workers' employment in regular salaried/wage employment increased over time.
- The share of agriculture employment declined faster for young workers than for adult workers as a whole.
- Unlike the adults, the share of industrial sector employment is higher than services for the employed youth.
- Half of the youth workers are self-employed and a little more than one-third are casual labourers.

- Job situation of the rural youth is more uncertain and they are lower paid.
- Unemployed youth make up 64.1 per cent of the total unemployed although their proportion in the total workers is 21 per cent.
- Unemployment among youth (8 per cent) is twice that of adults (for usual status).
- Unemployment levels increase with literacy and are highest for graduates (35.5 per cent).

Source: Dev and Venkatnarayana (2011, pp. 15–16, Table 4.4).

---

[20] Work participation rate (WPR) is defined as all those in productive work (excluding those available for work, i.e., unemployed).

[21] Dev and Venkatnarayana (2011). It covers the period from 1983 to 2004–05 unless otherwise specified.

[22] The discussion and chart is based heavily on Chandrasekar and Ghosh (2011).

Figure 2.15: Increase In education between 2004–05 and 2009–10

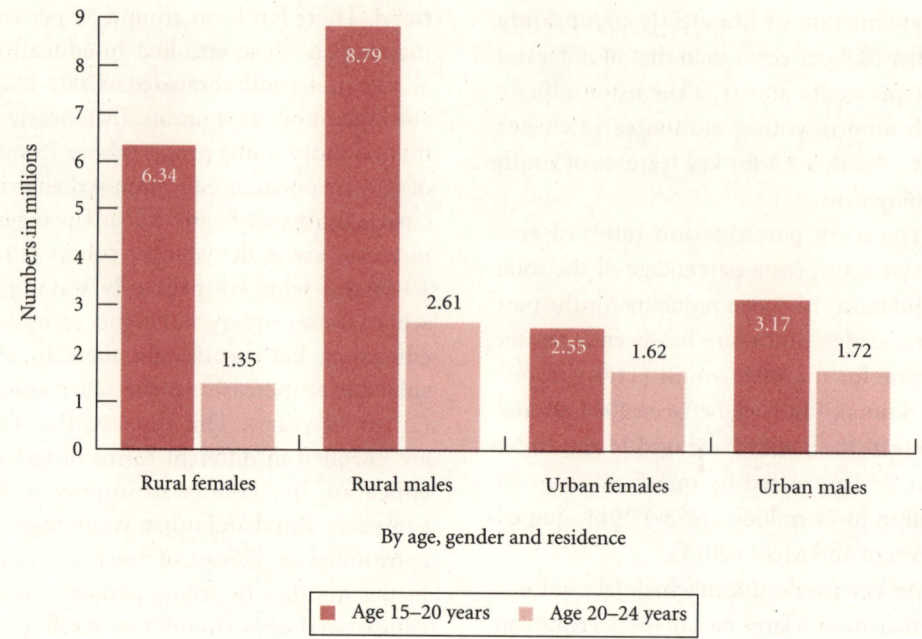

Source: Chandrasekar and Ghosh (2011, Chart 7).

The very fact that retention in education reduced labour force growth sharply between 2004–05 and 2009–10 points to a much larger increase in labour force in the next five years. Of course, this more educated labour force will also be more productive if employed, but ensuring that this does happen will require that the Twelfth Plan has a much clearer employment focus, beyond NREGA, than the Eleventh Plan did. (*Economic & Political Weekly* 2011)

However, greater numbers of youth in education does not by itself explain the extent of reduced youth workforce participation. The possibility that the young pull out of the job market because they fail to find jobs which suit them, must be seriously considered. The International Labour Organization (ILO) has coined the term 'jobless youth' to describe this new category of young people which includes not only those termed 'unemployed' by the NSSO definition,[23] but also those who are

neither attending school nor employed. In effect, what we are seeing is the discouraged dropout effect among the youth.

The creation of this new category of 'jobless youth' gives a clearer picture of the real situation for young workers. The ILO report on youth (International Labour Orgnization 2010, p. 6) argues that youth unemployment (due to discouraged dropout effect, or work under inadequate conditions)

…incur costs to the economy, society and to the individual, and the family. A lack of decent work if experienced at an early age threatens to compromise a person's future employment prospects, and frequently leads to unsuitable labour behaviour patterns that last a lifetime. … An inability to find employment creates a sense of uselessness and idleness among young people that can lead to increased crime, mental health problems, violence, conflicts, and drug taking.

Unemployed youth are an economic burden on their family; they do not augment the family's earnings; instead, families have to spend scarce resources on them. At the macroeconomic level unemployed do not contribute to the growth of the economy, do not give a return on investment made

[23] The NSSO definition of 'unemployed' (by the broadest 'usual status' category) is, after all, extremely limited, excluding even those who have a bare minimum of 30 days' work in a subsidiary activity over a year. See World Bank (2010, pp. 20, Figure 1.1).

on their education, instead governments have to spend more on crime and drug use prevention, on welfare and on social protection.

When this definition of joblessness is used in the Indian context, we see that in 2007–08, a quarter of the youth population—27.4 per cent—was 'jobless' (see Table 2.4; Dev and Venkatnarayana 2011, p. 19). Joblessness was distinctly higher among illiterates as compared to literates (38.7 per cent versus 22.8 per cent).

This is the reverse of the unemployment rate; unemployment rate was higher for literates—9.9 per cent versus 2.2 per cent for illiterates (see Table 4.7; Dev and Venkatnarayana 2011, p. 17).

The incidence of joblessness clearly shows the huge impact of the discouraged dropout effect on workforce participation. Joblessness was highest among those who had post-secondary level education (32.2 per cent) giving credence to the common sense understanding that those with some education are worse off as education makes them 'unfit' for the casual labour in agriculture and there are no jobs for them elsewhere. It puts them in the analogous situation of '*dhobi ka kutta na ghar ka na ghat ka*'.[24]

Table 2.4: Joblessness of youth in India by literacy status and educational levels, 1983 to 2007–08

Educational level	1983			1993–94			2004–05			2007–08		
	All	Rural	Urban	All	Rural	Urban	All	Rural	Urban	All	Rural	Urban
1	2	3	4	5	6	7	8	9	10	11	12	13
All	41.8	44.5	29.7	27.5	26.4	30.6	25.9	25.6	26.8	27.4	21.5	27.2
Not Literates	56.9	60.4	33.6	35.9	33.9	49.6	38.7	37.3	47.5	45.4	44.0	53.4
Literates	19.8	17.4	26.6	23.6	21.7	27.1	22.8	21.9	24.6	24.3	24.0	25.0
No Formal Schooling	–	–	–	–	–	–	–	–	–	45.2	43.8	52.6
Below Primary	13.5	12.0	26.8	29.5	27.2	37.7	30.1	28.8	36.3	35.6	35.0	38.5
Primary	20.8	18.1	29.1	27.5	24.3	37.1	26.4	24.9	31.6	31.1	29.6	37.5
Middle	21.8	20.1	24.0	21.3	18.8	26.9	21.4	19.3	26.7	22.8	21.3	27.0
Secondary	23.1	22.1	24.4	19.2	18.7	19.8	17.9	18.2	17.5	18.6	18.8	18.2
Post-Secondary	24.3	20.2	37.4	35.0	33.5	35.8	32.2	30.2	33.4	29.1	31.2	27.8

Source: Computed using NSS Employment and Unemployment Survey unit record data.
Note: 1. Figures presented are in percentages; 2. Usual status (including principal and suLisidiaiy); 3. *Youth* mean 15 to 24 year age group; 4. Secondary includes higher secondary below graduation.

Table 2.5: Unemployment rate of youth labour force in India by literacy status and educational levels, 1983 to 2007–08

Educational level	1983			1993–94			2004–05			2007–08		
	US	CWS	CDS	US	CWS	CDS	US	CWS	CDS	US	CWS	CDS
1	2	3	4	5	6	7	8	9	10	11	12	13
All	5.3	9.1	14.8	5.6	8.2	11.8	13.7	8.0	10.0	7.6	10.1	14.1
Illiterate	0.9	4.2	9.9	0.8	3.2	6.8	9.3	2.2	4.7	1.4	4.4	8.9
Literates	9.8	13.6	16.3	8.6	11.3	14.7	17.6	9.9	11.6	8.9	11.2	15.1
Below Primary	2.9	6.1	11.9	1.9	3.8	8.1	11.4	3.7	6.0	3.6	6.6	12.1
Primary	4.9	8.2	12.0	3.3	5.8	9.5	12.8	4.7	6.6	4.6	6.9	11.6
Middle	11.3	15.3	13.8	7.1	9.7	13.0	19.1	7.2	9.1	6.9	9.0	12.9
Secondary	21.0	26.1	21.4	16.0	19.2	21.9	28.2	16.9	17.8	12.6	15.0	18.1
Post-Secondary	30.2	35.2	38.1	36.0	40.3	41.7	35.2	35.5	36.2	27.2	28.2	29.1

Source: Computed using National Sample Survey unit record data.
Note: 1. Figures presented are percentages; 2. This table represents those who are employed or working; 3. *Youth* mean 15 to 24 years age group, 4. Secondary includes higher secondary below graduation; 5, Rural-urban and male-female combined; 6. *US*—Usual status (including principal and subsidiary), *CWS*— Current Weekly Status, *CDS*—Current Daily status.

---

[24] Translated it means that the washerman's dog neither belongs/has a home at the washerman's house nor does he belong/have a home in the washerman's workplace, the area adjoining the canals.

There are a disproportionately larger number of jobless youth, young workers as well as non-student youth in the poorer households. Additionally, the unemployment rate is lower for poorer households than for households which are better off. This information, in conjunction with the data on education and literacy, strongly suggests that illiteracy, lower level of education, high levels of youth workforce participation and joblessness go hand in hand. It suggests that uneducated youth—employed, unemployed and jobless—from the poorer households are in a highly vulnerable livelihood situation, and need urgent attention from policy-makers. See Figure 2.16 for distribution of vulnerable youth across employment status.

A key finding of NSSO 66th Round, that has emerged so far, is the reduction in the growth of the labour force. It turns out, this decrease is largely because a significant number of women and youth opt, or stay out of work.

Women's withdrawal, or lack of participation in the labour force remains largely unexplained except in gendered social–cultural terms of customs and as demands of 'household work'. The challenge is to get a better understanding of conditions under which women participate in the labour force, to ensure compliance with both—no discrimination and equality in wages—and to include women's unpaid productive activities for household consumption as 'work' within official statistics.

Among the youth, the underlying reasons for reduced labour force participation seem twofold, education and 'jobless youth'. The huge challenge ahead for policy and promoters here is in enabling the 'jobless' to get training for jobs they aspire to, ensuring that education and training translate to employability, and last but not least, creation of jobs for the huge numbers who will enter the workforce.

2.4. Global slowdown, inflation and informal economy

India escaped the ravages of the global slowdown relatively unscathed. Yes, the economy did show a slowdown from late 2008, but the brunt of the crisis was borne by specific exporting sectors (units), whose output recovered relatively quickly.

Figure 2.16: Vulnerable youth population

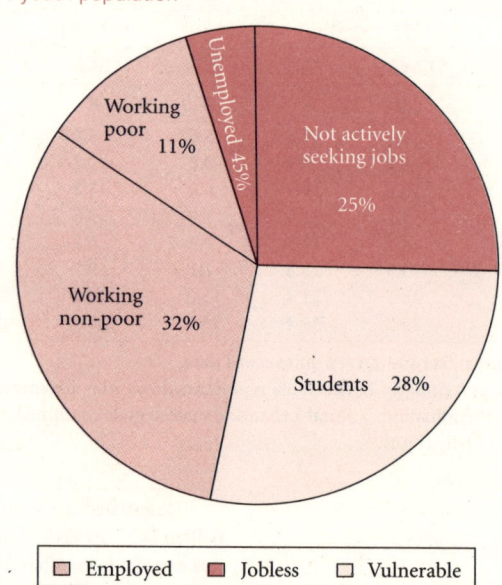

Employed   Jobless   Vulnerable

Source: Dev and Venkatnaryana (2011, p. 22).

Early expert predictions were that the informal economy, except for a few sectors, would not be much impacted by the global slowdown. Some economists even went so far as to predict that the informal economy would serve as a 'cushion' to those who had suffered losses in the formal sector. But microeconomic studies show the inaccuracy of these predictions.

Sinha (2010) reports that while the impact on the informal economy has not been uniform across the sectors, a few overall trends can be discerned: First, of the job losses, a large number were in the informal and casual segments of the formal sector, including a disproportionate number of migrant and women workers. Second, for certain category of self-employed workers, such as home-based workers, street vendors and waste workers, the impact has been shrinking markets, and decreasing incomes due to reduction in work orders, lower demands and falling prices for their products. Third, there has been a growth in the informal economy as many laid off from the formal sector have joined its ranks; this has led to overcrowding in the highly competitive informal market. Also, in certain sectors, such as traditional handicrafts, women were left with the responsibility of management of units as men left in search of alternative work (Banerjee 2010).

Inflation added to the woes of the working poor. Inflation, which refers to the change in prices, is officially measured in India through changes in the Wholesale Price Index (WPI).[25] WPI is the index that is used to measure the change in the average price level of goods traded in the wholesale market, and it is used as a measure of inflation at the macroeconomic level. For measuring inflation at the consumer level, an alternative measure, the Consumer Price Index (CPI) is used. CPI measures changes over time in general level of prices of goods and services that households acquire for the purpose of consumption. Rise in prices paid by the common person is reflected by the CPI.[26]

Inflation first kicked in, in the form of increased prices of food items, beginning in early 2008. The CPI shows an increase for two consecutive Financial Years (FYs)—2008–09 and 2009–10; it was at its highest of 16.22 per cent in January 2010, indicating a period of high price rise. It began a downward trend from April 2010 but continued to be above 9 per cent in the quarter ending June 2011 (see Table 2.6). The moderation in CPI in terms of prices at retail level merely meant a decrease in the rate of growth of the price rise; not a reduction in prices per se.

The WPI for 2009–10 was 3.8 per cent although average CPI[27] inflation during the

Table 2.6: Inflation rate chart (in per cent)

Year	Jan.	Feb.	Mar.	Apr.	May	June	July	Aug.	Sept.	Oct.	Nov.	Dec.
2011	9.35	9.54	9.68	9.70	9.06	9.44						
2010	16.22	14.86	14.86	13.33	13.91	13.73	11.25	9.88	9.82	9.70	8.33	9.47
2009	10.45	9.63	8.03	8.70	8.63	9.29	11.89	11.72	11.64	11.49	13.51	14.97
2008	5.51	5.47	7.87	7.81	7.75	7.69	8.33	9.02	9.77	10.45	10.45	9.70

Source: Reserve Bank of India (2011, p. 27).

[25] In India, a total of 676 commodities' data on price level is tracked through WPI. The index has two components—weights assigned for commodities and the price data collected at regular intervals.

[26] Consumer Price Index (CPI) in India is a measure of inflation that comprises multiple series classified based on different economic groups. There are four series, viz. the CPI Urban Non-Manual Employee (CPI-UNME), CPI Agricultural Labourer (CPI-AL), CPI Rural Labourer (CPI-RL) and CPI Industrial Worker (CPI-IW). While the CPI-UNME series is published by the Central Statistical Organisation (CSO), the others are published by the Department of Labour. The weights in the combined CPI (rural + urban) for the four major groups of commodities are as follows: food, beverages and tobacco—49.71 per cent; fuel and light—9.49 per cent; housing—9.77 per cent and miscellaneous (which includes items such as education, medical care, transport and communication)—26.31 per cent.

[27] CPI is used here interchangeably with CPI-IW which is the Consumer Price Index for Industrial Workers.

2009–10 was 14.86 per cent. In mid-2010, the government under pressure from global commodity prices of fuel passed on the hikes in fuel to the consumers. Soon, inflation spread to goods other than food items. In January 2011 WPI inflation overtook CPI inflation, for the first time in almost two years, since April 2009. In the first four months of 2011, the average CPI-IW inflation was 9 per cent while WPI was higher at 9.33 per cent and for 2010–11 the WPI climbed to 9.52 per cent. This increased WPI is a clear indication of the inflation shifting from primary articles to manufactured goods; contribution of food items to overall inflation declined as inflation became more generalized (see Figure 2.17).

As a result of the rise in generalized inflation, input costs have increased for the self-employed in non-farm sector. Several workers in the service sectors such as trade and restaurants have had to face declining demand, either as a reduction in their customer base, or volumes of sale or due to both. They are unable to increase prices to maintain profit margins because beyond a certain point increase in prices is counterproductive as the purchasing power of their clientele itself is limited. Competition from new entrants persists in many of the locales and sectors, and fluctuating prices impact input prices and market returns (Sinha 2010).

The recent study by the Women in Informal Employment: Globalizing and Organizing (WIEGO) (Horn 2011) in India, on the impact on the lives of home-based garment workers in Ahmedabad, and the waste pickers in Ahmedabad and Pune reinforces these general observations. Both sets of respondents experienced a decline in incomes. Waste pickers struggled with reduced volumes of recyclable wastes at their usual collection sites, and lower prices for their waste material. Home-based garment workers reported no significant increase in demand, a slight decline in contracts and shorter working hours per day although there was no decrease in the number of working days per week. The study underscores the lag in the recovery of the informal economy.

The increase in core inflation, coupled with the decrease in income and earnings has inevitably led to an impact on consumption and expenditure at the household level.

2.4.1. Impact at the household level

In the immediate aftermath of the crisis in late 2008, many families resorted to a reduction in the quantity and quality of food consumed. A study on waste collectors' household found that 80 per cent had reduced consumption on 'luxury foods', such as, milk, meat and fruit, and 41 per cent had stopped buying milk completely

Figure 2.17: Changing weighted contributions to increase in WPI

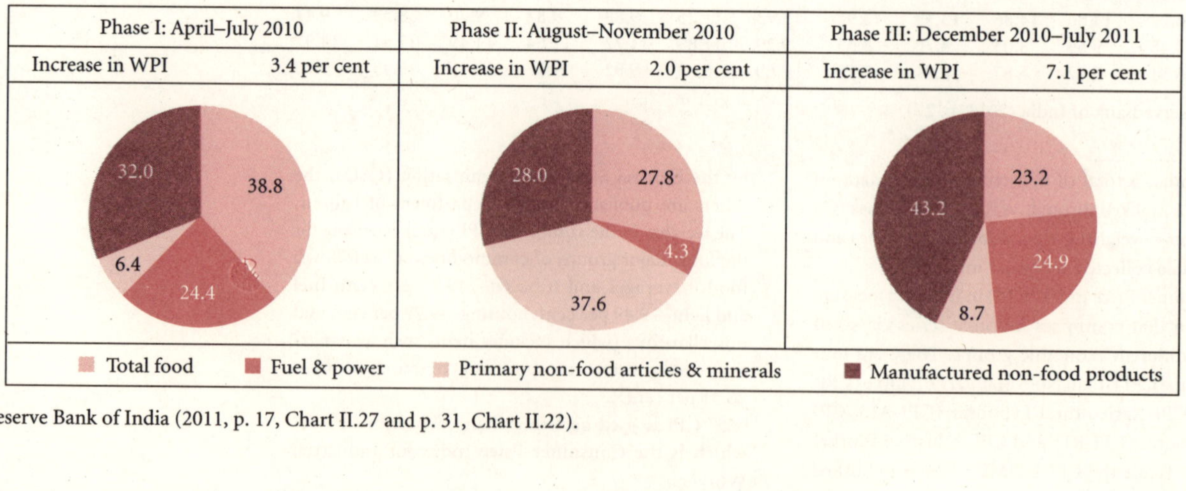

Phase I: April–July 2010		Phase II: August–November 2010		Phase III: December 2010–July 2011	
Increase in WPI	3.4 per cent	Increase in WPI	2.0 per cent	Increase in WPI	7.1 per cent

Legend: ■ Total food ■ Fuel & power ■ Primary non-food articles & minerals ■ Manufactured non-food products

Source: Reserve Bank of India (2011, p. 17, Chart II.27 and p. 31, Chart II.22).

(Chintan 2009 cited in Horn 2011). A worker laid off from a diamond factory in Surat captures the essence of the coping strategy at the household level (Kapoor 2009):

> In the earlier months we stopped consuming milk, it is our biggest luxury and we indulged in it uninhibitedly. We also stopped going out to eat, we used to every Sunday earlier. We don't eat meat or consume alcohol [ever] but the quality of food deteriorated just a little. I thought it was better to make these sacrifices instead of pulling my children out of school. If they keep going to school, at least they will have more of a chance at a better life. [Italics in the original]

In the Surat diamond industry, the rate of reverse migration was as high as 60 per cent. Some migrants from Delhi also chose to return home and take up work under NREGA on a temporary basis to tide over the crisis. Others who made a decision to stay shifted occupations—they became petty shop owners, vendors, rickshaw pullers and so on. A few experienced positive outcomes, as in Surat where one young diamond worker availed the skill upgradation programme that was offered as a special measure for the unemployed workers of the diamond factories, and as a result improved his prospects in the industry.

The uneven recovery, increasing food inflation and increased fuel prices have meant that families are adopting such coping strategies—to combat the short-term pressures—which would be harmful in the long term. An increasing number have even begun to withdraw children from school and put them to work. A home-based worker in Ahmedabad noted, 'I am a widow. My youngest daughter was studying in fourth standard but with the crisis I had to stop her schooling. Now she works as kitchen helper earning ₹5 a day' (Horn 2011). And households continue to reduce food consumption, further aggravating the already high levels of hunger and malnutrition. The next two sections examine the consequences of such strategies.

2.5. Food inflation and hunger

India had weathered the food crises that had affected the world in 2007–08 remarkably well. But in the fourth quarter of 2008, food inflation started to increase. Food inflation (primary and manufactured) went up from 10.14 per cent in April 2009 to 16.78 in March 2010, led by milk (17.64 per cent) and cereal (10.74 per cent). Food inflation was in double digits for 76 weeks from 5 June 2009. In December 2009, fuelled by India's worst monsoon in the past 25 years, the overall food inflation surged to a high of 22.6 per cent; primary food inflation at the time was 20 per cent, the highest since November 1999, and inflation of manufactured food was 26.7 per cent.

Rising food prices have disproportionate negative consequences for the poor because they spend a large share of their total expenditure on food; and a higher number of poor households are net buyers of staple food rather than net sellers. The differential impact of food prices on households in different classes is evident from the consumption expenditures (Dev 2010). As per the NSSO 2009–10, the share of food in total household expenditure was 57 per cent and 44 per cent in rural and urban India respectively. In rural India, this share in respect of the bottom 10 per cent of the population was 65 per cent, and 46 per cent for the top 10 per cent of the population. In urban India, the share of food was 62 per cent for its bottom 10 per cent population and 31 per cent for the top 10 per cent population.

The impact of food inflation on the poor is even higher than the one recorded by the CPI (see Box 2.5).[28] The reasons are twofold: First, the proportion of their income spent on food items is close to 60 per cent, which is more than the index weight for food at

---

[28] See n26 for details on CPI.

Box 2.5: *Food inflation: Greater impact on the poor*

A recent study in India, examined the impact of food inflation from 2005–07 across the high, medium and low categories of households. In 2006–07, while higher income households experienced food inflation at 4 per cent, the lower income household experienced it at 11.5 per cent. This period coincided with the times when the prices of essential items of the food basket (comprising of cereals, breads, oil and fat, and condiments and spices) increased at a faster rate than the price of discretionary food items (such as pulse, meat, fish, and egg; milk and milk products; fruits and vegetables). The food inflation impact was experienced the most by the lower income households.

Source: Munjal (2010).

46.2 per cent in CPI. Second, in times of higher food prices, the poor pay a higher price per unit of cost for a food item because they tend to buy even smaller quantities of food spread over a longer purchase period than at other times.

The percentage of contribution of food items to the overall inflation has varied over FY 2009–10 and FY 2010–11 (see Figure 2.18). Food inflation was the largest component of inflation for the entire FY 2009–10. Although the proportion of food inflation in total inflation decreased over 2010–11, it continued to remain high. It is only since February 2011 that food inflation has moderated. In March 2011 food inflation had decreased to 8.28 per cent, but this decrease was hardly reflected in reduced prices at the retail level. Food inflation is estimated to have pushed a great number of persons into poverty.

Figure 2.18: Contribution to overall inflation: Major groups

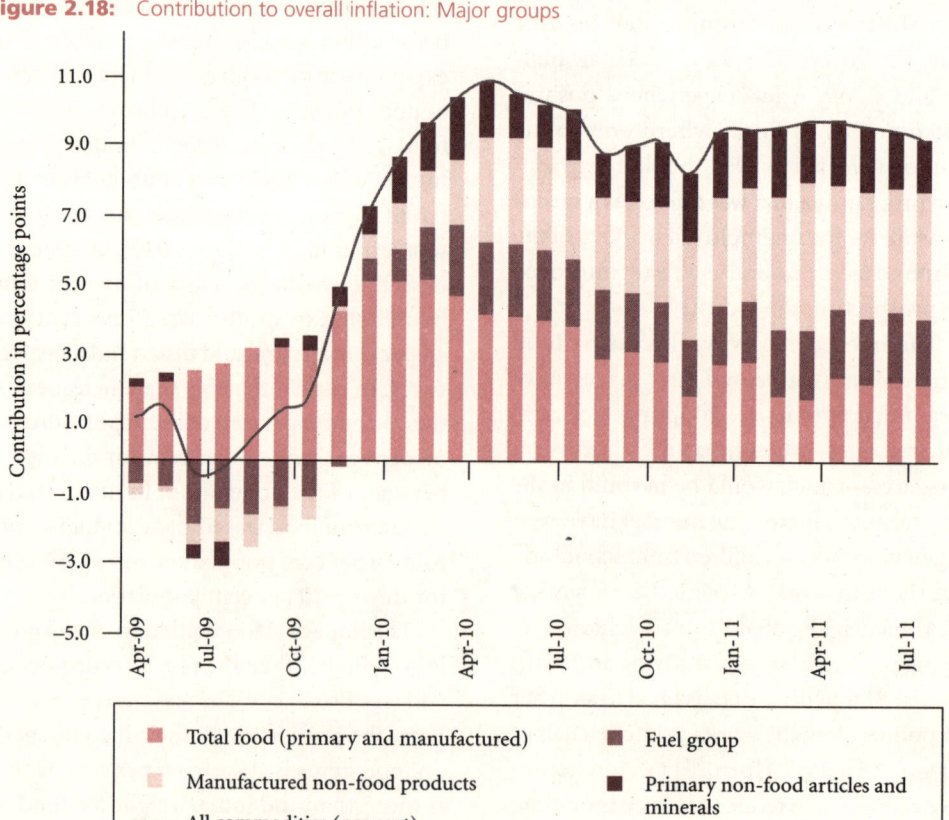

Total food (primary and manufactured)
Manufactured non-food products
— All commodities (per cent)
Fuel group
Primary non-food articles and minerals

Source: Reserve Bank of India (2011, p. 17, Chart II.27 and p. 31, Chart II.22).

A study by the World Bank estimated the poverty impact of food price increase between June and December 2010 in 28 low- and middle-income countries including India.[29] India showed a net increase of 0.77 percentage points in those under poverty at the US$ 1.25 per day level. As per the estimates of a recent Asian Development Bank (ADB) report,[30] in India, a 10 per cent increase in food price would add 22.82 million, an increase of 20 per cent would add 45.64 million and a 30 per cent increase would add 68.45 million to the number of rural poor. For urban India the corresponding figures would be 6.68 million for a 10 per cent increase in inflation, 13.36 million for a 20 per cent increase in inflation and 20.04 million for a 30 per cent increase in inflation.

The increase in prices of a few daily food items over a 36-month period, from January 2008 to December[31] 2010, given in Box 2.6, brings home the impact of inflation at the household level.

The increase in the prices of food items that are staples in the diet of Indian household (as noted in the box) has undoubtedly lead the poor to adopt the age-old coping strategy of reducing food consumption. This is especially so as, in more recent times, many of the non-food items in the food basket, such as, transport, education and health have become essential. Micro-level observations (see Box 2.7) show that discretionary items, such as, milk, milk products, eggs and meats were the first to be cut. Nutritious, but expensive staples had been substituted by high-calorie, non-nutritious foods. The next step was to decrease the total amount of food purchased. Box 2.7 shows the changes in food habits induced by inflation among a group of migrant workers.

Box 2.6: *Price increase from January 2008 to December 2010 in select daily food items (for which regular recorded data was available)*

- The price per kilo of the 'fair average' quality of rice has risen by an average of 42 per cent in 33 cities and towns.
- The average price rise for a kilo of *tur dal* is 46 per cent for 32 cities.
- Wheat prices increased by 30 per cent over three years in 10 of the 27 cities and towns.
- There was an average price increase of 10 per cent, 9 per cent, and 10 per cent in the three cooking mediums—groundnut oil, mustard oil and *vanaspati*—respectively, in the 37 urban centres.
- The average price increase for a kilo of sugar for the 32 cities and towns is 102 per cent; the range of increase was between 76 per cent and 125 per cent.

- The average increase in the price of milk was 37 per cent for 25 out of the 26 towns and cities (one city recorded a drop).
- The average increase for 100 grams of loose tea leaf is 38 per cent for 25 urban centres with regular price data.
- The average increase in price of onions for 29 cities is 197.5 per cent.
- The average increase for a kilo of potatoes was 39.5 per cent—this is the 36 month average increase recorded by 27 urban centres.

Source: Author's resources research: Food Inflation Crippled India's Households in 2010.

---

[29] Ivanic et al. (2011). The study factored in the differential and significant impact of food inflation on the poor in its estimations.

[30] Global Food Price Inflation and Developing Asia, ADB, March 2011. These estimations were arrived at by using the Oxford Economic Global Model.

[31] This data was sourced from Resources Research: Food Inflation Crippled India's Households in 2010. The primary source of the data is the monitoring cell of the Department of Consumer Affairs, Ministry of Consumer Affairs, Food and Public Distribution; it records the retail and wholesale prices of essential commodities in 37 cities and towns in India.

Box 2.7:   *Inflation impact on food consumption*

Sixty-five-year-old migrant brick kiln worker has stopped buying onions and garlic, key food staples for Indian families, and manages to save just 1,000 rupees ($22) per month to send his family of five back home. 'We have stopped having tea at work, and we add only red chilli to our vegetables as even oil has become too costly', said Nath, who hails from northern Uttar Pradesh state but has worked for 15 years in brick kilns in neighbouring Uttarakhand state. Five of his fellow workers whose 12-hour shifts heating bricks at the kiln earn them 150 rupees ($3) per day seconded the remark, with one jokingly adding that even 'donkeys would faint' near them as they couldn't afford to buy soap anymore. 'We are earning more now, but our living condition has actually gone down because everything costs so much more', said Shiv Kumar, who gets 220 rupees ($5) for every 1,000 bricks he molds, an increase of 20 rupees compared to two years ago.

Source: Lalmalsawma (2011).

That such coping strategies have contributed to the endemic hunger and malnutrition in India is widely accepted. The figures though vary as the measurement process is extremely sensitive to minimal changes in definition and methodology. The percentage ranges from a little above 20 per cent to as high as 60 per cent. The Food and Agriculture Organization (FAO) put the number of food insecure in India at 237.7 million; this was before the recent food inflation set in.[32] The M.S. Swaminathan Research Foundation (MSSRF) team of researchers who examined food insecurity in urban India contends that the multidimensional concept of food insecurity includes three broad dimensions—food availability, food access and food absorption. Thus, they developed a composite index based on indicators of each dimension to measure this multidimensionality.[33] Their findings for urban India suggest that smaller towns are significantly worse off than large cities and metropolitan areas with regard to the status of food security. At the all-India level there are improvements in some components of the index, such as, improved access to toilets, proportion of female workers having regular employment and percentage of underweight children. But some critical indicators such as the percentage of women and children suffering from anaemia show deterioration in 14 out of the 15 states. The percentage of urban children wasting has also worsened; it has increased in 12 states. Most importantly, the report emphasizes that many of the nutritional outcome indicators[34] 'suggest a high level of (food) insecurity'. This is not surprising given the levels and pattern of food intake.

The key facts of India's food intake are given below:

- Per capita food availability dropped from 480 g in 1994 to 440 g in 2006 (Saxena 2009).
- The cereal intake of economically poor has decreased from 12 kg per month in 1993 to 11.3 kg per month in 2005 (ibid.).
- The drop in per capita cereal intake in rural areas has not been substituted with an alternative source resulting in a decline in per capita calorie consumption (ibid.).
- Per capita calorie intake, as well as per capita protein intake in India has

---

[32] FAO 2009.

[33] These in turn are determined by elements such as extent and nature of employment opportunities available, accessibility to basic amenities, level and pattern of food consumption and nutritional status.

[34] The nutritional outcome indicators include the following: percentage of ever married women (14–59 years) with any anaemia; percentage of ever married (14–59 years) with chronic energy deficiency (CED); percentage of any children (6–35 months) with any anaemia; percentage of any children (6–35 months) who are stunted; percentage of any children (6–35 months) who are underweight for their age and percentage of any children (6–35 months) who are wasting.

systematically declined over the decade up to 2004–05.[35]

- The proportion of food in total consumer expenditure has fallen from 73 per cent in 1972–73 to 55 per cent in 2004–05 in rural areas, and from 64 per cent to 55 per cent in urban areas (Saxena 2009).
- In urban India, there has been a decline in average consumption of cereals, pulses, meat and sugar by an average urban consumer in the country as a whole in 2004–05 as compared to 1999–2000; this has resulted in lower levels of consumption than the recommended dietary allowance (RDA) (MSSRF 2010).

The consequences of the acute levels of food insecurity are reflected in the basic health indicators for adults and children. Some of these are given below:

- More than one in three Indian adults have been consistently underweight over the last decade (2000–10) (ibid.).
- More than one-third Indian women suffer from CED (having a Body Mass Index [BMI] of less than 18.5).[36]
- 56.6 per cent ever-married women in the age group of 15 to 49 were anaemic in 2005–06 (ibid.).
- 57.9 per cent pregnant women in the age group of 15 to 49 were anaemic in 2005–06.[37]
- Of the children in the age group of 0 to 3, 78.9 per cent are anaemic, 44.9 per cent are stunted, 40.4 per cent are underweight and 22.9 per cent are wasted (ibid.).
- Infant mortality rate (children under age of 1) is 50.[38]
- Child mortality rate (children under age of 5) is 66.[39]

- Forty-six per cent children in India are malnourished (UNICEF 2011).
- Wasting and stunting rates in children reflecting acute and chronic nutrition deficiencies are 48 per cent and 20 per cent, respectively.[40]

The government's nutritional intervention programmes, Integrated Child Development Sevices (ICDS) and Mid Day Meal (MDM) Scheme have targeted infants and pregnant women, and its safety net programme, Targeted Public Distribution System (TPDS), has the objective of mitigating hunger and malnutrition. But these programmes are plagued by leakages and inefficiencies, and have not been able to address the hunger and malnutrition in the population although they have been in place for several decades.

During the current crisis of high food inflation, and generalized inflation, except for some sporadic measures at price control, the government did not take any additional steps to address the expected decline in food consumption by the poor. No less a person than the Chief Economic Advisor to the GOI, Professor Kaushik Basu, has stated, 'In the case of recent Indian experience (second half of 2009), it is both true that food inflation is high and our foodgrain management leaves a lot to be desired' (Basu 2010, p. 10).

The government relied on a strategy of broad-based economic growth which was expected to raise incomes and reduce the vulnerability of households to sudden changes in food prices and mitigate periods of shock.

Let us examine the evidence from the various states to assess the success of such strategies which are based on economic growth. States with domestic product per capita greater than ₹25,000 in 2004–05 such as Tamil Nadu, Gujarat, Maharashtra and Haryana have a Hunger Index (HI) greater

[35] Deaton and Dreze (2008) cited in Saxena (2009).

[36] National Family Health Survey (NFHS-3) India 2005–06. International Institute of Population Sciences, Mumbai, India.

[37] Ibid.

[38] UNICEF 2009. Available at http://www.unicef.org/infobycountry/india_statistics.html

[39] Ibid.

[40] National Family Health Survey (NFHS-3) India 2005–06. International Institute of Population Sciences, Mumbai, India.

than 20. Even Andhra Pradesh and Haryana, states whose percentage annual real growth in per capita net state domestic product (PCNSDP) was greater than 5, between 1999–2000 and 2004–05, have an HI close to 20. Karnataka and Tamil Nadu, with annual real growth rate in PCNSDP hovering at 4, have a HI greater than 20—putting them in the 'alarming' category. Thus, we clearly see a co-existence between the state of high growth in the economy and high hunger and malnutrition.

The negative consequences of the current food inflation are reflected in the recent data on hunger.

- FAO estimates that 21 per cent of the total population was undernourished in 2009.
- The Global Hunger Index[41] for India in 2010 was 24.1, higher than it was in 2010 (23.31).
- UNICEF ROSA (2009) states that there were 20 million additional hungry people due to the 2008–09 food price crisis.
- In the 2010 Millennium Development Goals (MDGs) Progress Report, for MDG 1-hunger target, India was classified in the group of countries showing 'no progress or deterioration'.

That such food insecurity and hunger occurs in a period of robust growth, even in the wake of an economic crisis, once again provides distinctive proof that growth by itself will not take care of malnutrition, or food insecurity. Food insecurity and hunger will continue to have irrevocably harmful consequences for the health and livelihoods. The next section devotes attention to issues of health and its implications for livelihoods of the poor.

---

[41] The Global Hunger Index (GHI), an index developed by International Food Policy Research Institute (IFPRI) is used to describe a country's hunger situation. The GHI combines three equally weighted indicators: (a) The proportion of undernourished as a percentage of the population; (b) The prevalence of undernourished children under the age of five; and (c) the mortality rate of children under the age of five.

2.6. Health and livelihoods

'Health is wealth' may seem a trite observation, but its import is brought home clearly when one's health suffers. Several million poor Indians are at great financial risk precisely because of ill health, when families are dragged into poverty or remain entrenched in it. Ill health affects the livelihood in two ways, first, health expenses add to the household expenditure, and second, it leads to loss of working days and reduced earnings. Furthermore, malnutrition has intergenerational effects, such as, handicaps, stuntedness and so on.

Widespread hunger and the high level of malnourishment in India contribute to morbidity, ill health and a high burden of communicable and non-communicable disease. According to the World Health Organization (WHO) 2010 report, India is home to 23 per cent of the world's tuberculosis patients, 86 per cent of diphtheria patients, 54 per cent of leprosy patients, 29 per cent of pertussis patients, 42 per cent of polio victims and 55 per cent of malaria patients (WHO 2010). This is far in excess of the percentage of the world population (17 per cent) that India supports. In 2006, the percentage of childhood deaths in India that could be attributed to ill health was 69 per cent, which is the highest for any country in the world.[42]

Undernutrition also has severe economic and social costs. For example, it is estimated that 300,000 children are forced to drop out of school every year in India, because of an illness like tuberculosis in the family.

Health is also affected by the microenvironment in which one lives. Historically, the greatest advances in longevity and mortality reduction have not been the result of treatment of an individual disease, but from having well-maintained public health facilities, such as, modern drainage and sewerage systems, drinking water systems that produce and deliver disease free water

---

[42] Medico Friends Circle Bulletin February–March 2010. 'Hunger and Health: An Interdisciplinary Dialogue': Joint Statement from a Workshop.

and sanitation facilities. Let us take a look at the recent data (NSSO 2008–09)[43] on water supply and sanitation facilities in India to ascertain the vulnerability of the poor to disease and mortality on account of a lack of provision for basic amenities from the government.

Access to an improved source of drinking water was enjoyed by 88 per cent of the population in that year. In rural areas, their proportion stood at 84 per cent; tube wells/handpumps were the source of water for 55 per cent of the households, followed by water taps for 30 per cent of the households. In urban areas, the tap was the major source of drinking water for 74 per cent of the households and tube wells/handpumps served another 18 per cent households. Nearly two-thirds of urban dwellers in the bottom quintile used common drinking-water sources (community or building) while 63 per cent of the households in the top monthly per capita expenditure (MPCE) quintile class in urban areas had exclusive use of drinking water sources. In rural areas, as many as 71 per cent households in the bottom MPCE quintile class had community use of drinking water, even in the top quintile class 41 per cent of the households used community sources. Drinking-water facility within the premises was available to only about 41 per cent of rural households.

As per the Joint Monitoring Programme (JMP) Report for Water Supply and Sanitation (WHO 2010), only 21 per cent of the rural population had access to 'improved' sanitation facilities, while 69 per cent resorted to open defecation (in 2008). Overall nearly half (about 49 per cent) of households had no latrine facilities. This indicates the acute problem of open defecation in rural areas. In urban areas 11 per cent of households had no latrine facilities but the absence of latrine facilities is as high as 65 per cent. The absence of latrines is also significantly higher for the poorest 20 per cent of the population,

irrespective of rural/urban location. Nearly one-third of the households in the bottom quintile class in urban areas, and 85 per cent of the households in the bottom quintile class in rural areas had no latrine facility. Contrast this with the fact that more than 99 per cent of those in the top-quintile class in urban areas had latrine facilities. This clearly reflects the greater exposure of poor persons to unhygienic living environments, risk of disease and vulnerability to financial risk from ill health.

Nearly 59 per cent of the rural and 15 per cent of the urban households had no drainage arrangement. If you add the 19 per cent of rural and 6 per cent of urban households who had open *kutcha* drainage, then it is clear that drainage was a hygiene problem in about two-thirds of the rural and one-fifth of the urban households. The absence of garbage disposal system in 21 per cent of the urban and 76 per cent of the rural households further contributes to an unhygienic microenvironment.

2.6.1. Health expenditures

Unsurprisingly, given the malnutrition and high burden of communicable and non-communicable diseases, there is a high use of health services by the population. The average health care expenditure in India is about ₹3,000 per capita annually; this is around 6 per cent of its GDP. But, of this only about ₹450 comes from the public exchequer. In India, the state and central governments together spend about ₹52,000 crore annually, that is, 1 per cent of GDP. The central government's health budget has increased by about 20 per cent each year for the last four years (these increases are in National Rural Health Mission [NRHM]), but this is far short of the recommended 5 per cent of GDP expenditure on health recommended by WHO. Of the other 80 per cent of spending on private health care, only 4 per cent of it is currently covered by insurance, the other 96 per cent are out-of-pocket expenses. Public monies are minimal in addressing outpatient care expenses; 85 per cent of such expenses are out-of-pocket private expenses.

---

[43] NSSO (2010). The entire section on sanitation, drinking water and housing is based on data drawn from this report.

In the pre-liberalization period, the public hospitals provided services at minimal charges to all although the quality of care was uneven. Medicines were competitively priced because the government exercised significant drug-price control (over 300 drugs) in the essential, controlled price list, and the indigenous drug production industry was thriving in the absence of World Trade Organization (WTO) restrictions.

There is a significant shift in the government's stand from the 'universal provider' to an 'enabler in a market' in the period of economic liberalization. The government introduced user fees and two-tier services in public hospitals—those below the poverty line are supposed to get services free including drugs, but this is rarely the case (under-the-counter payments, and drugs have almost always to be purchased from outside). Also, there was a sharp reduction in the controlled drugs list leading to a significant increase in drug prices. Such a paradigm of health, of a very low share of public expenditure, and a very high share of unpooled expenditure (in the absence of health insurance) has exposed the poor to the risk of further impoverishment due to the high cost of health care.

The National Health Commission on Macroeconomics and Health headed by the then Finance Minister, P. Chidambaram, seconded the claim of the civil society health activists that out-of-pocket (OOP) expenditures often push the low-income households to catastrophic medical expenses and into poverty.[44] The Commission further noted the inadequate health expenditure by the central and state governments, inefficient delivery and poor utilization of public health care services, rising drug prices and a demand supply mismatch of medical professionals including paramedics and grassroots health workers. The Commission though failed to highlight issues such as the low access to health care, the devastating effect on households due to the aggregate cost of multiple episodes of less severe illnesses, and the expenditure in health being one of the top three reasons for pushing households into poverty. Box 2.8 shows the

---

Box 2.8:   *Expenditures on health by social group*

A recent study conducted during March 2008 and June 2009[45] in the rural areas of Uttar Pradesh, Rajasthan and Delhi's slums found that the OOP shares of rich and poor differ significantly with highest quintile (or top 20 per cent) of households according to their per capita monthly consumption expenditure (PCMCE) spending almost a quarter of their total consumption budget on health. In contrast, the same for the bottom 20 per cent is about 10 to 12 per cent in rural and urban areas. Almost a fifth (18.5 per cent) of the rural households and over a tenth (11.6 per cent) of the urban households spend more than a quarter of their total consumption budget on health care.

The situation is worse for lower caste SC households. SC and ST households incur a much higher OOP payment (15.8 and 13.8 per cent, respectively) than their upper caste counterparts (13.4 and 10.7 per cent for OBCs and upper castes, respectively). They also show very high percentages of catastrophic payments, 50.3 and 50.6 per cent for SCs and STs, respectively (versus 42.6 and 33.3 per cent for OBCs and upper castes, respectively), causing them to suffer from serious and highly disproportionate loss of well-being.

These findings of this study indicate a considerably higher OOP mean spending on medical bills than previous studies have found. The authors note that since these findings are a more accurate reflection of the situation in poor districts and slums, policymakers need to heed the critical scenario in areas with similar characteristics elsewhere in the country, and take immediate measures.

Source: Alam and Tyagi with Karan (2009).

---

[44] Crippling health costs also clog intergenerational health flows causing severe negative consequences for the co-residing old, especially women.

[45] Alam and Tyagi with Karan (2009). Data have been collected through a multi-stage sampling procedure from a total of 1,250 rural and 400 urban

disproportionate impact of health expenses for the poor and SC households.

When the poor are unable to pay the medical bills, their only option is to avoid treatment, reduce it, or discontinue it. A comparison of NSSO rounds till 2004–05 shows that there is a sharp increase in the percentage of persons, men and women, in both rural and urban areas choosing this harmful long-term option, between 1986 and 2004.[46] The percentage is as high as 40 per cent for women in the bottom quintile; there is almost a similar percentage of men in this quintile; as Sen (2010) notes, 'a closing of gender gap; a perverse catch up' (see Figure 2.19).

Financial considerations are cited more often than earlier by those in the bottom three quintiles (60 per cent of the population), as a reason for discontinuation of treatment (see Figure 2.20). That financial considerations have come into greater play in the decisions made regarding health care is not surprising given that there has been a considerable increase in the cost of care. Selvaraj and Karan (2009) show that on an average, private sector facilities are one and a half times more expensive than public facilities. For hospitalization, the cost per episode in private health facilities is twice that of public health. Figures 2.21 and 2.22 give information on the increase in the scale of expenditure on inpatient care and hospitalization since 1986–2004.

A significant increase in cost of health care is attributed to the cost of drugs. As much as 75 per cent of the total OOP expenditure for health, even in a normal situation is on drugs; in some instances it is

Figure 2.19: Persons never treated and discontinuing treatment

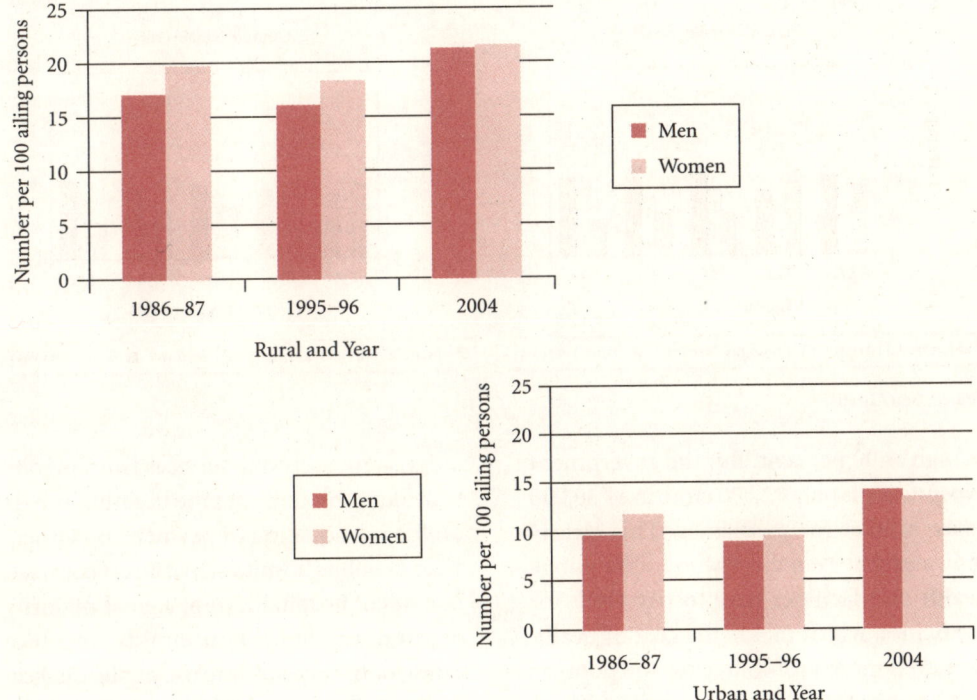

Source: Sen (2010).

---

households of UP and Rajasthan, and 360 households of Delhi. UP and Rajasthan were selected because of high poverty levels and weak demographic status.

[46] Sen (2010). The discussion and various figures that are used in this section are from the presentations made during this lecture.

Figure 2.20:   Reasons for non-treatment

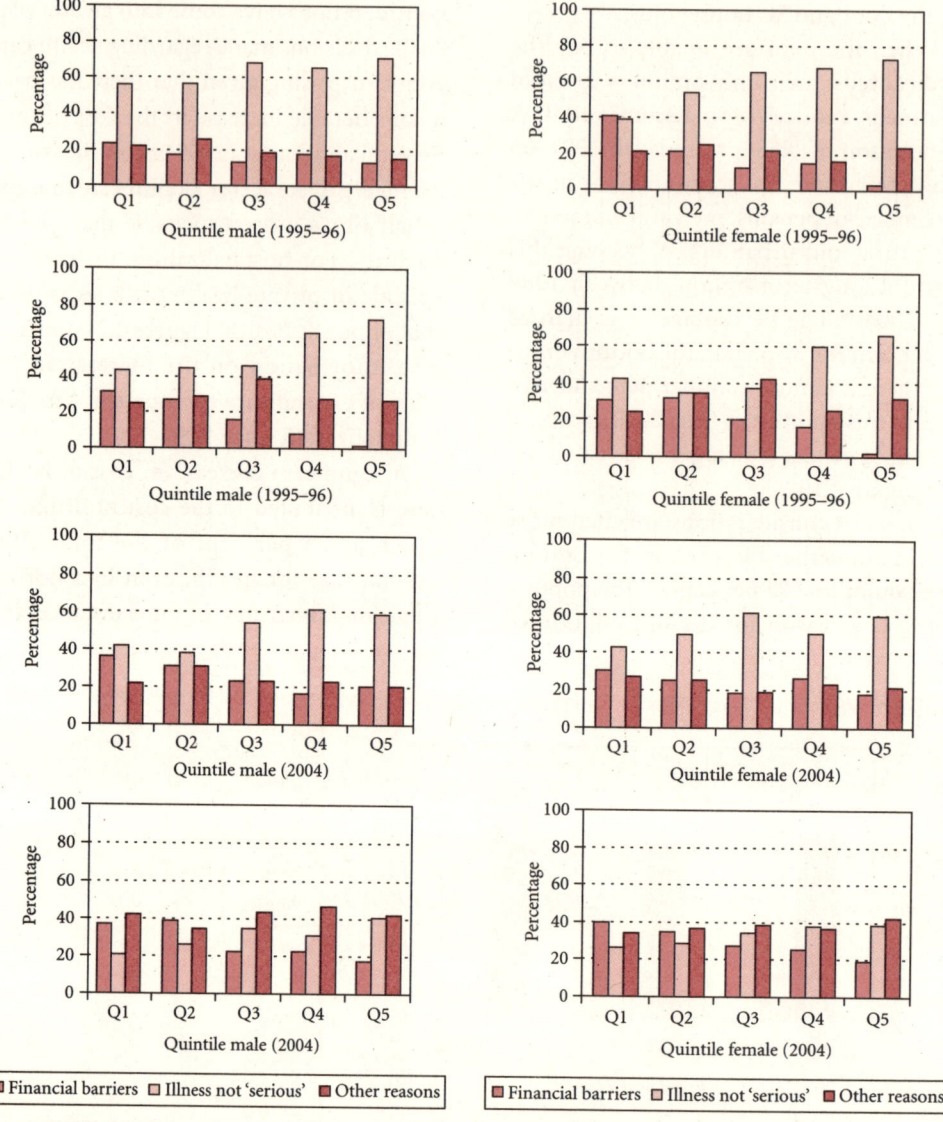

Source: Sen (2010).

as high as 90 per cent. But the government expenditure is only ₹2,000 crore in a ₹30,000 crore market for medicines. This clearly indicates that even those who utilize public health care facilities have to pay OOP for medicines, which makes the cost of health care even more prohibitive for the poor.

Catastrophic medical expenses are also a reason for the poor slipping into poverty. In the tri-state mentioned earlier (see n45), a little less than two-thirds to over 73 per cent of the total households who experienced catastrophic expenditures in non-hospitalization cases (in both rural and urban areas) were accessing services from private providers; this indicates the negative impact on the introduction of payment-based services in public hospitals. In a direct contrast, in cases of hospitalization, a good majority of rural and slum households who face catastrophic expenditure use public medical facilities. The reasons for this are likely to be either the inaccessibility of alternative health care facilities or the inability to pay the much higher costs of hospitalization in private hospitals; greater trust in public facilities is unlikely to be a reason given the heavy reliance on private facilities for in-patient care.

Figure 2.21: Expenditure on inpatient care: All India

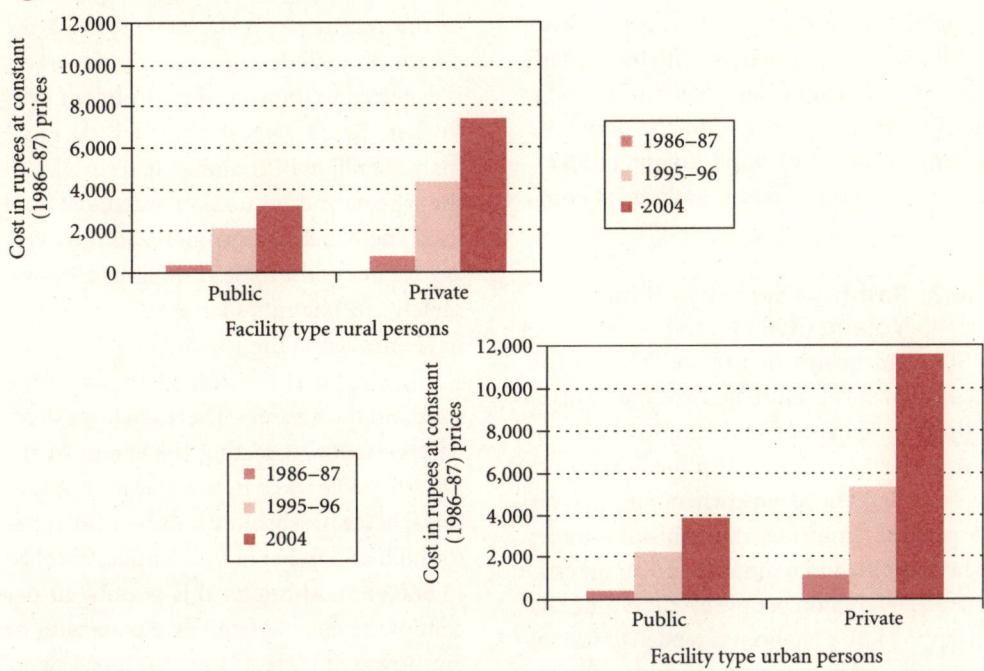

Source: Sen (2010).

Figure 2.22: Average expenditures on hospitalization at constant (1986–87) prices

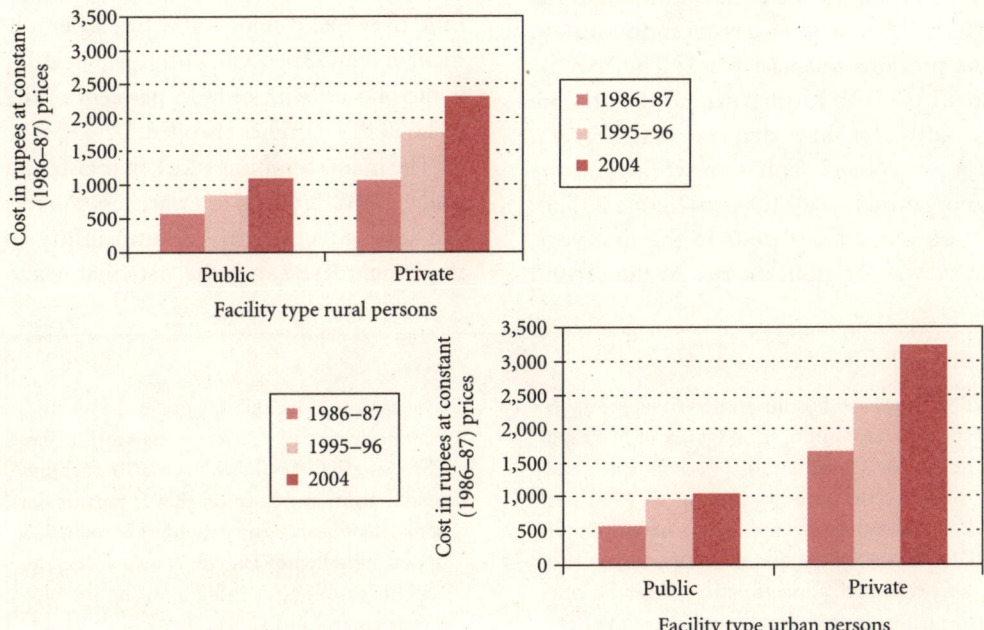

Source: Sen (2010).

Not surprisingly, more than one-fourth of the urban slum households and one out of every five rural household had borrowed to meet medical exigencies. A large proportion of those borrowings were from private money lenders (at exorbitant rates), further eating into the household earnings.

In light of the burden of health on the common people, the United Progressive Alliance regime had promised to increase its budgetary allocation from the current approximately 1 per cent to 3 per cent. While that commitment is yet to be fulfilled, the Government of India has introduced a health insurance scheme for the poor, the Rashtriya Swasthya Bima Yojana (RSBY). The next section takes a look at its components and impact.

2.6.2. Rashtriya Swasthya Bima Yojana (RSBY)

RSBY is a health insurance scheme for hospitalization, launched by the central Ministry of Labour and Employment on 1 April 2008 (see Box 2.9 for medical coverage details). The scheme when initiated was targeted at families of unorganized workers who fall BPL and it aimed to cover an estimated 300 million people by 2012. Since its inception RSBY has been extended to several categories of informal workers. As of now, the scheme includes construction workers, *bidi* workers, domestic maids, street vendors and the beneficiary families of the MGNREGA, with 15 days or more work in the previous financial year.[47] The government plans to further extend the scheme to auto rickshaw drivers, taxi drivers, rag pickers and sanitation workers in the unorganized sector (*Deccan Herald* 2011).

Enrolment was poor in the first year, there was a significant rise in the second year and there has been a staggering increase in the recent past. The extension of the scheme to include more groups of workers is expected to improve the enrolment even further. By 24 August 2011, a little more than 24 million BPL families had enrolled in the scheme and 2.3 million individuals had used the benefit of hospitalization coverage.[48] Thus of the total 51 million (approximately) BPL families targeted, almost half have enrolled in the scheme.

Enrolment is the responsibility of the state and the insurers. There is a huge statewise variation reflecting the extent of the proactive role taken by the state in accessing this scheme. In absolute numbers Bihar has the highest number of BPL families enrolled (5,660,683), although this is only 40 per cent of the eligible families. Kerala with its enrolment of 1,748,471 has the highest percentage of BPL families enrolled (66.5 per cent). Uttar Pradesh has one of the highest numbers of BPL families in the country—a little over one million—but has an enrolment of only 36 per cent. Enrolment in Delhi is the poorest with only 16 per cent of the 894,650 BPL families enrolled.

The main stumbling block in registering under RSBY is a lack of awareness. As it is the state governments' responsibility to implement RSBY, it is the state that has to

---

Box 2.9: *RSBY coverage details*

RSBY provides hospitalization coverage up to ₹30,000 per annum for a family of five on a floater basis. In addition, the scheme provides for transportation charges up to ₹100 per hospitalization covered up to a maximum of ₹1,000 per annum and coverage of pre- and post-hospitalization expenses incurred one day before hospitalization and up to five days from the date of discharge from the hospital. All pre-existing illnesses are covered and there is no age limit for eligibility under the scheme. Beneficiaries pay ₹30 as a registration fee. The beneficiaries have access to cashless service from any hospital that is part of the network of health care providers empanelled under the scheme. They may also access the benefits throughout India by using the biometric smart-card issued.

Source: Swarup and Jain (2011).

---

[47] The definition for each category of worker and the process to be followed are available at http://www.rsby.gov.in/Documents.aspx?id=1. The unorganized workers are required to show proof of their specific worker category and not of BPL status.

[48] These numbers were sourced from the RSBY site on 25 August 2011. Available at http://www.rsby.gov.in/Overview.aspx

make an investment in creating awareness and educating the target population either directly, or by putting pressure on and monitoring the insurers. Some state governments hired NGOs to promote awareness while others such as, Himachal Pradesh have organized health *mela*s and multi-speciality surgical camps.

Enrolment numbers are only a small part of assessing the success of the RSBY and utilization rate is critical to understanding the benefit of the scheme to the poor. Utilization rate in the first year was low[49] at 2.6 per cent, and burnout ratio[50] of insurers was about 73 per cent (below the national average of 80 per cent), implying that by and large insurance companies benefited. Critics claimed that this was because the incentive in the scheme was to maximize enrolments and minimize claims. However, within the second year itself there was a change in terms of insurers with regard to the beneficiary awareness requirements such as, health camps and IEC campaigns. The result of these was that by July 2010 the average rate of hospitalization was 3 per cent. This access to hospitalization is above the 1.7 per cent recorded for the poorest 40 per cent of population in NSSO 2004, clearly indicating that one of the objectives of the scheme—increase in access to health care by the poor is being achieved. Burnout ratio in the nine districts that had completed two years of operation also increased to a little above 84 per cent.

However, the average increase in hospitalization hides the enormous variations across districts, and also villages. This variation is a result of a combination of supply side and demand side factors. Supply side factors include availability of nearby empanelled hospitals, understanding and interest of the hospital administration (which may be a function of the package prices), transportation networks and promotional activities such as health camps and information campaigns. Demand-side factors include awareness and understanding of the scheme, morbidity rates, education and income levels. Poor people also accessed RSBY hospitalization based on the neighbour/villagers' hospitalization experience under the scheme—for empanelled hospitals of repute, and when the hospitals provided a wider array of specialized services that were in demand.

Supply-side constraints are severe. There exists an acute shortage of supply of health services, institutions, and personnel and transaction costs and transportation costs are very high. Thus, unless state governments take urgent additional proactive measures to improve the access to hospitalization, utilization will not increase to match their requirements. Poor persons will continue to not have access to hospitalization and the benefit of government spending will go to private insurance companies.

Some states such as Himachal Pradesh and Kerala have recognized these lacunae and taken steps towards improving the outcomes. Since 2009–10, Himachal Pradesh has organized health *mela*s and 11 multi-speciality surgical camps, increased the number of public hospitals empanelled and arranged for technologies for RSBY to be set up in these, has added an additional cover of ₹175,000 for critical illnesses and enhanced coverage for maternity and newborn child. Kerala has gone a step further. It has been a pioneer is achieving synergies between NRHM and RSBY (see Box 2.10).

The potential impact of RSBY on improved access to health services by the poor faces two important limitations. First, it does not cover any outpatient services. Enrolees and beneficiaries have expressed the need to have some coverage to outpatient services, and morbidity and disease patterns too indicate the urgent need for

---

[49] Swarup (2011). The findings are based on the study of 167 districts that had completed one full year of operation.

[50] 'Burn-Out Ratio' determines the outgo from Insurance Company in terms of percentage of expenditure incurred in payments made to the hospitals by way of settlement of claims, smart cards cost and service tax as against total premiums received.

Box 2.10:   *The Kerala experience: A successful instance of synergy of RSBY and NRHM*

Kerala leads all states in India with its low mortality and high life expectancy. However, high morbidity levels as a result of the shift from communicable diseases to chronic diseases and an ageing population are the challenges faced by Kerala in health care. Kerala shares the feature of high dependence on private health services and out-of-pocket expenses with the rest of India.

The state of Kerala and its health department in particular saw the RSBY/Comprehensive Health Insurance Scheme (CHIS) as a window of opportunity for mobilizing additional resources that were sorely needed to provide universal access to free health care, providing risk protection, and achieving improved health outcomes.

The Government of Kerala took radical reform initiatives for the supply and demand side to gear up the public health sector to meet the challenges of competing with the private sector. The insurance scheme was extended to the 'poor' BPL population and all others included under Above Poverty Line by introducing it along with the CHIS with a slight variation in the premium. The government of Kerala allocated a total of ₹76 crore—₹29 crore from Plan Budget and ₹47 crore from Arogyakeralam (name given to NRHM in Kerala)—and the RCH-II—to improve facilities at government empanelled hospitals. Moreover, the RKS/HMC fund distributed under Arogyakeralam was specially earmarked for upgrading logistics for implementation of RSBY in public health facilities. Arogyakeralam also provided services of ASHAs in all the empanelled hospitals, ensured drug distribution and logistics

management through Kerala Medical Services Corporation, took up NABH and NABL accreditation process for 19 government hospitals and 358 laboratories by signing an MoU with the Quality Control of India, and implementing hospital management information system with GIS Mapping and biomedical waste management.

For implementation purposes a separate agency 'Comprehensive Health Insurance Agency of Kerala' (CHIAK) was created. Labour and Rehabilitation Department is the nodal department, while, Health and Family Welfare, Local Self Government and Finance departments are the major participating departments.

Insurance in public health hospital has been perceived and practised as a combination of indirect and direct subsidy where, the government is paying the premium, staff salary (like retainer's fee), and the hospital is treating the patient as well as generating revenue, thus making a positive circle where the revenue generated is further used for the hospitals to improve the treatment facilities. Since the implementation of RSBY/CHIS scheme, October 2008 to February 2010 the revenue generated by the empanelled government hospitals (140) was more than that of the empanelled private hospitals (165). Public health institutions are used for treatment by 60 per cent of the enrolees' hospitalization requirements, and generate 53 per cent of the revenue through the scheme. The revenue generated until February 2010 was almost ₹18 crore.

Source: RSBY (2010).

such coverage. Second, in practice the migrants cannot utilize its portability feature in spite of the inherent promise of the scheme. Migrants are often absent at the time of enrolment in their native villages and thus do not get a smart card; split-card facility that allows them and their families to access health services at different locations is not well known, migrants' claims are not recognized by local administration in the destination areas and migrants do not have

the information of the empanelled hospitals at their destination.

Nevertheless, RSBY has been successful on several counts within its three years of operation. It has a far reach within its target population. Studies in different parts of the country show that enrolees fall in one or more of the following categories: they are unskilled and casual agricultural or non-agricultural workers, they live in *kutcha* households, they have poor drainage and sanitation facilities (indicating poor microenvironment); their earnings and expenditures are on a daily and not monthly basis; their annual income is not more than ₹45,000 and their average monthly expenditure is around ₹2,600.

There is evidence that in some regions the private health services sector is setting up health related infrastructure not serviced by it until now, and the public health hospitals are improving their capacities (in the wake of expected revenues from the demand by RSBY enrolees). In areas where health infrastructure exists, the poor now have a greater number of hospitals to choose from for accessing in-patient care. The OOP expenses of the poor have reduced. While in Kerala RSBY poor patients on an average spent six times less than the poor non-RSBY, in other places too there is a difference of at least ₹1,000 per hospitalization. These include the OOP expenses on medicines and diagnostics during hospitalization. Beneficiaries show very high levels of satisfaction with the hospital services, and less than 5 per cent rate the services as poor. Also, more than 80 per cent of those hospitalized confirm that their health has improved.

2.7. Concluding remarks

The gap between the jobs generated and new entrants in addition to the numbers already unemployed or underemployed (including jobless youth and women dropouts) does not show any sign of reducing at a greater rate. Jobs are not being generated in large numbers in agriculture and allied sector, or in the rural non-farm sector. The rural poor seeking work are either forced to eke out a living in the rural areas from an agriculture sector breaking at its seams, or migrate to join the millions of other poor in urban towns, cities and metros. In either case whether the poor work in cities or in rural areas the poor continue to be employed in low-paying, low-productivity jobs with little or no social protection in the ever-burgeoning informal sector. In such a

situation when they suffer shocks such as global slowdown, inflation and natural or manmade disasters, their livelihoods become even more precarious. A substantial percentage of the population of this country remains hungry, sick, in poor housing and unsanitary microenvironments. Malnutrition, morbidity and disease continue to compound the situation of the already fragile livelihoods. These conditions of the poor have persisted in spite of the phenomenal growth in the past few years.

The poor in India continue to look for succour from the welfare and social protection programmes of the '*maybaap sarkar*'. But the government welfare spending is unlikely to increase in the light of pernicious inflation. The Government of India has been unable to secure the livelihoods of the poor through its present policies. The attainment of the much-touted slogan 'inclusive growth' seems a distant dream.

References

Alam, Moneer, and R.P. Tyagi in Consultation with Anup Karan. 2009. *A Study of Out of Pocket Household Expenditure on Drugs and Medical Services: An Exploratory Analysis of UP, Rajasthan and Delhi*. Report submitted to Planning Commission.

Anant, T., and R. Mehta. 2011. Has employment fallen in India? Livemint.com. *Mint*, 30 June, New Delhi.

Banerjee, Nirmala. 2010. Integrating gender into the new employment policy. ILO-Asia Pacific Working Paper Series. ILO, Sub-regional Office for South Asia, New Delhi.

Basu, Kaushik. 2010. The Economics of Foodgrain Management in India. Ministry of Finance, Government of India.

Chandrasekar, C.P., and Jayati Ghosh. 2011. Latest Employment Trends in NSSO. The Hindu Business Line, 12 July. Available at http://www.thehindubusinessline.com/opinion/columns/c-p-chandrasekhar/article2219107.ece

Chintan (Chintan Environmental Research and Action Group). 2009. *Scrap Crash*. New Delhi: Chintan Environmental Research and Action Group.

Deaton, Angus, and Jean Dreze. 2008. Nutrition in India: facts and interpretations. Working Paper 1071, Princeton University.

Deccan Herald. 2011. RSBY extended to all of State. *Deccan Herald*, 25 August. Available at http://www.deccanherald.com/content/173108/rsby-extended-all-state.html

Dev, S. Mahendra. 2010. Rising food prices and financial crises in India: Impact on women and children and ways to tackle the problem. Working Paper No. 3, IHD-UNICEF Working Paper Series, Children of India: Rights and Opportunities.

Dev, S. Mahendra, and M. Venkatnarayana. 2011. Youth employment and unemployment in India. Available at http://www.igidr.ac.in/pdf/publication/WP-2011-009.pdf

Economic & Political Weekly. 2011. Don't shoot the messenger. *Economic & Political Weekly* XLVI (28).

Ghose, A. 2010. India's employment challenge. *The Indian Journal of Labour Economics* 53 (4).

Ghosh, Jayati, and C. Chandrasekar. 2011. Latest employment trends in NSSO. *Business Line*, 12 July.

Horn, Zoe. 2011. *Coping with Crises: Lingering Recession, Rising Inflation, and Informal Workforce*. A Sythesis Report, Inclusive Cities Study, Women in Informal Employment: Globalizing and Organizing (WIEGO).

International Labour Organization. 2010. Box 2, Why focus on youth? *Global employment trends for youth*. Geneva: International Labour Organization.

Ivanic, M., W. Martin, and H. Zamman. 2011. Estimating the short-run poverty impacts of the 2010–11 surge in food prices. Policy Research Working Paper 5633, World Bank.

Kapoor, Astha. 2009. Diamonds are for never: The impact of the economic crisis and coping mechanism in the diamond polishing industry in India. Research paper, International Institute of Social Studies, The Netherlands.

Lalmalsawma, David. 2011. Bholanath doesn't care much for India's growth story. Reuters. 26 January. Available at http://uk.reuters.com/article/2011/01/26/us-india-inflation-idUKTRE70P1PO20110126

Mahendra, Dev S., and M. Venkatnarayana. 2011. Youth employment and unemployment in India.Working paper, Indira Gandhi Institute of Development Research.

Mazumdar, Dipak, and Sandip Sarkar. 2008. *Globalization, Labour Markets and Inequality in India*. London and New York: Routledge.

Mitra, A. 2008. The Indian labour market: An overview. ILO-Asia Pacific Working Paper Series, International Labour Organization.

MSSRF (M.S. Swaminathan Research Foundation). 2010. *Report on the State of Food Insecurity in Urban India*. MSSRF, Chennai, India.

Munjal, Poonam. 2010. Inflation and its impact: The Distinct perspective. *Economy View*. CRISIL Ratings, May.

NSSO. 2010. *Housing Conditions and Amenities in India 2008–09*. NSS 65th Round, July 2008–June 2009, NSSO, Government of India.

———. 2011. *Key indicators of employment and unemployment in India*. NSS 66th Round, July 2009–June 2010. NSSO, Government of India.

Raveendran, G. 2010. Contribution of women to the national economy. ILO-Asia Pacific Working Paper Series. ILO, Sub-regional Office for South Asia, New Delhi.

Reserve Bank of India. 2011. Section II: Economic Review. *Annual Report Part I: The Economy Review and Prospects*. Available at http://rbidocs.rbi.org.in/rdocs/AnnualReport/PDFs/7IIECORE240811.pdf

RSBY. 2010. Towards alternative health financing: The experience of RSBY in Kerala. RSBY Working Paper No. 4, August. Available at http://www.rsby.gov.in/Documents.aspx?ID=14

Rustagi, Preeti. 2010. Employment trends for women in India. ILO-Asia Pacific Working Paper Series. ILO, Sub-regional Office for South Asia, New Delhi.

Saxena, N.C. 2009. *Call to action: Hunger, undernutrition and food security in India*. CLRA Policy Brief for Parliamentarians, Centre for Legislative Research and Advocacy (CLRA), New Delhi, India.

Selvaraj, Sakthivel, and Anup K. Karan. 2009. Deepening health security in India: Evidence from National Sample Surveys since 1980s. *Economic & Political Weekly* XLIV (40): 55–60.

Sen, Gita. 2010. Equity and health in an era of reforms. 4th Krishna Raj Memorial Lecture on Contemporary Issues in Health and Social Sciences. CEHAT/Anusadhan Trust, Mumbai, 9 April. Available at http://www.slideshare.net/essadmin/eq-healthsen

Sinha, Shalini. 2010. Global crisis, domestic impact: Impact of the global crisis on the Indian labour market. Draft version.

Swarup, Anil. 2011. Rashtriya Swasthya Bima Yojana (RSBY): The Evolving Scenario. Available at http://www.rsby.gov.in/Documents.aspx?ID=14

Swarup, Anil, and Nishant Jain. 2011. Rashtriya Swasthya Bima Yojana. In *Sharing innovative experiences: Successful social protection floor experiences*, 259–69. New York, USA: Global South-South Development Academy, UNDP.

UNICEF. 2011. *The situation of children in India: A profile*. New Delhi: UNICEF.

WHO. 2010. *World health statistics*. Geneva, Switzerland: WHO.

World Bank. 2010. *India's employment challenge: Creating jobs, helping workers*. New Delhi, India: Oxford University Press.

Reflections on Livelihoods Policies

3.1. Section I—Introduction

This chapter discusses the policies of the Government of India and some state governments like Bihar and Orissa, related to the improvement (and in some cases the destruction) of livelihoods of a vast majority of Indian citizens, both rural and urban. To be in tune with the annual character of this report, the chapter focuses on new and emerging issues instead of trying to capture the entire canvass of policy domain. A policy is defined as any, or a mix of, mission, scheme, act and policy declaration, no matter in which way it is presented in the public domain. Thus, it treats Mahila Kisan Sashaktikaran Pariyojana (MKSP), Mukhya Mantri Balika Cycle Yojana, MGNREGA and National Rehabilitation and Resettlement (R&R) Policy as the same ontological category.

For an individual household, livelihood is the challenge of trying to make many ends meet: food, nutrition, income, savings, credit, insurance, education, health, shocks, status, dignity, equity, and the like. While many challenges manifest themselves to the entire household, there are some that manifest to members of the household in a particular way; the wife, daughter, children, old, disabled, and so on. As the nation tries to meet these multidimensional and multilayered challenges, it leads to formulation of policies related to credit, savings, wages, employment, education, health, agriculture-horticulture, forestry, non-farm livelihoods, markets, trades, prices, displacement, rehabilitation-resettlement, migration, food security, nutrition, children, gender, disabled, transgender, etc.

However, livelihoods, and particularly that of the poor get affected not only by the affirmative actions of the state, a large number of macroeconomic measures taken to stabilize and orient the economy in certain directions also affect livelihoods. This chapter will not discuss those macroeconomic issues. For example, the food inflation and overall inflation have remained too high affecting livelihoods of people. Increase of diesel and kerosene prices have a direct bearing on poor households. Liberal import policies, allowing forward trading in some commodities, shrinking flow of credits from mainstream financial institutions and crises in micro-finance have affected livelihoods. It must be said though that most macroeconomic policies in recent times have affected livelihoods negatively, and at this point, it is not possible for us to clearly say if affirmative actions have the ability to minimize the negative effects of macroeconomic policies.

Before embarking on the discussion of how livelihoods is conceptualized in the planning process, let us first offer a rough estimate of the universe of people whose livelihoods are being discussed in this chapter. Table 3.1 describes the various constituencies that need livelihoods interventions.

As the nation tries to meet the multidimensional and multilayered challenges of its population, it formulates policies related to credit, employment, education, health, agriculture, forestry, markets, prices, displacement, migration, food security, nutrition, children, gender, disabled and so on. However, in doing so, the nation also has to meet the macro-challenges of the economy and society: growth, inflation, pressures emanating from globalization, fiscal consolidation, governance, corruption, accountability and broad-based equity. Therefore, the overall challenge in the national planning process is to determine the issues of livelihoods within the overall framework of achieving growth, employment and equity. As we see elsewhere in this report (Chapters 1, 2 and 5), the connection between growth, employment and equity remains complicated; for example, livelihoods support and affirmative action is often offset by the negative impact of the macroeconomic policy. Strong commitment and robust strategies are needed to ensure a triple-win process for growth, employment and equity.

The chapter is organized in five major sections: Section II—discussion on the 11th Plan, Union Budget and approach to the 12th Plan, followed by examples of some attempts at improving governance, including attempts of the civil society to demystify the budget process; Section III—discussion on some new initiatives that are in various stages of formalization; Section IV—critical case studies on challenges of livelihood and its policy issues and Section V—an attempt to formulate a Livelihoods Schemes Coverage Index.

3.2. Section II—Livelihoods in current plan and budget

3.2.1. 11th Five Year Plan: What is different?

The difference in the 11th Five Year Plan is visible right in its name, 'Inclusive Growth'. While it recognized the challenge of macroeconomic growth in terms of GDP growth, growth in investment, domestic savings of

Table 3.1: Constituency that needs various livelihoods interventions

Description	Percentage of population and numbers
Persons below official income poverty line	27% of population (Planning Commission 2005)
Persons who can be termed as poor	77% of population (NCEUS Report 2006a)
N.C. Saxena Committee defined poor	50% of rural population (PIB 2010a)
Tendulkar Committee defined poor	41% of rural population (PIB 2010b)
Scheduled Caste population	16.23% of population (Census 2001)
Scheduled Tribe population	7.5% of population (Census 2001)
Muslim minorities population	13.4% of population (Census 2001)
Households without any land or homestead sites	10.04% of population (Rawal 2008a)
Household with only homestead sites	41.63% of population (Rawal 2008b)
Financially excluded families in India	70% of population (Yeswanth 2007)
Families not covered by health insurance	89% (PWC 2007)
Persons engaged in the informal sector	92% of 457million (NCEUS 2006b)
Number of backward districts under Backward Regions Grant Fund (BRGF)	30% (250 of 640 districts)
Number of disabled persons	2.13% of population (11th Plan Approach Paper 2006a)
Crop insurance coverage of farmers	4% of farmers' population (11th Plan Approach Paper 2006b)
Vocational education outreach	3% of rural and 6% of urban Youth (11th Plan Approach Paper 2006c)

Source: Compiled by the authors from the sources mentioned in the table.

households (HHs) and fiscal consolidation which are necessary determinants of the progress of an economy, it also explicitly recognized the challenge of including all sections of the population in this growth pathway.

Agriculture poses the gravest of challenges, and is in urgent need of revival through new policy initiatives of water, land reforms, credit, insurance, price control, land improvement and diversification. The industrial growth also faces manifold challenges in terms of lack of generation of appropriate skills, financing and creation of supportive infrastructure. Improving environment and biodiversity, universalizing joint forest management (JFM) and implementation of Forest Rights Act 2006 (FRA) are other priorities.

While the canvas of policy is vast and complex, 'inclusive growth' has been rendered in the Plan in the form of particular schemes and services: reorienting Integrated Child Development Services (ICDS), with more emphasis on pre-school education, reducing dropout rates of schools, substantially improving educational attainments at schools, universalizing Mid Day Meals (MDMs) and new initiatives for child labour and migrant labour. Emphasis has been placed on vocational education leading to skill formation, in which direction the country has far to go. Adult literacy and health were other major agendas under the 11th Plan. NRHM sought to integrate all kinds of health services like preventive health care, secondary and tertiary health care, water and sanitation, vector control, curative health care and alternative systems of medicine.

The national targets set under the 11th Five Year Plan and its achievements as observed in the mid-term appraisal (MTA) are presented later. This is compiled by culling the data from each sector in MTA and putting it across the national targets of the 11th Plan. As the 11th Five Year Plan

ends in March 2012, a fuller understanding of its achievements will only be possible at a later date. So our understanding of the achievements (and failures) of the 11th Five Year Plan will be based on the MTA report submitted in 2009.

A reading of the MTA shows that many of the targets set in the 11th Plan documents (pages 23–24 of the 11th Plan document) have not been measured in terms of achievements. Indeed we have MTA data only for 9 out of 27 national parameters set out in the Plan; for some sectors like infrastructure, there is no data at all. Instead, only investments have been discussed, not outputs and outcomes. In every sector, some of the declared national targets could not be measured, either due to non-availability of data, or due to un-smart indicators which were not defined by an objective and measurable data which can be collected in national surveys.

Table 3.2 shows the progress as recorded in MTA on the national targets set by the 11th Five Year Plan on the basis of the first three years of progress. It clearly reveals the enormous gap in available data. It has been clearly stated where no data could be found.

The central message of the MTA is:

1. Agriculture must grow at 4 per cent for the next few years.
2. There is a major concern for the manufacturing sector that it is growing at 3 per cent only.
3. PM's Task Force (TF) recommendation on MSME must be implemented immediately.
4. Poverty estimates need to be revised.
5. The number of dropouts and very low educational outcomes are major concerns.
6. Major emphasis on skill education must continue.
7. Health expenditure must reach around 2 to 3 per cent in the near future.

Table 3.2:   National objectives of the 11th Plan and progress as per the MTA

11th Plan national parameters	11th Plan target	Information on progress as per the MTA
Growth and employment		
• GDP Growth	9 per cent	• 9 per cent (projected)
• Agriculture GDP growth	4 per cent	• 3.2 per cent (projected)
• Job creation	58 million	• No data
• Reduction in educated unemployment to	5 per cent	• No data
• Increase in real wage by	20 per cent	• No data
• Reduce Head Count Ratio by	10 per cent	• No data
Education		
• Reduce drop out to	20 per cent	• 14 per cent (primary)
		12 per cent (secondary)
• Reduce gender gap by	10 per cent	• 7 per cent points
• Increase literacy to	85 per cent	• No data
• Increase cohort going to college by	15 per cent	• No data
• Determining standards of educational attainments	No indicator	• No discussion
Health		
• Reduce IMR to	28 per cent	• 53 per cent (2008)
• Reduce MMR to	1/1,000	• No data
• Reduce total fertility to	2.1	• 2.6 (2008)
• Clean drinking water to	All	• 478 habitation left
• Reduce 0–3 malnutrition to	Half	• No data
• Reduce anaemia by	50 per cent	• No data
Women and child health		
• Improve 0–6 sex ratio to	935	• 915 (2006–08)
• Direct and indirect beneficiaries of all govt programmes	33 per cent women	• No data
		• No data
• Safe childhood to	All	
Infrastructure		
• Ensure electricity to villages	All villages	• No data
• Ensure electricity to BPL	All BPL HHs	• No data
• Rural roads to 1,000 population habitation	All	• No data
• Telephone connectivity to	All villages	• No data
• Broadband connectivity to	All villages	• No data
• Provide homestead sites to	All	• No data
Environment		
• Increase forest cover by	5 per cent	• Unrealistic/difficult
• WHO standards of air quality	All major cities	• No data
• Treat urban wastes	All	• No data
• To increase energy efficiency by	20 per cent (2016–17)	• 7.5 per cent (2009)

Source: MTA Report of Planning Commission.

8. Emphasis on RSBY is to continue.
9. Poor implementation of the Tribal Sub Plan is a cause for concern.
10. Improving governance is a major concern, especially in Maoists-affected and Panchayats Extension to Scheduled Areas (PESA) areas.
11. Thrust on improving the Management Information System (MIS) at all levels.
12. Push has to be made for greater devolution towards local self-governments.

Exclusion is defined as an HH's inability to access services, participate in social or political processes, represent her constituency in public domain, enjoy dignity as an equal member of society and feel empowered, as a consequence of economic, social and political factors. Excluded groups are differentiated on the basis of their social identity (such as caste, gender, race, or ethnicity), or some other parameter that sets them apart from the normative majority such as a disability, language, profession, HIV status and so on (UNICEF 2010, p. 3). Therefore, inclusion would mean a combination of institutions and processes leading to improved access, participation, representation, dignity and empowerment (PRDE).

Looking at the 11th Five Year Plan through this lens one cannot but notice the strong emphasis on improved service delivery of all kinds—education, health, infrastructure, employment and income supplements. The special emphasis placed on pre-school education, residential schooling for first-generation learners, abolition of child labour and bringing them back in school, universal access to primary preventive health care, clean drinking water to all hamlets, rural roads to all habitations, homestead sites to all, electricity supply to all villages, shelter for the abandoned, mainstreaming separated women, etc., is the commitments of an access-driven inclusion framework.

However, in contrast, there is a conspicuous absence of other dimensions of inclusion, such as PRDE. None of these can be achieved even with improved services; these require intervention at another level. The available examples of inclusion suggest that PRDE results from strong institutions of various forms. Country wide examples of Mahila Samkhaya, self help group (SHG) Federations, workers' unions and peoples' movements bear testimony to the fact that PRDE can be achieved through strong institutions dedicated to the respective constituency they represent. Since some of these initiatives have been taken up by the Union and state governments, one would have expected their inclusion in the core agenda. This did not happen. Instead, all emphasis was placed on improving services.

The approach paper to the 11th Five Year Plan sought to have inclusion as a major development agenda. It was obvious that Indian economy is growing, but not all sections of the society are experiencing this as positive growth. So the slogan was to have 'inclusive growth'—growth that touches all, positively. The approach paper to the 12th Plan recognizes that inclusion is taking place, but not at the desired pace, so the nation is going to miss the MDG except perhaps for poverty (Planning Commission 2011). Even this claim is no longer true since the definition and head count average of the country is now pegged at 46 per cent of rural population, close to a double of 27 per cent, which was the last such estimate (*The Hindu* 2011a).

3.2.2. Budget allocation on livelihoods in 2011–12

In keeping with the basic thrust of the 11th Plan, the annual budget of 2011–12 stuck to its focus on growth, fiscal consolidation, inflation, agriculture and higher allocation to the social sector (see Table 3.3). While the economic results of the previous year were encouraging, with an overall high growth, agriculture back on a growth track, and fiscal consolidation on expected lines, inflation, high food prices, corruption and weak governance were key concerns.

A few key issues can be determined by looking at the Budget 2011–12 from a livelihoods perspective. It must be said at the outset, that budgeting is an allocation exercise; it reflects the dynamics of the government's emphasis in view of emerging realities, and conscious prioritization of a particular sector. However, the budget speech often promises new policy initiatives and to that extent, budgeting does fall within the scope of a policy discourse.

The three key aspects of the budget are: Allocation to existing programmes, new programme initiatives and new policy initiatives.

Allocation: Allocations to the sectors that have a direct relationship with livelihood enhancement are shown in Box 3.1. In all cases, the increase seems substantial with respect to the last year. However, the

Table 3.3: Increase in budget allocations with respect to last financial year (₹ crore)

Key areas	2011–12	2010–11	Per cent change
Agricultural credit	475,000	375,000	27
Social sector	166,887	137,510	21
Sarva Shiksha Abhiyan	21,000	15,000	40
Primitive tribal groups	244	185	32
Health	26,760	23,300	15
Rashtriya Krishi Vikash Yojana	7,860	6,755	16
Bringing Green Revolution to the agriculture of the eastern region	400	400	same
Improving agriculture of 60,000 villages	300	300	same

Source: Compiled by author from 'Key Features of Budget 2011–2012', pp. 5–10. Available online at http://indiabudget.nic.in

---

Box 3.1: *New programme initiatives announced*

1. Promotion of oil palm—new allocation of ₹300 crore to bring 60,000 ha of land under palm cultivation to reduce imports.
2. Allocation of ₹300 crore to promote vegetable clusters near major urban centres.
3. Allocation of ₹300 crore for improving production of *bajra*, *jowar* and *ragi* in 1,000 compact blocks covering 25,000 villages of semi-arid regions.
4. ₹5,000 crore to be provided to SIDBI for incremental lending to MSMEs.
5. Accelerated Fodder Development Programme in 25,000 villages in 1,000 compact blocks.

Source: Budget Highlights published by Press Bureau of GOI.

---

calculation of per HH or per capita allocation can only be made if the denominators are adequately and accurately known, in all the cases, which is beyond the scope of this chapter. Among the sectors, agriculture seems to have received a major thrust in terms of allocation and its diversity.

New Programme Initiatives: Much of the new programme initiatives are for agriculture and allied sectors. This sector started receiving the governments' attention from the previous financial year (2009–10), which continued into the last year. Fodder, vegetables, oil palm and millets expect some boosts in production from these initiatives. The other thrust area is lending to MSMEs.

New Policy Initiatives Announced: Perhaps the most important announcement has been about initiating a national mission on sustainable agriculture, and expanding the scope of the Swasthya Bima Yojana. However, certain other smaller initiatives are worth mentioning too, like the SHG Development Fund and Microcredit Equity Fund.

The most important single sectoral thrust in the Budget 2011–12 is on agriculture. This had started in the previous year, and helped achieve a growth of over 5.4 per cent, and with this year's support mechanisms, a growth of around 5 per cent is expected again. The support to agriculture included enhancing agricultural credit, continuing with interest subvention, and specific subsector intervention on vegetables, fodder, millets, rice intensification and so on. After almost a decade of policy neglect of agriculture, these are certainly welcome initiatives (see Box 3.2).

Most of the central sector programmes have a cost sharing mechanism with the states. Table 3.4 gives the cost sharing formula for major livelihood impacting programmes funded jointly by the Centre and the states. It is clear that the cost sharing formula remains the same for most states except the North Eastern Regions (NERs) where the Centre funds 90 per cent of the costs. This is due to the fact that the tax and other revenues collected by the states are

---

Box 3.2: *New policy initiatives announced*

1. National Commission on sustainable agriculture.
2. Scope of RSBY expanded.
3. Old age eligibility to access IGNOAPS reduced from 65 to 60, and an increase in the pension amount for old above 80 years.
4. Setting up of the National Innovation Council.
5. National Food Security Bill to be introduced this year.
6. Agricultural Produce Marketing Act to be introduced.
7. A women's SHG development fund to be created with a corpus of ₹500 crore.
8. An India Micro Finance Equity Fund to be created with SIDBI with a corpus of ₹500 crore.
9. Exit norms under co-contributory pension scheme' 'Swavalamban' 'to be relaxed.

Source: Budget Highlights published by Press Bureau of GOI.

---

simply not enough to be able to take the usual share of costs. On the other hand, some states like Tamil Nadu have actually put in additional funds on ICDS programmes over and above the stipulated share to make the programme a success.

The Budget is an exercise in balancing receipts and payments of the government, and orienting its priorities. Its merit can be assessed from a number of perspectives.

First, from a public finance perspective, let us see how the expenditure fares as a percentage of GDP over the years. The Union Government's expenditure for the social sector has hovered around 1.5–2 per cent of GDP for several years now. While adding all states together, it hovers around 6–6.5 per cent of GDP (CBGA 2011, pp. 5–10). Therefore, the oft-repeated claim that the social sector receives the highest importance is not true.

The second approach is to look at the budget promises over the years. Table 3.5 from a study by Centre for Budget and Governance Accountability (CBGA) illustrates how the budget promises and even the language and emphasis have gradually shifted. On two of the budget elements, namely, on starting model schools and universalization of ICDS, CBGA actually computed the cost required to fulfil the objectives. For example, if the government declares that setting up one model school requires ₹A, then setting up one each in 6,300 blocks would require ₹$A \times 6300 = 6300A$. Then it compares the budgetary allocation of B as a percentage of $6300A$. In the same fashion CBGA computed the cost of universalization of ICDS and the food subsidy, and showed the mismatch in allocation versus the need. In case of model schools, this was ₹39,100 crore against which the allocation is just ₹425 crore. In case of universalization of ICDS, the cost was calculated as ₹41,400 crore against which only ₹8,300 crore have been allocated. The budgetary allocation has yet to be made for the Food Security Act and for access to education for dalits and adivasis.

Another perspective on the budget is trend analysis for outlays for each important

Table 3.4: Cost sharing for various central sector programmes

Programme	Centre:State
Tribal Sub Plan	50:50
MGNREGA	75:25 (specific)
IAY	75:25 (non-NER)
IAY	90:10 (NER)
SGSY	75:25
ICDS (G)	90:10
ICDS (SNP)	90:10 (NER)
ICDS (SNP)	50:50 (non-NER)
MDM	90:10 (NER)
MDM	75:25 (non-NER)
SSA	65:35 ('09)
TSC	75:25
MKSP	75:25 (Non-NER)

Source: Compiled by author from each of the programme guidelines.

Table 3.5: Budget promises over the years on the same or similar issues

Subject	Promises in Congress manifesto 2009	Promises addressed in Budget 2009–10	Promises addressed in Budget 2010–11	Promises addressed in Budget 2011–12	Comments
Health	Health insurance for BPL families	RSBY allocation ₹350 crore	RSBY for NREGA workers	Scope of RSBY expanded	Scheme in place; implementation started
Education	Two model schools in each block	Scheme for model school launched with ₹350 crore	Allocation increased to ₹425 crore	This is integrated with SSA	Allocation far short of budgetary need
Education	Free education access across stages for dalits and adivasis	Not addressed	Post-matric scholarship rates to be revised for SC/ST/OBCs	A pre-matric scholarship started for SC/ST/OBCs	Issue not addressed
Employment	100 days for work at ₹100 per day	Budget allocation increased but wages became fixed	Debates on wages continues	MGNREGA wage pegged with CPIAL	Budget issue addressed
Social security	Social security for high-risk groups	High-risk groups identified and action initiated	National Social Security Fund called Swavalamban initiated with ₹1,000 crore	Eligibility of IGNOAPS reduced to 60 years; people aged more than 80 to get more pension	Scheme in place; implementation just started
Food security	National Food Security Act and universalization of ICDS	No allocation	Food Subsidy reduced by ₹1,000 crore, and allocation to ICDS increased by ₹2,000 crore	Food Security Bill to be introduced, budget for ICDS	NFSA yet to start, universalization is far short of budgetary need

Source: CBGA Report (2011, pp. 9–10).

sector, like education, health, water sanitation, rural development and so on, and the fundamental message is captured here. For example, the budgetary outlay for the centre and states together has remained more or less constant for education at 3.5 per cent of GDP, on an average, from 2000–01 to 2009. Similarly, health outlay too has remained constant at around 0.9 per cent of GDP from 2002 to 2009. Water sanitation has remained more or less constant at 0.80 per cent of GDP for the last seven years. In contrast, the rural economy and agriculture has seen a significant increase in the budget allocation from 1.5 to 2.5 per cent of GDP, and from 1.1 to 2.0 per cent of GDP respectively. Another contrast is the continuous decline in food subsidy from 0.82 per cent to 0.66 per cent of GDP in the last six years.

3.2.3. Allocation and fund utilization: A case study of Orissa

The Union Government allocates funds, but it is mostly up to the state governments to decide how to utilize them. Therefore, the efficiency, equity and quality of spending by the state governments greatly affect and impact the states' welfare. Since the monitoring is still mostly limited to spending, it is worthwhile to look at the state of affairs in this regard (see Table 3.6).

We will present a case study of funds utilization by one of the poorest states, namely Orissa. For the past 10 years, the state has been unable to fully spend the funds received from the GOI under the Centrally Sponsored Plan (CSP).

In the last financial year (2010–11), the state government received an as-

Table 3.6: Central sector plan funds utilization by Orissa

Year	Utilization
2006–07	54.01 per cent
2007–08	75.97 per cent
2008–09	92.00 per cent
2009–10	87.30 per cent
2010–11	68.70 per cent

Source: Business Standard (2011).

sistance of ₹527.09 crore from the GOI under CSP but has managed to spend ₹360.05 crore only, meaning an achievement of 68 per cent on the expenditure front. The performance was better in 2009–10; the state had managed to spend ₹995.49 crore out of the Centre's assistance of ₹1,143.83 crore received under CSP, an achievement of 87.03 per cent. In 2008–09, the spending was ₹1,118.89 crore as against the receipt of ₹1,164.76 crore. In 2007–08, the expenditure by the state under CSP was ₹850.04 crore which is an achievement of 75.97 per cent of the total receipt of ₹1,118.81 crore. In 2006–07, the state government's expenditure under CSP was ₹396.03 crore out of an actual receipt of ₹733.17 crore, which marks an achievement of only 54.01 per cent.

The expenditure figures are as per the data provided by State Minister for Planning and Coordination A.U. Singh Deo in the state assembly.[1]

To improve expenditure levels, the state finance department introduced the Cash Management System in 10 departments in the last fiscal year. According to this system, up to 60 per cent of the expenditure as per the Plan would be spent by the end of December, and the expenditure for the month of March shall not exceed 15 per cent. The total expenditure, Plan as well as Non-Plan, from April to December in the last fiscal (2010–11), at ₹21,615.73 crore has been 54.18 per cent of the total Plan provision of ₹39,896.60 crore for the current

fiscal year. In the fiscal year 2009–10, 48.35 per cent expenditure was achieved till the end of December 2009.

Though, it must be said that fund utilization is only an initial indicator of a good performance. The best example again is MGNREGA, where even in those states that have spent high, the number of HHs that got work are just about 50–60 per cent, and the number of HHs that got 100 days' work is extremely meagre—just about 3–4 per cent.

The Planning Commission has started widespread consultations with 900+ Civil Society Organizations, several think tank organizations, and through its website for the approach paper which got 32,000 hits and several thousand responses.

The following are the key points for the approach paper:

- Improve implementation, accountability and service delivery.
- Objectives of the government programmes are generally all right, institutional structure is weak and greater devolution is needed.
- Government programmes need a new architecture—greater localization, breakdown of silos, feedback from citizens and mechanisms for learning and sharing of best practices.
- Create an environment for nurturing enterprises, improving markets, supporting innovation, improving access to finance and inculcating respect for common pool resources.

Section 6.2 of Chapter 6 discusses this in more detail.

3.2.4. New policy on monitoring implementation: Performance and social audit under Comptroller and Auditor General (CAG) fold

Livelihood policies and programmes of the government are largely meant for the poor and ultra poor HHs. So how to institute a process by which the programme outreach

---

[1] A.U. Singh Deo in Orissa Assembly in 2010 Winter Session.

and quality can be ensured has to be determined. Participatory monitoring, systemic monitoring of outputs and outcomes by the implementers, performance audit on programmes, citizen charter, citizen report card, community score card, social audit, public hearing and the usual compliance audit done by the CAG to check misuse of tax payers' money are a few well-known tools that can be used for this purpose. Most of these tools are technically complex and require experts, except perhaps the social audit process, which has become the new buzzword in programme monitoring. Social audit process is intrinsically less technical and more mobilizational; it involves the programme recipients, has a more or less open simple format and can also involve the illiterate and socially excluded people. This section will briefly deal with the policy efforts to institutionalize the social audit processes.

The CAG of India, the constitutional body of public audit in the country has always been in the business of doing compliance audit of all state and central government departments, and parastatal bodies. Compliance audit is essentially a mechanism to ensure that cost of governance remains low and at worst, optimal. However, in recent times, the CAG has also started doing performance audit of social-sector programmes, and have audited the NREGA, NRHM, Accelerated Rural Water Supply Programme (ARWSP), MDMs and so on, from time to time. Performance audit goes beyond compliance and looks at output, outcomes and cost effectiveness. The power of performance audit can be seen in the unearthing of the 2G scam (CAG 2010), that shook the nation in the current year.

Recognizing the growing popularity, importance and criticality of social audit, the CAG set up a Task Group in May 2009, to come up with recommendations as to how the social audit can be mainstreamed in the public audit system. This TF submitted its report on January 2010 (CAG 2010). Its major observations were:

1. The recognition that CAG audit is essentially a governmental process involving public functionaries, auditors and legislators. In the present era of citizen participation in governance processes, it is important to take the audit process to the public domain, and involve all stakeholders.
2. With increasing importance of Panchayati Raj Institutions (PRIs) in programme implementation, it raises the question of their audit. However, CAG's jurisdiction on PRI audit is still nebulous, and PRI audit being a state subject further complicates the situation.
3. Since social sector programmes now receive massive budget support from central and state governments, it is imperative to involve the civil society and community in determining whether the programmes are being received well and having any impact on their lives.

The Task Group came out with 15 recommendations; the major ones are listed in Box 3.3. The highlights are:

1. A clear recommendation to adopt social audit as a component of performance audit and compliance audit.
2. Clear pathways of how the synergy can be developed by usual audits and social audit.
3. Setting up of a committee mechanism.
4. Easy training modules for the use of CSOs.

The most critical aspect of this report is the recognition that audit can no longer remain a closed door governmental and legislative affair. The larger citizenry have a critical stake in affairs that affects their lives and so must have enough right and voice to make it happen, not only for programmes and policy designs, but also in programme implementation. However, the policy domain has yet to see this happen in case of mainstreaming social audit.

While these are welcome steps, we have yet to see the start of the process of

Box 3.3: *Major recommendations of the Task Group of CAG on social audit*

1. Incorporation of Social Audit in performance and compliance audit of social sector programmes.
2. Social Audit reports of Civil Society Organizations to be used to prioritize and make risk assessment.
3. Social Audit reports of Gram Sabha and/or CSOs to be included as part of CAG's performance audit.
4. To make CAG's reports and social audit reports available in public domain.
5. A coordination committee of central and state-level officers to anchor the process.
6. Develop easy training modules for conducting audit and make it available to CSOs through ICTs.
7. Legislative mandate necessary to improve local fund audit of PRIs.
8. Maintain structural and process uniformity in social audits of all social sector programmes.

Source: Report of the Task Group on Social Audit, Office of the Comptroller and Auditor General of India, January 2010.

institutionalization of social audit in the public audit system.

3.3. Section III—New policy initiatives

3.3.1. National Food Security Act

In 2001, the Supreme Court of India recognized the Right to Food as an inalienable fundamental right under Article 21 of the Constitution. It established a clear set of actions to be taken by the central government to improve the food distribution system all over the country. Thereafter, a series of measures were taken to improve the Public Distribution System (PDS), ICDS and MDMs, the three major avenues of food distribution.

PDS in India provides subsidized grains to the two target groups—BPL families and Antyoday[2] families—and offers grain, free of cost, to destitute families comprising of the old.[3] The subsidy amount differs for BPL and Antyoday families. The National Food Security Bill is the latest attempt by the state to institute some kind of a universalsation based on legal entitlement rather than on availability of resources. 2010 has seen intense debate on various ethical and instrumental issues around this bill. The following paragraphs make an attempt to capture the debate's essence.

The National Food Security Bill proposes to roll the three schemes into one, offering a standard rate of 25 kg of foodgrains to all poor HHs per month at a flat price of ₹3 per kg. The three key words here, 25 kg foodgrains, poor HH and ₹3 per kg, have given rise to all the debates.

National Advisory Ccouncil, the supreme policy advisory body of the country took the view that entitlements have to be better structured, the term 'poor' has to be better defined and the price has to be poor friendly (NAC 2010). It came out with an alternate proposal, defining the poor slightly broadly to cover 75 per cent of the total population (90 per cent rural and 50 per cent urban). This population is then divided into two broad categories, like 'Priority' population, which constitute 46 per cent of the rural population and 28 per cent of the urban population; and 'General' population—44 per cent in rural areas and 22 per cent in urban areas. The figures were arrived at by adding 10 per cent beneficiaries (to cover those on the margins) to the Tendulkar Committee's poverty estimates of 41.8 per cent of the rural poor and 25.7 per cent of the urban poor. NAC suggested that the 'Priority' group should get 35 kg of foodgrains at the rate of ₹1 per kg for millets, ₹2 per kg for wheat and ₹3 per kg for rice. And the 'General' group should get

---

[2] Antyoday Anna Yojana is meant for bottom 38 per cent of families below the poverty line, who are given grains at nominal prices.

[3] Annapurna Anna Yojana is meant for individuals over 65 years of age, of BPL families, who do not have any one to look after them. They are given a weekly quantum of rice free.

20 kg per HH at 50 per cent of the minimum support price (MSP) for the grains. Further, NAC also recommended the conversion of the provisions of nutrition supplements and food distributed under MDMs into a legal entitlement. Moreover, the NAC took clear cognizance of the fact that reducing leakages in PDS is as much a priority as the supply itself.

Professor Jean Dreze, a member of NAC, took a different view (Dreze 2010). He argued that targeting is unreliable and divisive. At least three independent surveys (the National Sample Survey [NSS], the National Family Health Survey [NFHS] and the India Human Development Survey [IHDS]) show that about half of all poor HHs in rural India did not have a BPL card in 2005. The identification of poor families can be improved, but ultimately, it is bound to be a hit-or-miss affair. When it comes to food security, 'exclusion errors' are unacceptable—everyone has a right to protection from hunger.

The government appointed the C. Rangarajan Committee to examine the recommendation made by NAC. The Rangarajan Committee took the view that the above poverty line (APL) population should be kept out of the subsidized PDS on principle. It also argued that the food procurement and even the food production system are not ready to absorb the increased demand for foodgrains if NAC's proposal is accepted. Also nearly ₹10,000 crore will be required to implement NAC's recommendation. The Rangarajan Committee also recommended linking the BPL price with inflation and CPI, and the APL price with the MSP.[4]

If it is really impossible to accurately determine the number of poor and identify them, then, it raises ethical questions about the basis of applying a BPL/APL divide. Limiting the state's responsibility towards its citizens to providing 25 kg grains to each family per month which will just about keep them from destitution is also questionable.

If the state can invest nearly US$ 1 trillion in infrastructure which is 10 per cent of GDP, reluctance in investing 1 per cent of GDP for food security cannot be ethically acceptable.

At the time of writing the SOIL Report, the Food Security Bill is with the Parliament, with the Rangarajan Committee recommendations. We have to wait to see what the Parliament decides on the bill.

3.3.2. National Policy on Skill Development Policy

India is set to have the largest working population in the world by 2030. At present, the Indian workforce stands at 459 million, of which 26 million are in the organized sector and the rest 433 million are in the unorganized sector. About 12.8 million people add to the workforce every year. Skill development has recently come out to be of great importance after the World Bank published its report in 2006 delineating several critical gap areas. The current capacity of all skill development programmes stands at only 3 million. The policy goal of skill development is twofold, (*a*) to make new entrants to the job markets employable for decent work, and (*b*) to help the existing workforce to acquire new skills to survive and move up in the job market.

The existing gaps in the skill developments are, (*a*) inadequate institutional capacity to handle existing skill requirements, (*b*) lack of private sector investment in skill development, (*c*) new and emerging skill development requirements unmatched by an institutional investment, (*d*) total disconnect of skill with school education, (*e*) no focus on quality assurance of the institutions, etc.

Government of India formulated the National Skill Development Policy that set out an ambitious target of skilling 500 million people by 2022. The task is clearly stated in the Policy as follows (NPSD 2009).

1. Increasing capacity and capability of the existing system to ensure equitable access to all.

---

[4] *Business Standard*, 12 January 2011.

2. Promoting lifelong learning, and maintaining quality and relevance according to changing requirements, particularly of the emerging knowledge economy.
3. Creating an effective convergence between school education and various skill development efforts of the government, and between government and private sector initiatives.
4. Capacity building of institutions for planning, quality assurance and involvement of stake holders.
5. Creating institutional mechanisms for research development, quality assurance, examinations and certification, and affiliations and accreditation.
6. Increasing participation of stakeholders, mobilizing adequate investment for financing skill development, and attaining sustainability by strengthening physical and intellectual resources.

Several institutional mechanisms have been proposed to take this policy forward. They include, (*a*) a National Skill Development Council for policy direction and review, (*b*) a National Skill Development Coordination Board for inter-departmental, inter-sectoral and inter institutional coordination, (*c*) a National Skill Development Corporation for sector developmental work, and (*d*) a National Council for revitalizing vocational training. All these institutions have become operational of which NSDC has already tied up with private sector players to run 30+ projects of skill formation, apart from identifying sector specific detailed needs of various skills in an elaborate skill sector report. The study identified a skill-gap in 21 critical sectors among 244 million; whereas 120 million more will be added to the workforce. The central challenge is to quickly shift from a supply driven model to a demand driven model.

A critical challenge would be to bridge the regional gap in skill development interventions. For example, Kerala has provisions for training 15 per cent of its workforce,

whereas, Bihar has provisions for only 0.5 per cent. Another critical challenge would be to connect literacy and school education with skilling; the present approach of having vocational education is simply not the model for future as it's a totally supply driven model.

3.3.3. Micro, small and medium enterprises

MSMEs[5] remain a very important livelihood sub-sector. They contribute 8 per cent to GDP, 45 per cent of manufactured output and 40 per cent of exports. They employ 60 million people in 26 million enterprises. The labour to capital ratio is much higher in MSMEs relative to large industries, and the geographical spread of MSMEs is far greater than that of large-scale industries. A glance at the MSME statistics reveals a few important characteristics.

While 66 per cent of the manufacturing units are registered, 73 per cent of service sector units are unregistered. Seventy-one per cent of all units are in the service sector, and the rest are in the manufacturing sector. This implies a large number of persons employed in MSMEs belong to the unregistered (informal) sector.

SC/ST/OBCs constitute 52 per cent of the employed workforce in the MSME sector. Muslims are not included in this list, so their inclusion would make the percentage share substantially higher.

---

[5] MSME definition: MSMEs are categorized on the basis of investment in plant and machinery and equipment. Also, they are classified into two: Manufacturing units and service units. Micro Manufacturing Unit is defined as having investment less than ₹25 lakh, Micro Service Units are defined as having investment less than ₹10 lakh. Small Manufacturing Unit is defined as having investment less than ₹5 crore. And Small Service Unit is defined as having investment of less than ₹2 crore. Medium manufacturing unit is defined as having investment less than ₹10 crore. And a medium service unit is defined as having investment less than ₹2 crore. In all cases, the investment means that in plant-machinery and equipment.

Box 3.4:   *Major issues before MSMEs*

Financial/taxation

- Lack of availability of adequate and timely credit
- High cost of credit
- Collateral requirements
- Limited access to equity capital
- Issues relating to taxation, both direct and indirect, and procedures thereof

Marketing

- Problems in supply to government departments and agencies
- Problems of storage, designing, packaging and product display
- Lack of access to global markets

Infrastructure/technology/human resources

- Inadequate infrastructure facilities, including power, water, roads and so on

- Low technology levels and lack of access to modern technology
- Lack of skilled manpower for manufacturing, services, marketing and so on
- Procurement of raw materials at a competitive cost

Institutional/legal

- Multiplicity of labour laws and complicated procedures associated with compliance of such laws
- Absence of a suitable mechanism which enables the quick revival of viable sick enterprises and allows unviable entities to close down speedily

Source: Compiled by author from a whole list of problems as identified and published in http://business.gov.in/enterprises/problems.php

---

Ninety-four per cent of all such MSME enterprises have proprietary ownership, 95 per cent of the units are running perennially, and women make up only 17 per cent of the workforce.

In the past, several committees have looked at the issues faced by MSMEs, and recommended measures to the government, a key measure being the financial stimulus package (Government of India 1996; National Commission 2007; Reserve Bank of India 2004). Responding to the call of 19 national level MSME associations, the Prime Minister formed a TF in August 2009 to look into the issues of MSMEs, and recommend immediate measures, to resolve these issues, to the government.

The issues identified by the Committee are shown in Box 3.4; these can be classified into four broad groups:

1. Finance/taxation
2. Market access
3. Infrastructure/technology/HRs
4. Institutional/legal

The recommendations made by the TF also fall under these categories. The main features of the recommendations are discussed below.

Finance/taxation:

1. Stimulus package should continue for one more year.[6]
2. Creation of an Exclusive Risk Capital Fund of ₹2,000 crore within Small Industries Development Bank of India (SIDBI) to cater to MSMEs.
3. Additional budget support of ₹3,000 to 5,000 crore over five years to support infrastructure upgrades.
4. States to be supported in funding the rehabilitation of MSMEs.
5. Commercial banks to adhere to the target of 20 per cent of their lending to MSMEs, out of which 60 per cent must be apportioned for micro-sectors.

---

[6] Stimulus Package for MSMEs refers to four financial stimulus packages announced by GOI on 7.12.2008, 2.1.2009, 24.2.2009 and 26.2.2009. This refers to a series of measures starting to reducing Cenvat, to support measures in exports, easing import restrictions, and duties, provision of working capital and sector-specific measures for textiles, leather, housing and so on. For a complete picture of all the stimulus packages, see www.rajind.rajasthan.gov.in/Stimulus_Packages.pdf that compiles all of them together.

6. Government should increase the equity base of the National Small Industries Corporation (NSIC), to cater to the demand-side requirement of the MSMEs.

Market access:

1. There is a recommendation for 20 per cent procurement by all departments and PSUs from MSMEs.
2. The government's offset policy especially for the Defence and Aviation Sectors should give priority to MSMEs.

Infrastructure/technology HRs:

1. DICs should be converted to Industrial townships that are better equipped to serve the sector.
2. The government should encourage corporatization of the MSMEs.
3. New clusters of MSMEs should be created.
4. Setting up a ₹1,000 crore fund was recommended to encourage the concept of business incubators.
5. Another fund of ₹1,500 crore may be created to utilize green technologies in the MSME sector.

Institutional/legal:

1. There is a need to create a national-level institution for promotion and development of MSMEs, over and above the institutions like SIDBI, NSIC, Development Commissioner (MSME), that already exist.
2. An expert group may be formed for the above to determine the overall mandate for the institution.
3. Creation of an MSME exchange.
4. New legal entities like a single person company or limited liability partnerships should be given wide publicity.

These recommendations are more than a year old, and their implementation remains sluggish (Ramkrishnan 2011). NSIC has taken the initiative to implement a few of the recommendations that refer to them, in terms of setting up a cell on market intelligence, organizing sector-specific trade fairs, improving raw material procurements for MSMEs, enhancing the equity base of NSIC and so on. But none of the other recommendations have seen the light of day. The recommendations themselves are disquieting as none of them refer to any mechanisms for improving labour and its welfare, other than encouraging green technologies.

3.3.4. Conditional cash transfers

The central challenges of all redistributive programmes are:

1. Identifying the deserving population.
2. Reaching the deserving population.
3. Avoiding leakages due to hijacking of resources and corruption.
4. Streamlining procedures to avoid inefficiency.
5. Establishing administrative accountability.
6. Controlling costs of delivery.

Redistribution expenditures and subsidies exceed the states' share of the central taxes (Mukhopadhyay 2008). Besides leakages and inefficiencies, there are difficulties in identifying and ensuring access to the poor, as highlighted in Section 3.3.1 on the National Food Security debate. For example, the 61st Round of the NSS reports that only 44 per cent of the poorest of the poor and overall only about 39 per cent of the poor have BPL cards to access redistributive programmes. In 2007, there were 151 central-sector schemes targeted at the poor that required ₹72,000 crore per annum, of which 90 per cent was required for just 30 such schemes. This apart, the subsidies for fertilizers and food (under PDS) constituted more than ₹61,000 crore in 2007–08. Various studies have shown that the leakage is very high, and the ratio of disbursement by central government to receipt by the beneficiary can be as low as 11 per cent to

21 per cent (Mukhopadhyay 2008). In a hypothetical situation, if this entire money were to be sent to the bank account of the poor, each BPL family would receive a monthly cash of ₹2,140 for an entire year.

An alternative approach to the transfer of goods and services is to transfer cash directly to the poor families. The Janani Suraksha Yojana, in which pregnant mothers are given cash incentives to have safe institutional deliveries of their first two children, is currently a major cash transfer programme in India. There have also been a plethora of cash transfer programmes in the past which were mostly geared towards incentivizing birth of a girl child and girl education.

Building upon earlier works (Dutta 2010; Mukhopadhyay 2008) the Planning Commission proposed five different ways of CCTs (see Box 3.5) by the end of 2010, and identified a few prerequisites for their successful implementation, which are:

1. Correct targeting—there are two types of targeting at work, NREGA works on the principle of self targeting, and all other programmes work on the principle of targeted intervention. Since targeting interventions have always been abysmally inaccurate, the Planning Commission proposed a new way of simplifying, and thereby improving the system-driven targeting (see Box 3.5).
2. Biometric identification—it is already being piloted under the unique identification (UID) programme of the country.

3. A system of electronic transfer to the bank account of the poor. Fortunately, the MGNREGA has already created nearly 90 million bank or post office accounts. If these banks and post offices are modernized, then electronic cash transfers are entirely feasible.

Several critics have pointed out that wherever CCT has worked best, it has worked:

1. Only in combination with other types of transfers, that is, goods and services (Dreze 2011).
2. When supply of service provisions are adequate to absorb the heightened demand. That cannot be said to be true in India; therefore, cash transfers in lieu of other transfers and provision of services can be completely counterproductive.

The Bihar Mukhya Mantri Balika Cycle Yojana is selected for its critical importance as a pilot of CCT, which is being cited as a success, and is described in Box 3.6.

3.3.5. Corporate Social Responsibility (CSR) as national mandate

In purchasing power parity terms, India's GDP is the fourth highest in the world after USA, China and Japan (World Bank 2010), and this phenomenal growth has occurred mostly due to the efforts of the private sector. The Indian corporate sector in general has greatly benefited from the liberalization era over the last one and a half decade.

Box 3.5: *Planning Commission proposal on CCTs*

1. Cash Transfer to provide a minimum monthly income guarantee to each household—₹500 per family per month
2. Cash Transfer to pregnant and lactating mothers to encourage institutional delivery—₹700 for three months before, and ₹1,000 for three months after delivery

3. Cash transfers to replace ICDS cooked SNPs—₹5,376 crore subsidy component of its full expenditure of ₹8,000 crore
4. Cash Transfer to replace food subsidy in PDS
5. Cash Transfer to youth for skill development—stipend to attend vocational education, and expenditure subsidy to the institution

Source: Planning Commission (2010).

Box 3.6: *Bicycles through cash transfer: Success in Bihar*

Students dropping out of school is an all India phenomenon, starting at the upper primary level. The work done during the last decade in terms of improving access to education has resulted in a near 100 per cent enrolment and close to 80 per cent retention at the primary level. However, retention beyond that appears to be a massive challenge. More significant is the girl children's dropout rate. One particular reason is the average distance of an upper primary or secondary school from each home and the cost and availability of local conveyance. Most often, the local bus services are inadequate, and even when available, they are expensive. Lack of motorable roads could also be a reason.

In an effort to combat this situation, the Bihar government introduced a scheme in 2006, and initially sought to provide a bicycle to all girls who enrolled in class IX. This was a self-targeted scheme, with no preference to BPL families. Any girl who enrolled in class IX was given a bicycle. Later, 2009 onwards the modalities were changed, and ₹2,000 were given as a cash grant to buy a bicycle and ₹700 to buy a school uniform. A total of 871,000 girls benefited from this scheme in the three years from 2007–08 to 2009–10. The scheme was extended in 2009–10, to girls studying in madrassas, and aided minority schools in addition to Rajkiya and Rajkiya Krit High Schools.

In 2010 A.N. Sinha Institute of Patna, found in its evaluation that while targeting was 100 per cent, in 92 per cent cases, bicycles and uniforms were indeed purchased. Peer pressure from girls who have cycles and uniforms ensured that a large percentage of the money was used as intended, though the report lamented the purchase of poor quality cycles in some cases. Additionally, scholarships were provided to girls who scored 60 per cent in secondary exams. The result has almost been miraculous. In 2009, dropout rates in the 11 to 14 age groups came down from 17.6 per cent to 6 per cent only. A political fallout of this as pointed out by the media was, that these bicycles were used by families to come and vote for Nitish Kumar's party, as women voters came out in bulk and voted for him.

Source: *The Hindu Business Line* (2011, p. 4).

For example, Tata Groups' annual turnover was about ₹50,000 crore around 1994, whereas it was ₹313,000 crore in 2009, two-thirds of which was earned from business interests outside India.

Therefore, large corporates are expected to share the burden of the social sector development. The Ministry of Company Affairs, Government of India formulated a voluntary guideline for the corporate sector on its social responsibilities. The document named, 'Corporate Social Responsibility, Voluntary Guideline 2009' made a serious attempt to define CSR as distinct from philanthropy, and a clear commitment to:

1. care for all stakeholders,
2. function 'ethically',
3. uphold the dignity of workers,
4. protect the environment,
5. respect human rights, and
6. contribute to social sector development.

While these are laudable goals in themselves, the guidelines did not ask for a measurable commitment, and kept it voluntary. However, as the Ministry of Company Affairs were introducing a Companies Act (Amendment) Bill, the Parliamentary Standing Committee on Finance came out with a strong recommendation of making the CSR provisions mandatory and measurable. Its suggestion is summarized in Table 3.7.

The Ministry of Company Affairs accepted the recommendations of the Parliamentary Standing Committee on Finance and agreed to introduce a bill in the coming session of the Parliament to this effect. The onus has been placed entirely with the company board and its shareholders. The Board shall have to formulate a CSR policy and publish it, as well as report to the shareholders with regard to compliance.

This approach was criticized by a section of the corporate world. They believe that

Table 3.7: CSR as corporate mandate

Company category	Mandate for CSR as per cent of net profit
Private companies having net worth of ₹500 crore or having turnover ₹1,000 crore or PAT ₹5 crore, whichever is more	at least 2 per cent
PSUs having net profit less than ₹100 crore	3–5 per cent
PSUs having net profit between ₹100 and ₹500 crore	2–3 per cent
PSUs having net profit more than ₹500 crore	0.5–2 per cent

Source: Press Information Bureau (2010).

commitment to CSR policy should be voluntary, while disclosure norms can be made stringent. It is felt that making it compulsory may result in a 'tick the box' approach or lip service with little effectiveness.

3.3.6. New policy on land acquisition, resettlement and rehabilitation

Concerns over destruction of livelihoods has been on the national agenda from the time the large infrastructure and SEZs started being developed, and in particular, as people's resistance against land and forest acquisition started spreading, inspired by the Narmada Bachao, Singur, Nandigram and other resistance movements. The issue of land and livelihood became a central agenda on charting development pathways of the nation. The government's policy response took the shape of a Land Acquisition (Amendment) Bill, 2007 (later modified in 2009) and a national R&R Bill (2009) that in some ways tried to accommodate the public concerns of lost livelihoods, keeping the eminent domain framework of the state intact. These two policies are discussed below.

Land acquisition for public purposes is done by various wings of the governments, like the Indian Railways, National Highway Authorities, Port Trusts, Metropolitan Development Authorities and others on the strength of specific Acts. But the most well-known and far-reaching consequences have always been the result of acquisition of land by the Land Revenue Department of the state governments on the strength of the Land Acquisition Act 1894 (as modified from time to time), and the recent SEZ Acts.

The government in the wake of a number of land rights related resistance struggles, and the consequent debates in the media and academia came out with a Land Acquisition (Amendment) Bill 2007, which was hotly debated in the public domain, resulting in another revised version in 2009. Further, a related bill, namely R&R Bill 2009 has also been drafted and introduced in the Parliament to address the specific issues of compensation and rehabilitation of the affected people.

The 2007 draft bill on Land Acquisition was also riddled with defects, just like its predecessor the Land Acquisition Act 1894. First, the Act grants absolute power to the state to acquire private land, while placing it under no obligation to rehabilitate the families affected by the acquisition. Second, the public purpose has not been clearly defined, and even land acquisition for private companies was included under public purpose. The principle of compensation, based on land ownership rights, was a very narrow interpretation of who the users are, and how they incur costs of being excluded from the land. 'Common property resource'—land, ponds, pastures, forests that belong to the community and are often absolutely critical to their lives—were excluded. Further, landless agricultural labourers and even unrecorded tenants and sharecroppers were not entitled to compensation in this scheme. Also, the principle of computation of compensation, based on the market value that precedes acquisition, is faulty on two counts; the registry records always show less value than the actual prevailing market price, and market price actually jumps manyfold, immediately after acquisition, the benefit of which is received by the buyer and not the seller.

The policy debates that ensued on this draft and on land acquisition in general have taken three major stands.

1. No acquisition of forest land for mining for environmental reasons, and for protecting lives of the poor, especially the tribals.
2. No large construction projects like big dams that destroy environment and livelihoods, and do not offer commensurate benefits in the long term.
3. Adequate compensation and rehabilitation for all the people affected by land acquisition. While the first two are being propounded by civil society activists, environmentalists and a section of the radical academia, the techno-bureaucracy, economists and policy planners preferred the third strand, and came out with a revised draft of the LAA Bill and a separate R&R policy in 2009.

The new draft of the LAA Bill (see Box 3.7) defined the public purpose with some clarity, covering only works related to defence, infrastructure and vital works of the state, and completely abolished land acquisition for private companies. The 'Other' public purposes clause refers to a situation where the government can only acquire 30 per cent of the land after 70 per cent has been bought directly by the buyers. This 30 per cent will only be acquired for public purposes. The tribals and other traditional forest dwellers (OTFDs) are included in the 'interested persons' list, land records have

to be updated mandatorily before the final decision on acquisition is taken and land transactions are disallowed after land acquisition proceedings have started. The market value is to be calculated on the intended future use of the land, and compensation has to be paid within 60 days after the award, for which a compensation authority is to be constituted.

However, many of the critical flaws remained as they were. For example, the absolute power of the state allowing it to forcibly acquire land without the consent of the affected people remains intact. This is in a sense in contravention of the 73rd and 74th Amendments to the Constitution and PESA Act 1996 that allows the citizens a say in the planning and implementation of the projects that affect their lives. The clarity on public purpose is not enough; there are loopholes in the definitions that can bring in land acquisition for private companies through the back door. There is an undefined urgency clause in Article 17(1) of LAA Bill that empowers the government to bypass all acquisition procedures and forcibly acquire land within 15 days, and in some cases, within 48 hours. The compensation scheme continues to exclude fishermen, agricultural labour, artisans, unrecorded tenants, sharecroppers and so on. Compensation for loss of common property resource continues to be out of the ambit of the Bill. Rehabilitation rights arise only in case of a threshold number of 400 affected persons in general and 200 affected persons in forest and hill areas. Projects affecting less number of persons do not have to meet this clause. No provision is made in the

---

Box 3.7: *Public purpose as defined in LAA Bill 2009*

1. Defence purposes of military, navy, air force or any other works vital to the state.
2. Government infrastructure projects that benefit the general public, where infrastructure means—electricity, highway, ports, airports, railways, bridges and so on.

3. Any other purpose useful to general public, in which 70 per cent is already acquired by the private party, and 30 per cent remains to be acquired.

Source: Compiled by author from Draft Bill (2009).

Bill to return the land to its previous land owners for unutilized acquired land.

The issue of Tribals and OTFDs is a case in point. The LAA Bill considers them as interested persons. However, the rights enshrined upon them under FRA 2006 and PESA 1996 are not built into the process of acquisition nor do they have a place in the R&R Policy. The processes related to Social Impact Assessment (SIA) and Environment Impact Assessment (EIA) have not been made an integral part of the LAA and R&R Bills either.

The R&R policy makes a commitment of allocation of land, as per Article 36, to a maximum of 1 ha of irrigated and 2 ha of un-irrigated land to the affected HH, but only if government land is available in that area. Similarly, the clause of preferential treatment, in employment is subject to 'if available' and 'as far as possible' clauses. The benchmarks of 400 and 200 affected persons as the threshold for any resettlement seem arbitrary. It has also been argued that resettlement as a principle of welfare by the state has to be based on citizenship. Further, while a time frame has been drawn to complete the compensation and reimbursement process within 60 days, no such time frame is fixed for completing the R&R process. Another lacuna is neither LAA Bill nor the R&R Bill has any penalty clause for violation of provisions of the law. This means that the cost of compliance remains much more than the cost of violation, a situation that risks encouraging non-compliance.

Looking at both the Bills together, one gets the impression that these aim at making the acquisition process faster. They are mainly designed to meet the requirements of the rural areas and do not pay enough attention to the urban displacement, and remain elusive about the larger goals of improving livelihoods of the poor people (Saxena 2009).

At the time of writing this chapter, the NAC seems to have formed a set of recommendations on the entire issue of land acquisition and rehabilitation and resettlement (*The Hindu* 2011b). These are:

1. Compensation should be pegged at six times the market price as defined before acquisition.
2. Fisher folks, agricultural labourers, artisans and forest dwellers should be included as affected persons.
3. Instead of two separate acts there should be a single Land Acquisition, Resettlement and Rehabilitation Act.
4. The acquired land should be returned to the original owners if it is not used for the purpose as laid out during acquisition within five years.
5. Setting up of a National Commission on land acquisition, resettlement and rehabilitation.

However, the issue of protection of affected persons under land purchase for private purposes by private parties remains unresolved.

3.3.7. Policy developments in agriculture

The agriculture sector supports livelihoods of about two-thirds of the Indians and is considered critical for the economy. In this context, the Prime Minister is considering an annual agriculture survey from next year to analyze policy issues and evaluate various schemes and their impact on farm economy. Agriculture has remained under tight central government control, and the first stirrings of farm sector reform came only last year, with the unshackling of fertilizer prices—urea prices have been raised by 10 per cent.

Some recent successes of the government in agriculture are:

- Queries received by the revamped Kisan Call Centres have tripled during the last one and a half years.
- Introduction of Internet and SMS-based advisory services to farmers is gaining acceptance.
- Extension reforms provides for 20,800 dedicated extension functionaries down to the block level and one farmer friend for every two villages.

- Loans to farmers have increased from ₹86,981 crore (2003–04) to ₹426,530 crore (2010–11 provisional).
- Due to state incentives under Rashtriya Krishi Vikas Yojana (RKVY) and greater outlays by the centre, the total allocation to agriculture has increased by ₹27,309 crore in five years (i.e., an increase of 97 per cent).

The new initiatives being proposed by the government are summarized in Box 3.8.

In the recent years, India has experienced a large number of farmers' suicides, due to depression, and losses of animals and crops as a result of climate change; high food inflation (see Chapter 2) and ongoing shortages in basic commodities which have compelled a rise in imports. But the slow growth in agriculture has turned. As per the latest Economic Outlook report of the Government of India (India's Economic Outlook 2011), agriculture grew at 6.6 per cent in 2010–11 and is projected to grow at 3.0 per cent in 2011–12. Laying emphasis on agriculture has, once again, become central to India's inclusive growth strategy.

While presenting the Union Budget 2011–12 in February 2011, the government outlined a four-pronged strategy covering agricultural production, reduction in wastage of produce, credit support to farmers and a thrust to the food-processing sector.

The measures announced include an increase of ₹1 lakh crore for farm credit at subsidized rates, removal of production and distribution bottlenecks in food items and a second Green Revolution in the east. The government has also directed the banks to step up direct lending for agriculture and credit to small and marginal farmers at a heavily subsidized rate of interest, that is, 7 per cent, but with a 3 per cent subvention if loans are paid back on time. Box 3.8 lists the new agricultural policy initiatives for 2011–12.

One of the challenges for the Ministry of Agriculture is that its total annual outlay of ₹15,034 crore is disbursed across about 51 schemes. It has decided to reduce the number of central schemes to 10, including the flagship RKVY, and a new variant of the scheme that will focus on infrastructure and agriculture statistics. The total allocation for RKVY has been increased from ₹6,755 crore in 2010–11 to ₹7,860 crore and has been warmly welcomed by the states as it provides them with the flexibility to formulate state-specific strategies while being administered by the centre, and it has also been proved more efficient, and is beneficial to farmers. The centre monitors the state initiatives which could range from responses to agro-climatic conditions, to natural resource management, to technology, livestock, poultry, fisheries and land

---

Box 3.8: *New initiatives in agricultural policy*

- Extending Green Revolution to Eastern India (seven states) by tapping ground water potential and using appropriate technologies.
- Rainfed Areas Development Programme (RADP) in 424 districts, covering arid, semi-arid and sub-humid regions.
- Programme of integrated development of 60,000 villages in 11 states with more than 5 lakh hectares of area under pulses.
- Initiatives for nutritional security through intensive millets production, and value addition by processing.

- Accelerated Fodder Development Programme to enhance fodder availability throughout the year to benefit 25,000 villages.
- Vegetable Initiatives Scheme in peri-urban areas to enhance production, improve supply chain and ensure direct sales around major urban centres.
- Special programmes on oil palm area expansion to augment oil-palm productivity by 3 lakh million tonnes (mt) in five years.

Source: Compiled by author from the Budget 2011–12 speech of Pranab Mukherjee, Minister of Finance, Government of India.

reform. Given the RKVY's vast scope, more than a third of all funds for agriculture are expected to be invested here by the end of the 11th Plan (2012).

One of the key features of the government's agricultural policy has been the signal given to the farmers from time to time in the form of a MSP offered to them for various crops (see Table 3.8). The centre's decision to raise the MSP, sharply for oilseeds, and moderately for rice and pulses, is considered right in the customary sense as they are hardly ever implemented. But the government's capacity to procure produce is limited outside north-west India, causing market prices to frequently crash below the MSPs, as occurred recently for wheat and maize.[7] To complicate matters, following the government's initiative to extend the Green Revolution to the country's eastern region, the states which are covered under the initiative have refused to offer procurement prices for paddy and wheat to the farmers. To boost the procurement drive, the Ministry has already held consultations with officials of Bihar, Orissa, Jharkhand, Chhattisgarh, Uttar Pradesh, West Bengal and Assam.

One particular feature of the Indian agriculture is that it's increasingly becoming female-centric. The national level data suggests that women form 33 per cent of the agricultural labour force, 48 per cent of self-employed farmers and 18 per cent of farm families are headed by women (MKSP 2010).

If we do away with the narrow definition of productive workers, rural women have always been engaged in some farm activity or the other, such as, sowing, harvesting, ground preparation, de-weeding, post-harvest processing and so on. However, women were never recognized as farmers, a policy lacuna due to which all farm credit, extension services, training, subsidies, seeds, pesticides, etc., are received by men, since these supports are mostly given on the basis of land asset, which are almost totally owned by men.

MKSP is the first such attempt in the history of independent India, to encourage and invest in women as farmers. It aims to provide skills, extension services, finance, seeds and other inputs to help the women engage in agriculture more productively and develop their ownership. Eight expected outcomes are listed in the programmes that are shown in Box 3.9. The MKSP is conceived as a sub-programme under NRLM.

MKSP hinges on a few core strategies of interventions, such as:

1. Identifying strong community-level organizations of poor women.
2. Harnessing locally adaptable, resource saving and sustainable agricultural technologies.
3. Technical skill building for women.
4. Providing other inputs to make them sustain their production, sale and income.

Table 3.8: Major shake-up planned in farm funding

	Agriculture Department Allocation (₹crore)	
	2010–11 (RE)	2011–12 (BE)
Agriculture & cooperation	17,695	17,522
Agri research and education	3,818	4,957
Animal husbandary, dairy & fishers	1,356	1,696
• The govt currently has 51 schemes which will be pared to 10	• Govt tried to streamline plans in 2007, however the changes were insignificant	

Source: Banerji (2011).

---

[7] The dearth of maize which resulted, prompted poultry feed manufacturers to start using wheat instead of maize as the base.

Box 3.9: *Expected outcomes in MKSP*

1. Net increase in the incomes of women in agriculture on a sustainable basis.
2. Improvement in food and nutritional security for the women and their families.
3. Increase in area under cultivation, cropping intensity and food production by women.
4. Increased levels of skills and performance by women in agriculture.

5. Increased access to productive land, inputs, credit, technology and information.
6. Reduction of drudgery for women through use of gender friendly tools/technologies.
7. Increased access to market and market information for better marketing of their products.
8. Increased soil health and fertility to sustain agriculture-based livelihoods.

Source: MKSP (2010, p. 2).

The targets have been clearly designed for families headed by women, single-women families, primitive tribal groups, women groups engaged in agricultural activities and resource poor SC/ST HHs.

Just like the SGSY special project, the proposal has to be routed through Panchayati Raj and Rural Development Department of the state. The funding support for the project is divided between the centre and state in the ratio of 75:25 for non-NER and 90:10 for NER states.

The project design elements include strong women groups that are already engaged or ready to engage in agriculture, enhanced access to productive assets by way of purchase or lease of land or pond, use of locally known sustainable agri-horticultural techniques, improved market access for the produce, training for women on technology, post harvest techniques, and marketing and so on.

This is a demand-driven project, and the onus is on the state governments to submit appropriate proposals to the Ministry of Rural Development (MoRD) while seeking funds. Although the guideline tacitly suggests that the Project Implementation Agency (PIA) can be a non-government organization and even a community organization, the conditionality of 25 per cent state share is likely to limit the PIA to Panchayat and Rural Development (P&RD) Department of the state governments. While the planned outcomes are laudable, they seem ambitious for a single project.

3.4. Section IV—Challenges to livelihood: Policy issues

People's existing livelihoods are threatened and eroded by a number of factors, like natural disasters, political conflicts, shocks, contingent poverty and so on. There may or may not be a direct causality between these factors and public policy which can help mitigate and minimize negative effects. The most critically emerging challenge specifically to the poor people's livelihoods is from public policy on land acquisition for industrial development and infrastructure. Large-scale mining, SEZs, big dams, megaports and other infrastructure development projects need vast tracks of land and forest, which are inhabited and being used by the poor. In the past the land acquisition related policies have worked towards destruction of livelihoods, instead of improving it. Here we will present two case studies from Orissa to illustrate and describe the political and social processes fighting against public policy.

3.4.1. The case of Vedanta

The story of Vedanta has been unfolding for nearly eight years. It sought a license to construct an aluminium refinery, a power plant and a mining lease to extract bauxite (the primary raw material for aluminium) from Niayamgiri hills of Lanjigarh in Kalahandi District in Western Orissa, way back in 2003. The mining lease component was to cover an area of 7 sq km in Kalahandi and the adjacent Raigada Districts. The proposed mining lease request was challenged in the Supreme Court, which after some deliberations, in its interim order agreed to stall the mining project pending an investigation on environmental issues, but gave permission for the refinery. In its final order in 2008, the Supreme Court gave clearance to the mining lease subject to fulfilling conditions regarding sustainable development, environmental protection and conservation of wildlife, the onus of which was on the state government. However, Ministry of Environment and Forests' (MoEF) Forest Advisory Committee made an inspection of the sites and noticed that gross violations have taken place in all the three environmental and livelihood aspects of the project. On the basis of their report the MoEF constituted a four-member committee in June 2010 to look into the issues of environment, livelihoods and wildlife. The Committee headed by N.C. Saxena submitted its report in August 2010 (Saxena 2010).

The report came out as a damning indictment of the Orissa government for failing to comply with provisions of the law, and in some cases, even questioned the trustworthiness of its official reports. It observed that Niyamgiri Hills are a part of a greater bio-reserve that extends to the Kalhandi, Raigada and Koraput Districts. It tried to measure the ecological, human and other costs of mining here. The area of 7 sq km (700 ha approx.) is inhabited by the Dongria and Kutia Kondh tribes, recognized as Primitive Tribal Groups, of which a total of 1,453 Dongria Tribe families will be displaced, about 121,353 trees would have to be cut, 3.63 lakh shrubs and ground level flora will have to be cleared and an uncounted number of four-horned antelope, barking deer, rare variety of lizards, etc., would perish. Apart from this, it will also destroy 41 villages in the area.

The Committee took strong exception to the fact, that the state government and its district authorities flouted all legal provisions made under the PESA, FRA and other relevant laws. The district authorities not only failed to protect the rights of the tribes and the community forest reserve, they actually produced false certificates of Gram Sabha in some cases. The Committee in its report observed:

> From the evidence collected by the committee, we conclude that the Orissa government is not likely to implement the FR Act in a fair and impartial manner as far as the PML area is concerned. It has gone to the extent of forwarding false certificates and may do so again in future. The MoEF is advised not to believe the Orissa government's contentions without independent verification. GoI should therefore engage a credible professional authority to assist people in filing their claims under the community clause for the PML area with the state administration.

Based on its observations about the impact on the different aspects of livelihoods, wildlife and ecosystem; failed implementation on the part of the Orissa government making its commitment to its tribal community questionable and flouting of all norms by Vedanta, the Committee concluded:

> In view of the above this committee is of the firm view that allowing mining in the proposed mining lease area by depriving two Primitive Tribal Groups of their rights over the proposed mining site in order to benefit a private company would shake the faith of tribal people in the laws of the land which may have serious consequences for the security and well being of the entire country.

Based on this damning report, the MoEF cancelled the mining lease of Vedanta on 21 October 2010. However, it is interesting to note that the Orissa government filed an appeal with the Supreme Court, against this order. Therefore, at the time of writing the SOIL Report, the livelihoods of nearly 1,500 primitive tribal families hang in the fine balance of the court briefs and legal arguments.

3.4.2. The case of POSCO

The case of POSCO is in some ways similar to the case of Vedanta. POSCO's proposal was about setting up an integrated steel plant and a captive port in Jagatsinghpur District in coastal Orissa. Both Vedanta and POSCO are minerals-based projects, both are situated in declared forest land and both displace people. While POSCO wanted 1,621 ha area of which 1,253 ha is forest land, Vedanta wanted 621 ha of mining lease.

The dissimilarities are also striking: the Vedanta plant was being set up in hill areas covered under a dense forest. The land belongs to the Forest Authority, and the area was inhabited by primitive tribal groups, who enjoy various constitutional protections. There is substantial environmental and ecological destruction in this case. The POSCO plant is situated in a coastal district, not in a scheduled area and has no ST people. Some part of it is forest land, but another part is *ryoti* land, where about 700 predominantly agricultural families doing betel vine and paddy farming, as well as fishermen, many of whom are SCs, will be displaced. While the Vedanta project would affect the hills and forests, the POSCO project would affect the coast. In the case of Vedanta, the project, including the works without any environmental clearance, was almost nearing completion, whereas the land has not yet been transferred to POSCO and work has not started at the proposed site.

Just as the MoEF appointed the N.C. Saxena Committee to look into the violations of the FRA 2006 and Forest Conservation Act 1980 in the case of Vedanta, it also appointed a four-member committee headed by Meena Gupta to look into the environmental and livelihood issues of the inhabitants in the context of the POSCO project. The committee submitted its report on 18 October 2010 (Gupta 2010).

One striking feature of the report is that there was gross disagreement between members of the panel so that two reports were submitted, the first by the chairperson and a separate report by the other three members of the committee. There was broad agreement on the need to repeat the exercise of claiming forest rights of the communities, as it was not done in the desired manner the first time round. The issue of environmental clearance, Coastal Regulatory zone clearance and paying compensation to affected farmers were more contentious issues. The panel differed on this, and so, two separate reports were presented to the MoEF. Meena Gupta was not in favour of cancellation of the EC, CRZ clearance as wanted by the other members.

The MoEF actually gave the clearance to POSCO, with certain conditions. The conditions were to ascertain whether there are OTFDs, and their constitutional rights are adhered to. There have been protests and anger has been expressed by the civil society on this decision. The resistance movement that started four years ago is still continuing, and more than 700 farmers' and fishermen's families face an uncertain future.

3.4.3. Onion crisis: A case of policy failure

Onions are an essential ingredient in cooking across many parts of India. Its use is not limited only to middle- and upper-class homes, nor is its use limited to exotic dishes. The use of onions is very much a part of rural and urban HHs across many classes and castes almost on a daily basis. Therefore it is not surprising that India is the second largest producer of onions after China. Onion is a political product too, and it is often said that it influenced election decisions in Delhi and Rajasthan in 1998, and in 1980 as well.

About 45 per cent of onions come from the two states of Maharashtra and Karnataka. September 2010 saw heavy rainfall in the onion producing areas of Maharashtra, Karnataka and Rajasthan, which somewhat disturbed the sowing season. However, despite some initial hiccups, according to Nafed Chairman, Sanjeev Chopra, the onion production was almost 20 per cent more than the previous year. But the supply of onion to big markets was less, and consequently the prices shot up from ₹25 to

₹30 per kg to ₹88 to ₹100 per kg in just one week in December 2010, in all metropolitan cities and even in rural areas. Even in Nasik, one of the core onion-producing areas, the price was 50 per cent higher. The Food and Agricultural Minister announced that the price increase was due to crop loss, and would continue for another three weeks. The situation was grave, as the public opinion was quickly turning sour, it was further aggravated by the sudden announcement by the Union Commerce Minister that there were no shortages of stock, and the crisis was due to large-scale hoarding.[8]

This sudden price rise in mid-December 2010 was not anticipated, nor did the government's price control mechanism has any handle on it at any time during the two weeks in which this saga was played out. This news was in the headlines of almost every newspaper, building pressure on the government, when BJP, the main opposition, called for a demonstration in Delhi for which more than 20,000 people assembled at very short notice. The government, after an initial disarray, realized the gravity of the situation and its possible political fallout, and took two important decisions on 20 December 2010. All onion exports were banned till 15 January 2011, and quick imports were made from Pakistan where the price was about a third of the Indian prices, at zero customs duty, implying a quick and cheap supply of onions to the market. This helped as the prices fell and stabilized at ₹45–₹50 per kg in about 10 days. However, *The Times of India* claimed that the hoarders made about ₹10 lakh a day, and in a period of 15 days' time, made about ₹1.50 crore each.

The policy failure was on three major counts:

1. The inability to institute an effective price monitoring and control mechanism,

having efficient market intelligence inputs.
2. Failure to act swiftly and decisively to catch the hoarders, and, if necessary, take appropriate actions to ensure adequate supply and bring down the price.
3. The government's intervention brought the price under control for the consumers, but did nothing to address the plight of the onion farmers.

3.5. Section V—Towards a livelihoods schemes coverage index

Livelihoods-related programmes of the central and state governments run into hundreds, of which about 30 consume 90 per cent of the resources. Is there a way we can compare inter-block, inter-district and inter-state performance for any given set of livelihoods scheme? Is it at all possible to determine and index the reach of the schemes to the desired population? If possible, what could be the ways to approach the issue? Developing a composite index of coverage of livelihoods schemes and testing it with available data is beyond the scope of this section; instead, we intend to outline some of the principles that need to be applied in developing such an index.

It is well known that most livelihood schemes target families, members of families and in certain cases, a community. For example, Indira Gandhi National Old Age Pension Scheme (IGNOAPS) targets old age persons in a family; ICDS targets children between the ages of 0 to 6 years, lactating mothers and pregnant women; JSY targets pregnant women; MDMs targets primary and upper-primary school children attending government schools; whereas NREGA targets the HH, water supply and sanitation. Loans and subsidies to SHGs are targeted towards the SHGs, village electrification targets villages, Pradhan Mantri Gram Sadak Yojana (PMGSY) targets habitations with a population of 500 and above. Therefore, indexing has to first delineate the constituency.

---

[8] This paragraph is a short summary from all the reports published in *The Times of India* and *The Hindu* from 15 to 23 December 2010, that tracked the story on a everyday basis.

The target constituency is further classified in categories like BPL, SC, ST and minorities. Many livelihood programmes target BPL HHs, like the PDS, IGNOAPS, Antyodaya, JSY and so on. There are some programmes like ICDS and MGNREGA that are self selecting, and not limited to BPL families. Similarly, there are specific programmes for SCs, STs and minorities, which are not limited to BPL families. So perhaps the first step in any indexing procedure should be to define the target constituency. A constituency thus defined may look like the following:

JSY : pregnant women of all BPL families irrespective of caste, ethnicity and religion

ICDS : all children between 0 to 6 years of age, irrespective of caste, ethnicity and religion

MDM : all school-going children of primary and upper-primary government schools, and aided schools but not private schools or coverage of schools only irrespective of number of students

MGNREGA : all rural households willing to do manual unskilled labour

The second aspect is to consider the geographical areas. For those livelihoods schemes that are pan-Indian, this may be a block, a district or a state. The reason being that much data is desegregated at the block level, and some is available only at a district level. So the geography can be determined, depending on the level at which the primary data is collected.

The third aspect is to decide the period under review. It may be practical to consider a year and preferably a financial year to conduct the computation. However, ideally, subject to availability of resources and if possible, it should be done at even shorter intervals.

The fourth aspect is about defining coverage. Coverage is defined as the number of constituents registered under the programme. For MGNREGA, it is the number of HHs having a job card; for JSY, the number of BPL women having a JSY card; for IGNOAPS, the number of persons included in the official list; for PDS, the number of HHs having a PDS card and for MDM, the number of schools brought under the MDM programme.

The fifth issue is about defining the service. In case of MDM it's apparently a simple, cooked mid day meal. However, it is possible to ask if the quantum and the meal components are as stipulated. For MGNREGA, for example, the service may be defined as being given job cards, getting 100 days of work, per HH in a year, and getting paid for the work. Similarly, for IGNOAPS, the service may be defined as the inclusion of the name in the IGNOAPS beneficiary list and getting a pension as stipulated for all the 12 months.

The sixth issue is determining a method to compute and index the service coverage for a target constituency for a given scheme for the service(s) defined. Let us assume the target constituency is called A. The number of such constituencies in a district is N. So the total target constituency is NA. Now let us consider the time period is one financial year. And coverage is defined as the number of constituencies that are included in the programme in terms of registration. So in case of JSY the coverage is those BPL pregnant women who have been issued the JSY Card; for MGNREGA, those who have a job card; for MDM, those schools that are registered under it and for IGNOAPS, those whose names are in the official list. Let us say that the coverage number in a district is B. Now comes the tricky part of determining how to compute the service. We could propose that a three-level service inclusion be defined, as those who got the minimal level, those who got the middle level and those who got the maximum level. For MGNREGA, this may mean the number of persons who got work (minimal level), and the number of persons who got work and got paid for 100 days in a year (maximum level). This may alternatively be called the degree of service.

So if the coverage is C = B*100/NA, and we have a minimal degree of service as *Wm*, and maximum degree of service is *Wx*, then the percentage of *C* getting covered by *Wm* and the percentage of *C* getting covered by *Wx* over a year is the value of coverage and the degree of service. This may then be indexed to 100 for coverage, a minimum degree of service and a maximum degree of service.

3.6. SECTION VII—Conclusion

Livelihood policies in India encompass a broad variety of thematic areas, with focus on large-scale transfer of goods and services, and creating conducive conditions for augmenting livelihoods. The focus has remained largely fixed on the poor, with its usual challenges of identification, leakage and lack of accountability. New and emerging trends are geared towards inclusion, entrepreneurship, skills formation, gradual shift from goods and services to cash, citizen participation and better governance. Though, the issue of land, in shaping our development agenda, continues to be of particular concern.

There is a certain disquietude, even over the affirmative action of the state, about the government's capacity to deliver, which is increasingly getting manifested in poor functioning of the state systems, delays and ineffectiveness, and loosening control of the lower arms of the governments. A new category is now being invented in the West to describe the state of India, as a 'Flailing State' (Pritchett 2011), where quality, capacity, intent and desires for social–economic transformation though strong at the upper level, have no control over its development army at the lower levels.

There is one trend that can reinstate our hope in change for the better. The Indian electorate is maturing day by day, and all the signs point towards it seeking less rhetoric and better performance on the ground. And the second is the hope placed on the emerging civil society that has already demonstrated its might. These two together are our hope for the future.

References

Banerji, Devika. 2011. Farm schemes to have states in lead role in XIIth plan. *The Economic Times*, 23 May.

Business Standard. 2011. Quoting U. Singh Deo's statement in Orissa Assembly. *Business Standard*, 18 March, p. 3, column 3–4.

CAG. 2010. *Report of the Task Group on Social Audit*, pp. 7–10, submitted to the India Parliament on 24 October.

CBGA (Centre for Budget and Governance Accountability). 2011. 'Study of Budget 2011'. New Delhi: CBGA.

Dreze, Jean. 2010. Middle class has lost track of how poor the country is. Interview with Tahelka.com, 6 November.

———. 2011. The cash mantra. *Indian Express*, 11 May.

Dutta, P. 2010. Small but effective: India's targeted unconditional cash transfers. *Economic & Political Weekly* 45 (52), 25 December.

Government of India. 1996. *Report of the expert committee on small enterprises*, chaired by Prof Abid Hussein.

Gupta, M. 2010. *Panel Report*. 18 October 2010.

Mahila Kisan Sashaktikaran Pariyojana (MKSP) 2010. Guidelines, p. 1, 24 December. Ministry of Rural Development, Government of India.

Ministry of Labour. 2009. *National Policy on Skill Development*, p. 3. Ministry of Labour, Government of India.

Mukhopadhyay, P. 2008. More on direct cash transfers. *Economic & Political Weekly* 43 (47), 27 November.

NAC (National Advisory Council). 2010. *Communications to the Government*, 23 October.

National Commission. 2007. *Report of the National Commission for enterprises in unorganized sector, 2006–2007*.

NCEUS. 2006a. *Report on Conditions of Work and Promotion of Livelihoods in Informal Sector*. pp. 4 and 6, submitted to Government of India in 2006–07.

———. 2006b. 11th Plan Approach Paper, p. 29. Planning Commission, Government of India.

———. 2006c. 11th Plan Approach Paper, p. 60. Planning Commission, Government of India.

———. 2007. Poverty estimates of 2004–2005. Press release by PIB, March.

NPSD (National Policy on Skill Development). 2009. Formulated by the Ministry of Labour and Employment, approved by the Cabinet in its meeting held on 23 February 2009.

Planning Commission. 2006. 11th Plan Approach Paper, p. 78. Planning Commission, Government of India.

———. 2010. Introducing conditional cash transfers in India: A proposal for five CCTs, 12 March, pp. 11–20.

———. 2011. Issues for the approach paper to 12th plan: PPT, 3rd slide.

Press Information Bureau (PIB). 2010. Press Release, 10 September. Ministry of Corporate Affairs, Government of India.

Pritchett, L. 2011. Is India a flailing state? Detours on the four lane highway to modernization. Unpublished paper personally communicated to author.

PWC. 2007. *Health Care in India-Emerging Market Report*, p. 7.

Ramkrishnan, D.E. 2011. Speech of the President. *IIA News*, 30 March.

Reserve Bank of India. 2004. *Report of the working group on flow of credit*, submitted to the SSI Sector, Reserve Bank of India, Rural Planning and Credit Department.

Saxena, K.B. 2009. Earth sale. *Tahelka Magazine* 6 (7), 21 February.

Saxena, N.C. 2010. *Report of the Four Member Committee*, 16 August.

The Hindu. 2011a. NAC recommends compensation six times the registered value. *The Hindu*, 26 May.

———. 2011b. BPL head count capped at 46%. *The Hindu*, 20 May.

The Hindu Business Line. 2011. Bicycles through cash transfer: Success in Bihar, *The Hindu Business Line*, 22 February.

UNICEF. 2010. *Inclusion by design: Unicef India's approach to equity*. New Delhi: UNICEF.

Vikas, R. 2008. Ownership Holding of land in rural India. *Economic & Political Weekly*, 8 March: 43–47.

World Bank. 2010. *World economic indicator data base*, 15 December.

Yeswanth, D. 2007. Financial inclusion: Road ahead. *IRMA Network* 11 (3).

State as the Largest Livelihoods Promoter

4.1. Introduction

The year 2011–12 is a turning point for Indian planning. It marks the end of the 11th Five Year Plan and sets the direction and strategies for the next five years. Two significant changes are taking place. First, there is a significant change in the population growth rate of the Empowered Action Group (EAG) states[1]—Rajasthan, Uttar Pradesh, Uttarakhand, Bihar, Jharkhand, Madhya Pradesh, Chhattisgarh and Orissa. These states have traditionally been characterized by high population growth, low literacy and poor health indicators. After decades of high growth pre-1990 and stagnation thereafter, these states, for the first time, have been experiencing a significant fall in population growth of about 4 per cent between 2001 and 2011. Second, the recently published NSSO 66th Round data indicates that the employment generation rate is higher than the rate at which the labour force is growing, which is no mean accomplishment, given the significant increase in the number of persons joining the labour force in the past decade. On the other hand, as discussed elsewhere in this report, there has been an acceleration of a broad-based growth during the year which is seen in all the three sectors—agriculture, industry and services.

India's relative as well as absolute poverty is becoming a major concern, and inequality is increasing rapidly with growth. To fulfil its potential, India has to ensure that growth is inclusive as projected in its 11th Five Year Plan and the current ongoing preparatory process for the 12th Five Year Plan—to ensure that the poorest households and the backward regions of the country are integrated in India's growth.

There are many taxonomies of poverty alleviation schemes, but one way to categorize the enormous landscape of government schemes is suggested in a forthcoming book by Mehta and Pratap (forthcoming) (Mehta et al. 2011). They argue that schemes fall into three broad categories (though many overlap):

- Those which prevent entry into poverty.
- Those which enable people to escape from poverty.
- Those which ameliorate persistent poverty and improve quality of life.

Table 4.1 categorizes the various schemes.

The government's efforts in schemes have played their role, though with mixed

[1] In India, the eight socio-economically backward states of Bihar, Chhattisgarh, Jharkhand, Madhya Pradesh, Orissa, Rajasthan, Uttaranchal and Uttar Pradesh are referred to as the Empowered Action Group (EAG) states.

Table 4.1: Poverty alleviation schemes and poverty dynamics

Programme/scheme	Prevent entry into poverty	Enable escape from poverty	Ameliorate persistent poverty/improve quality of life
Enjoyment and self-employment			
Mahatma Gandhi National Rural Employment Guarantee Act			x
Swamjayanti Gram Swarozgar Yojana		x	
Swama Jayanti Shahari Rozgar Yojana			
Urban Self-employment Programme		x	
Urban Wage Employment Programme			x
Support to Training and Employment Programme for Women		x	
Self-help groups and microfinance	x	x	
Nutrition and education			
Targeted Public Distribution System			x
Integrated Child Development Services Scheme			x
Mid day meals		x	x
Sarva Shiksha Abhiyan		x	
Health and health insurance			
National Rural Health Mission	x		x
Janani Suraksha Yojana	x		x
National AIDS Control Programme III	x		x
Aam Admi Bima Yojana	x		x
Rashtriya Swasthiya Bima Yojana	x		x
Infrastructure and basic services			
Pradhan Month Gram Sadak Yojana		x	
Indira Awaas Yojana			x
Total Sanitation Campaign	x		x
Bharat Nirman		x	
Jawahar Lal Nehru Urban Renewal Mission		x	
Accelerated Rural Water Supply	x		x
Integrated Watershed Management Programme	x	x	
Backward Regions Grant Fund		x	
Programmes for specific groups			
Scheduled Caste Sub-plan and Tribal Sub-plan		x	x
Integrated Child Protection Scheme			x
National Old Age Pension Scheme			x
Kishori Shakti Yojana		x	

Source: Mehta and Pratap (forthcoming).

results. Since the 1990s, their perceived role in poverty alleviation has been largely overshadowed by the belief that poverty will be eradicated when economic growth trickles down to the poor, rather than through targeted welfare and services. More recently, there has been a shift in focus in the poverty literature away from 'trickle down' towards the idea of inclusive growth. The shift towards inclusive growth has been accompanied by a shift from targeted welfare to an entitlement and rights-based approach, whereby the poor are not the beneficiaries of subsidies or services, but are citizens whose capacity must be developed to enter the markets and access existing entitlements, irrespective of the provider.

This approach recognizes that the supply side (both public and private) cannot be made more efficient in terms of including the poor except in response to a strong demand by the poor themselves.

Broadly, the poverty alleviation programmes launched from time to time can be classified under two heads—self-employment programmes and wage employment programmes:

1. The self-employment programmes started with the introduction of the Integrated

Rural Development Programme (IRDP) in 1978–79, Training of Rural Youth for Self-Employment (TRYSEM) (1979), Development of Women and Children in Rural Areas (DWCRA) (1982–83), supply of improved toolkits to rural artisans (1992) and the Ganga Kalyan Yojana (1996–97). To remove conceptual and operational problems in the implementation of these programmes, a holistic programme was developed to cover all the aspects of self-employment, such as, organization of the poor into SHGs, training, credit, technology, infrastructure and marketing. This was the SGSY, started on 1 April 1999 and which continued into the 11th Five Year plan.

Based on the feedback provided and recommendations made by the various studies, NRLM was launched during 2009–10 to facilitate effective implementation of the restructured SGSY in a mission mode. NRLM aims at reducing poverty in rural areas through promotion of diversified and gainful self-employment and wage employment opportunities.

2. The wage employment programmes aim to provide livelihoods during the lean agricultural season as well as during droughts and floods. Wage employment programmes were first started during the Sixth and Seventh plans in the form of the National Rural Employment Programme (NREP) and Rural Landless Employment Guarantee Programmes (RLEGP). These programmes were merged in 1989 into JRY. A special wage employment programme—Employment Assurance Scheme (EAS)—was launched in 1993 for the drought-prone desert tribal and hill area blocks in the country. The different wage employment programmes were merged into the Sampoorna Grameen Rozgar Yojana (SGRY) in 2001.

NREGS,[2] which was launched in 2006, aims at enhancing the livelihood security of people in rural areas by guaranteeing hundred days of wage-employment in a financial year to a rural household whose adult members volunteer to do unskilled manual work.

India's recent scale-up of skills marks a departure in wage employment from public works to the market for jobs. India faces a major skill development challenge due to the lack of skill development opportunities for 80 per cent of the new entrants to the workforce. The existing training capacity can accommodate only 3.1 million per annum against the need of 12.8 million[3] new entrants per annum. Only 2 per cent of the workforce has skill training.

Besides, there are a plethora of programmes launched by the government with other objectives, which include:

1. Food security programmes under which the Public Distribution System (PDS) is the key safety net.
2. Social security programmes which include, the National Social Assistance Programme (NSAP), Annapurna and so on for the BPL.
3. Urban poverty alleviation programmes that include the Nehru Rozgar Yojana, Urban Basic Services for Poor (UBSP) and so on, involving participation of the communities and non-governmental organizations.

The other initiatives undertaken to alleviate poverty include price supports, food subsidy, land reforms, area development

---

[2] In this chapter, MGNREGS, NREGA, MGNREGA, MGNREGP and NREGS have been used interchangeably. The NREG Act was named as MGNREGA in 2009. The Act also makes it mandatory for states to formulate Schemes and Progammes, thus adding S and P for usage by many.

[3] Planning Commission website.

programmes, improving agricultural techniques, free electricity for farmers, discounted water rates, Panchayati Raj Institutions (PRIs), growth of rural a banking system, grain banks, seed banks and so on. These initiatives and programmes aim not only at reducing poverty but also at empowering the poor to find solutions for their economic problems. In this respect, the government has set up more than 50 programmes and schemes that benefit the farming community and strengthen their livelihoods. Most of the people are unskilled, food insecure and lack assets, and some are dependent on others.

This chapter attempts to highlight the shifts and drifts in three government flagship programmes which impact the life and livelihoods of the poor the most. In this chapter, the focus lies on bringing out the various facets of and breakthroughs made by these programmes during the last one year.

While Chapter 3 described broad shifts in the budget and ways to evaluate budget decisions, here we present allocations for special flagship livelihood programmes for 2010–11 and 2011–12. Table 4.2 shows

Table 4.2: Budget allocation (plan) for major flagship programmes (₹ crore)

Sl No.	Programmes	2010–11	2011–12	Percentage increase over 2010–11
1.	MGNREGS	40,100	40,000	−0.2
2.	IAY	10,000	10,000	0
3.	National Social Assistance Programme (NSAP)	5,762	6,158	6.9
4.	PMGSY	12,000	20,000	66.7
5.	NRHM	15,672	17,840	13.8
6.	ICDS	8,700	10,000	14.9
7.	MDM	9,440	10,380	10
8.	SSA	15,000	21,000	40
9.	JNNURM	12,685	13,700	8
10.	RKVY	6,722	7,810	10
11.	AIBP	11,500	12,650	10
12.	NRDWP	9,000	9,350	3.9

Source: Extracted from an article published in Kurukshetra, April 2011 written by K.K. Tripathy. Sourced from Budget documents, GOI, 2010–11 and 2011–12.

that in this year's budget allocation for the major flagship programmes, 9 out of the 12 high-budgeted development programmes witnessed a hike of less than 15 per cent over the previous year allocation. Rural housing programme—Indira Awaas Yojana (IAY) has not seen any increment over and above last year's budget allocation. MGNREGS also experienced a slight fall in its budget allocation. Allocation for the National Rural Drinking Water Programme increased only by 3.9 per cent. The three major programmes which have witnessed more than 15 per cent increase include the Pradhan Mantri Gram Sadak Yojana (PMGSY) with 66.7 per cent; Sarva Shiksha Abhiyan (SSA) with 40 per cent and Rashtriya Krishi Vikas Yojana (RKVY) with 16.2 per cent.

For the sake of deliberation, the chapter covers only the major government initiatives wherein these are engaged as livelihoods promoter, each at different stages of evolution. The three flagship programmes discussed are:

1. MGNREGS: It aims at providing at least 100 days of guaranteed wage employment a year to every household that seeks it, while mandating 33 per cent participation for women. 52.6 million households were provided employment in 2009–10, and data indicates that the poorest states benefited the most.

2. NRLM: In response to the limitations of the SGSY, the Government of India converted the SGSY into NRLM in 2010 for poverty alleviation and employment generation in selected areas. The objective of the NRLM is to reduce poverty by providing gainful self-employment and skilled wage employment opportunities to the poor rural households.

3. Skill Development Initiative: In the Budget 2011–12, the government made provisions of an additional ₹500 crore for the National Skill Development Corporation (NSDC), which is likely to create a skilled workforce of an additional

Box 4.1:   *NREGA since inception 2006–07*

- Approximately 988 crore days of work generated with a total expenditure of approximately ₹128,000 crore till 2010–11.
- During 2010–11, provided employment to over 5 crore household.

- Opened about 9.8 crore bank and post office accounts for wage distribution.
- Average wage per person days increased from ₹65 to ₹100 during 2010–11.

Source: Data compiled from various sources, including www.nrega.nic.in and government presentations.

40 million across the country in the next 10 years. NSDC, a joint venture between the government and industrial associations was formed in 2010 and has a mandate of creating a skilled workforce of 150 million by 2022, in 21 focus sectors identified by the government through a funding of training ventures for profit and not-for-profit organizations.

The task of improving the livelihoods of the poor is so diverse that most of the government's policy instruments have a direct and indirect bearing on this. For very specific reasons, this chapter restricts its propositions to capturing the cases relating to the economic well-being and livelihoods aspects promoted by the government which includes the centre, state, district administration and loosely the decentralized PRI system.

4.2. Evolution of MGNREGS

Mahatma Gandhi National Rural Employment Guarantee Programme (known as NREGA)—the flagship programme of the Government of India under the Ministry of Rural Development (MoRD)—has a budget allocation of ₹400,000 crore (US$ 8.8 billion) for 2011–12, an allocation almost unchanged since last year. The annual budget allocation and expenditure under NREGA since 2006–07 to date is detailed in Table 4.3. Since 2005, the programme has promised 100 days of work per year for unskilled labourers to build rural infrastructure like irrigation ditches and roads. Costing 1 per cent of GDP, the MGNREGS is India's largest welfare scheme.

A recent World Bank report on welfare programmes in India, including MGNREGS, said they did not give the 'bang for the rupee' warranted from such huge spending (World Bank 2011). The report says that the allocation for MGNREGA programme was approximately 0.6 per cent of GDP, up to 2009. It also lauds the inclusion of the poorest—the scheduled castes, tribals and women—in the programme. However, it also underlined the fact that the MGNREGA implementation across states was uneven, with states such as Andhra Pradesh, Chhattisgarh, Madhya Pradesh and Rajasthan as high performers with respect to the percentage of participating households, as well as person days of employment generated per rural household. Rajasthan was at the top with around 90 per cent in fund utilization rates, and Punjab at the bottom with around 5 per cent fund utilization for programme implementation.

NREGA has now been in operation for about five years. The policy focus remains anchored in achieving the twin objectives set out in the Act, of which, in practice, the second objective of creating productive

Table 4.3:   NREGA funds allocation and spends, 2006–07 to date

Year	Budget allocation (₹ crore)	Expenditures (₹ crore)
2006–07	11,300	8,823
2007–08	12,000	15,857
2008–09	30,000	27,250
2009–10	39,100	37,910
2010–11	40,100	39,377
2011–12	40,000	provisional

Source: Data compiled from various sources, including www.nrega.nic.in and government presentations.

assets that can kick start and energize the rural economy has been neglected, and the emphasis is almost completely on creating person days of work and paying wages.

In this section, we review the policy process and implementation issues which have risen as the programme reaches its maturity. First, the wage controversy—NREGA wages have been falling in real terms constantly over the years, and we describe how a policy correction has been made through an institutional process. Next, we look at the efforts to address seasonal job demand and labour supply, for the poor and for the farmers, respectively. Third, we review initiatives to improve the transparency and efficiency of the scheme. Finally, we look at the capacity limitations at the state and panchayat level, and the efforts being made to address these.

4.2.1. NREGA wage controversy

When NREGS was implemented in 2005, the central government set the wage rate at ₹60 per day or the minimum wage rate set by a state, whichever was higher. Gradually, state governments realized that NREGS—putting cash directly in the hands of the poor—was a great way to build political capital and willingly began raising their minimum wages (reflected in NREGS wage). The escalation in rates led the central government to cap the rate at ₹100 per day January 2009, in clear violation of the MGNREG Act which stipulates that the wages be pegged to the Minimum Wage Act. This act of the government led to a nationwide controversy and a Policy Working Group was convened to assess the wage issues in detail. The Working Group reported the following serious lacunae (Working Group on NREGA Wage 2010):

1. The MGNREGA wage is falling in real terms on a continuous basis year after year.
2. There is no clarity as to how the wages are determined, no process of how those would be revised from time to time, and no guarantee of a statutory wage, let alone a living wage.

3. In many states the NREGA workers are earning less than the statutory wage.
4. Rampant delays in wage payment.
5. Entitled compensation is never paid by the government.
6. Very little is done to acknowledge the crisis and there is little willingness to do something about it.

The Working Group made three emergency recommendations and 29 other recommendations to be implemented in the medium term (see Box 4.2). It sought an immediate redressal of the issue of real-wage loss by asking the Rural Development Ministry to peg the MGNREGA wage with the Consumer Price Index of Agricultural Labourers (CPI-AL) with 1 April 2009 as the base, at ₹100.

Around the same time the MoRD appointed the Chief Statistician of India the task of determining a national index of wages for MGNREGA workers. This came under criticism from the Working Group, as well as others, who argued that prices may vary greatly depending on geographic areas and other local conditions, so a national index can never truly represent the real wage situation. After talks, listening to protests, and receiving other recommendations, the prime minster ordered an immediate implementation of the Working Group's recommendations. This lead to a 17–30 per cent increase in NREGA wages to match the state minimum wage. Notwithstanding the wage issue, MGNREGA remain yet another unfulfilled promise of the state to its citizens. When it was linked to each state's minimum wage rate, NREGA set the floor of labour earnings and lifted wages. Now that it is delinked, Table 4.4 shows that NREGA wages are lower than minimum wages in seven states.

4.2.2 Job demand and labour supply

Ashok Gulati,[4] Chairman, Commission on Agricultural Costs and Prices (CACP) argues that, NREGS has pushed up farm

---

[4] *The Economics Times*, 11 April 2011.

Box 4.2: *Three emergency recommendations by the Working Group on NREGA wages*

1. Immediately peg the NREGA wage with consumer price index of agricultural labourers with 1 April 2009 as the base, at ₹100. If the central government decides to fix the minimum wage, then this should be reviewed every six months.

2. MGNREGA Wage policy should always be consistent with the Minimum Wage Act, and cannot override it.

3. Reduce the working hours of the NREGA labour from 9 hours to 7 hours.

Some of the other 29 recommendations made by the Working Group

1. Every state must take measures to ensure clear timelines for each step towards timely payment of wages like Andhra Pradesh and Tamil Nadu.

Source: NREGA (2010).

2. The possibility of interim payment to the extent of 80 per cent of the wages by the end of the week may be explored.

3. Payment of an extra day of wage for a delay of each week may be instituted to incentivize on time wage payment.

4. Every state government must immediately notify setting up of a competent authority for compensation of wages to NREGA workers.

5. RBI's guideline of 'know your customer' (KYC) must be followed by all banks in setting up bank accounts and payment of wages through banks.

6. New technologies like the business correspondent model or biometric recognition systems should be used for payment services. These may be introduced after careful piloting.

---

wages and heightened the availability of farm labour since its inception. Rising farm wages, which have a major impact on food prices, may force the government to devise a blueprint in which agricultural work is included under a widened ambit of MGNREGP. In the Punjab–Haryana belt, wages have gone up by over 20 per cent in 2010–11. In Kerala, the rise in farm wages has been the highest, at almost 300 per cent. While some have argued that there is no adverse impact of the NREGA on agricultural production and costs, a study undertaken by Tata Energy Research Institute (TERI) in March 2011 (NREGS and Agriculture: Manifestations and Opportunities) maintains that employment guarantee schemes have led to an increase in the bargaining power and labour shortages at critical points in the agricultural cycle. The study recommends 'a proper work calendaring' so that MGNREGS works are done during the agricultural lean season to reduce peak season labour shortage problems.

The MoRD has responded, informally at least, by advising the states to suspend and consider deferring NREGS work particularly keeping in mind sowing, transplantation and harvesting seasons in the region. This is primarily intended to free up rural labour to take up work in fields and check the rising cost of agricultural labour. This informal advice is made keeping in view the legal aspects of the NREGA guaranteeing 100 days of work on demand and the concerns expressed by the Ministry of Agriculture on farm labour availability in the key and peak farming season.

On the other hand, the scheme has also been hobbled by an under-supply of funds, when they are most required. Release of funds from centre to state has been on the basis of expenditure in previous months, which meant disbursement for subsequent months did not reflect increased seasonal demand. Following suggestions by Bihar, the norm was adjusted in February 2011, so that disbursement reflects the demand projected in the labour budget made by each state government.

4.2.3. Improving transparency and efficiency

In an effort to improve the efficiency of administration, the MoRD is taking steps (including holding consultations with the

Table 4.4: From convergence to divergence

	NREGA wage rate		
	2006–07	2009–10	Min agricultural wage rate
NREGA above minimum wages			
Maharashtra	47	127	100–120
Gujarat	50	124	100
Orissa	55	125	90
Arunachal Pradesh	55–57	118	80
Uttar Pradesh	58	120	100
Tripura	60	118	100
Chhattisgarh	63	122	122
Madhya Pradesh	63	122	110
Assam	66	130	87
Nagaland	66	118	80
Bihar	68	120	109
West Bengal	69	130	96
Jammu & Kashmir	70	121	110
Meghalaya	70	117	100
Manipur	72	126	81
Uttaranchal	73	120	114
Himachal Pradesh	75	120–150	110
Jharkhand	77	120	111
Tamil Nadu	80	119	85–100
Sikkim	85	118	100
Haryana	99	179	167
NREGA below minimum wages			
Karnataka	69	125	134
Rajasthan	73	119	135
Andhra Pradesh	80	121	125
Mizoram	91	129	132
Punjab	93–105	124–130	143
Kerala	125	150	200
Goa	NA	138	157

Source: Ministry of Rural Development.

Comptroller and Auditor General [CAG]) to ensure that the findings of the social audits be taken seriously by the state governments. As a way forward, transaction-based management information system (MIS) as practiced in Andhra Pradesh, and the habitation-level MIS as demonstrated in Rajasthan (Mazdoor Kisan Shakti Sanghatan [MKSS]), are considered a solution as every transaction from the application for work to the payment slip can be stored in the MIS and it will restrict fudging of any data.

An ongoing CBI probe in Orissa is investigating the allegations of corruption in implementing the scheme. The probe follows a 2007 report by the Centre for Environment and Food Security (CEFS) which alleged a ₹500 crore scam in the implementation of the NREGS in Orissa. Reports from the CAG of India and National Institute of Rural Development indicated a misappropriation of 88 per cent of the funds in some districts of Orissa. About 77 per cent of the very poor in Orissa did not get even a single day's work under the rural employment scheme in the previous year. The report further reveals that the yearly average employment per household in the district of Ganjam (Chief Minister's district), which was declared the 'Best Practice District' in MGNREGS, and was declared the 'Best Performing Model District' by the central government, was less than half a day. Similarly, in another case, the MoRD has sought a detailed report from the Government of Madhya Pradesh on alleged financial irregularities worth several crores of rupees in works done under MGNREGS, and is considering a CBI enquiry.

4.2.4. Improving capacity at state and panchayat level

As required by NREG Act, the government must make MGNREGP more open to scrutiny and empower its beneficiaries by getting panchayats (village councils) to periodically disclose information about the scheme's functioning in that area, including, status of work, purchases made and from where, number of days worked and by whom, and payments made. To this end, the MoRD has issued an advisory to village panchayats, making it mandatory for them to convene regular Gram Sabhas (village general bodies). The initiative is also aimed at making the scheme less centralized. The Act mandates that at least half the tasks under the programme should be executed by the panchayat, making the body key to its success. The CAG performance audit of the scheme found that the lack of mandatory proactive disclosures by local bodies was a key failing. In reality, the panchayats grossly lack the capacity to undertake all these tasks at the decentralized government level.

Most of the states were unable to utilize even half of the funds slotted for administrative expenses, stalling the administrative reforms that are expected to increase the efficiency of the scheme. The states can use 6 per cent of allocation under the scheme for administrative purposes, to build capacity for the scheme's purpose of providing an income support to the poor. But the overall utilization of funds for administrative costs under the scheme was 40.3 per cent (of this 6 per cent) in 2010–11. The most cited reason for the low use was the lower demand for work because of the good monsoon. But the lower utilization is also apparently due to the lack of capacity to build the context to undertake public works at panchayat level. The scheme suffers from major human resource constraints in its planning and administration at this level. Some states like Andhra Pradesh and West Bengal have spent the most towards improving administrative issues. Bihar has taken some initiatives towards enhancing the administrative capacity of the human resources by establishing a Bihar Rural Development Society that has started an extensive recruitment and training programme.

Finally, the central government is looking at ways to rework its development programmes and its delivery mechanisms in the affected districts. One of the key changes that is expected to take place in MGNREGS is to consider resource allocation not linked to the size of the population in the Left-Wing Extremism (LWE) districts. The MoRD is devising a new strategy to better implement social and economic development programmes in the 60 districts affected by Maoist militancy. These districts are mainly spread across nine states including Orissa, Jharkhand, Chhattisgarh, Bihar and West Bengal. An example of how the district administration of Kandhamal saw MGNREGS as a way to bridge the widening divide between the tribal majority and the SC community after the riots can be seen in Box 4.3.

The Ministry of Rural Development, as the nodal agency for the development schemes (including the MGNREGA, the IAY, the PMGSY and the NRLM), has been allocated ₹87,800 crore in 2011–12 to implement these programmes. The Rural Development Ministry has identified infrastructure and governance deficit as the two main hurdles in implementation of the programmes in these areas, and laid emphasis on addressing these issues in a more structured manner. With regard to MGNREGS, there is a need to enhance administrative expenditure to 10 per cent of the total allocation from the current 6 per cent, to strengthen the bank and post office infrastructure and give an additional 50 days of work in a year, after the completion of the 100 days guaranteed by law.

4.2.5. Towards better implementation of MGNREGS

In 'The Battle for Employment Guarantee', edited by Reetka Khera[5] (IIT Delhi), the

[5] *The Economic Times*, 21 July 2011.

Box 4.3: *District administration in Kandhamal—Best work out of MGNREGS*

Three years ago, due to the communal riots, Kandhamal District in Orissa was India's shame. This district, received the award on 2 February 2011, through the dedicated work of the District Collect Krishan Kumar which made it one of the top 10 districts in the country for innovations in MGNREGP implementation (the others are Churachandpur [Sikkim], North Sikkim, Dharwad [Karnataka], Sant Ravidas Nagar [Uttaranchal], Rajkot [Gujarat], Jalpaiguri [West Bengal], Barmer [Rajasthan], Anupur [Madhya Pradesh] and Thiruvannamalai [Tamil Nadu]). The significant work has covered building of roads, farm ponds and integration of natural resources. The district has showed a steep rise in expenditure, spending ₹64.20 crore in 2009–10 (an increase of 284 per cent) as compared to ₹22.57 crore in 2008–09. It has reported a sevenfold increase in the number of families who got at least 100 days work (7,305 in 2009–10 as compared to 1,020 in 2008–09). More than 56 per cent of the eligible families, mostly from the excluded communities, have

Source: Financial Express, 31 January 2011.

been covered, while the national average is only about 23 per cent.

Kandhamal is ranked among the 30 districts in Orissa which are categorized as 'food insecure' (as per the report 'Food Security Atlas of Rural Orissa', IHD, 2008). The district administration saw MGNREGS as a way to bridge the widening divide between the tribal majority and the scheduled caste community after the riots. The district administration launched a youth programme called 'Antaranga: Celebrating Diversity' and mobilized 7,500 youths representing each panchayat as workers for MGNREGS. To quell the tribal resentment over the non-tribals usurping their land, the district administration dovetailed MGNREGS with improving the quality of their lands secured through the Forest Rights Act. In the process, each tribal household received monetary help for farm ponds, land development, wells and plantation. This not only helped in creating social capital but also in building an asset base for rural households which was eroded during the conflict from 2007 to 2008.

---

factors that have contributed to the better implementation of NREGS in a few states, as compared to others have been well summarized. According to her, the four things that matter most are:

1. Demand for the programme in terms of poverty
2. Public mobilization
3. Administrative capacity
4. Political will

She has cited the examples of the states that have done well, like, Tamil Nadu, Rajasthan and Andhra Pradesh, which have a prior experience in implementing drought relief works backed by political will. States like Uttar Pradesh initially dismissed MGNREGS as a populist programme of the central government, but slowly changed its approach by increasing the minimum wage from ₹58 to ₹80 to ₹100, and issuing orders to the district magistrates to ensure at least

one ongoing MGNREGS work in each gram panchayat.

Despite drawbacks, the MGNREGS has undoubtedly provided a safety net for the rural poor and boosted incomes. The MoRD is working on including rural infrastructure such as rejuvenation of water storage systems (Watershed Management Programme) and convergence of MGNREGA with programmes under RKVY of the Ministry of Agriculture.

4.3. National Rural Livelihoods Mission

In 2010, the Government of India approved the restructuring of its SGSY programme into the NRLM. The move reflects recommendations from stakeholder consultations and lessons from the World Bank-financed rural livelihood projects in seven states, and many others by civil society organizations. These programmes showed that investing in self managed institutions of the poor, and aggregating those institutions beyond the community level yields impressive returns for poverty reduction. The programme recognizes that the poor people have the potential to come out of poverty with proper handholding, training and capacity building and credit linkage.

The NRLM is, perhaps, the largest poverty programme in the world with its goal of reaching nearly 7 crore rural households in 60,000 villages across 600 districts in the country. Thus, it has been touted as the most important and ambitious programme next to NREGS. The NRLM also recognizes that poor people have multiple livelihoods—wage employment and self-employment—and aims at stabilizing and enhancing incomes from both. The NRLM depends on the banks as a source of credit for the poor at reasonable rates with the smart use of subsidy. The NRLM places a stress on the participation of women.

In a clear break from the SGSY, the NRLM puts local mentors at the frontline. It utilizes the services of these mostly female Community Resource Persons (CRPs) who have experience in coming out of poverty and are members of self help groups (SHGs). As frontliners, they are expected to spread the concept of NRLM at the village level as well as across districts, and help make NRLM a people's movement. It allows flexibility in formulating context specific action plans at the state level, since, the level of development and availability of local resources is different for each state.

NRLM combines the triple objectives of social, financial and economic inclusion of the poor. Social inclusion involves enabling SHG members to build their skills to better access services such as education and health, entitlements like PDS, NREGS and other safety net programmes, and to gain a voice in local governance institutions. Financial inclusion involves ensuring access to financial services such as savings, credit and insurance. Economic inclusion involves developing skills for self-employment so that they are no longer dependent on safety net programmes and can build productive assets.

The NRLM entails these distinct features:

1. Universal social mobilization through SHGs which ultimately brings each and every BPL household under the SHG network.
2. SHG Federations are envisaged to act as second-tier institutions.
3. The goal of universal financial inclusion through SHGs linked to banks.
4. Allocation of up to ₹7,500 per beneficiary towards capacity building and training.
5. There is a provision of basic orientation training for all the *swarozgaris*, and skill training for the ones who are entering the micro-enterprise level.
6. Institutional arrangement for skill development, for self-employment and wage employment.
7. At least one training institute—Rural Self-Employment Training Institute (RSETI)—is to be set up in each district.
8. These RSETIs are to be set up in partnership with banks and with grants received from the MoRD and state governments.
9. A provision of an enhanced Revolving Fund of ₹15,000 per SHG.
10. A provision of a capital subsidy of ₹15,000 to individual Swarozgars of the general category, and ₹20,000 to SC/ST and people with disabilities, subject to a maximum of ₹2.5 lakh per SHG. Also a provision of professional support—at present the DRDAs/blocks only have a skeleton staff and are over burdened with a multiplicity of programmes.
11. Special projects—Under the NRLM, 20 per cent of allocation is earmarked for special projects, which combines 15 per cent for placement-linked skill development projects, and 5 per cent for innovative projects.

12. Improved evaluation and monitoring—evaluation of SGSY was done by commissioning studies and through an online Monthly Progress Report, regular meetings of the Performance Review Committee, visit by area officers and so on. In addition to these, NRLM plans:

- A comprehensive MIS encompassing a database of SHG profiles, federations, training institutions and activities, placements of trained beneficiaries, marketing of products and so on.
- Social accountability practices like social audits to bring in transparency.

13. Involvement of states for state-specific action plans.
14. Above all, a mission-mode approach is envisaged for its implementation, to enable time bound achievement of the goals of NRLM in partnership with civil society, industries, educational institutions and other resource organizations.

In a recent Solution Exchange[6] led group discussion to comment on the framework of NRLM implementation, done on behest of the Working Group constituted by the Planning Commission, many suggestions were made to lay focus on the cluster approach and value chain in primary, secondary and tertiary sectors; natural resource management; convergence with MGNREGS; making use of 'product champions' and separate funding for demonstration units for successful livelihoods models. The Planning Commission while formulating the 12th Five Year Plan is looking at incorporating these ideas and strategies to roll out NRLM on a large scale.

The Government of India has come out with a phase-wise approach to implement NRLM in the whole of the country, and the states are also expected to fulfil certain norms, before transiting from SGSY to NRLM, like:

1. Setting up of state level agencies and the district/sub-district level units.
2. Training and placement of professional staff and formulation of State Poverty Reduction Strategy for each state.
3. Formation of a State-Level Core Team with a nodal officer.

Many states have launched NRLM by promoting independent livelihoods promotion societies. Through these societies (a company in case of Gujarat), the state governments are looking at getting desired results from the social-benefit schemes which would provide a platform for formation of village groups, and support in fine-tuning existing government schemes. The government's expectations from NRLM stems from the instances of success in some districts in Andhra Pradesh, Bihar and Orissa, that have been able to use the village-community groups to further government entitlements to the poor.

As NRLM follows a demand-driven strategy, all the states have the flexibility to develop their livelihoods-based State Perspective and Implementation Plans (SPIPs) for poverty reduction, determined by the allocations for the respective states based on *inter se* poverty ratios, and in the process, it is envisaged that all the states/UTs would have to transit to NRLM within a period of one year, and thereby funding under SGSY will cease to operate (see Figure 4.1).

With a loan of ₹50 billion from the World Bank,[7] the Government of India is strengthening its ambitious NRLM to start a comprehensive rural livelihood mission to support the 12 poorest states which account for about 85 per cent of the total poor population in the country. The World Bank has invested about ₹30 billion in livelihoods missions in the state of Andhra Pradesh

---

[6] Solution Exchange for the Microfinance Community and Solution Exchange for the Work and Employment Community—consolidated reply dated 23 July 2011.

[7] *The Economic Times*, 13 June 2011.

Figure 4.1: NRLM delivery system in two phases

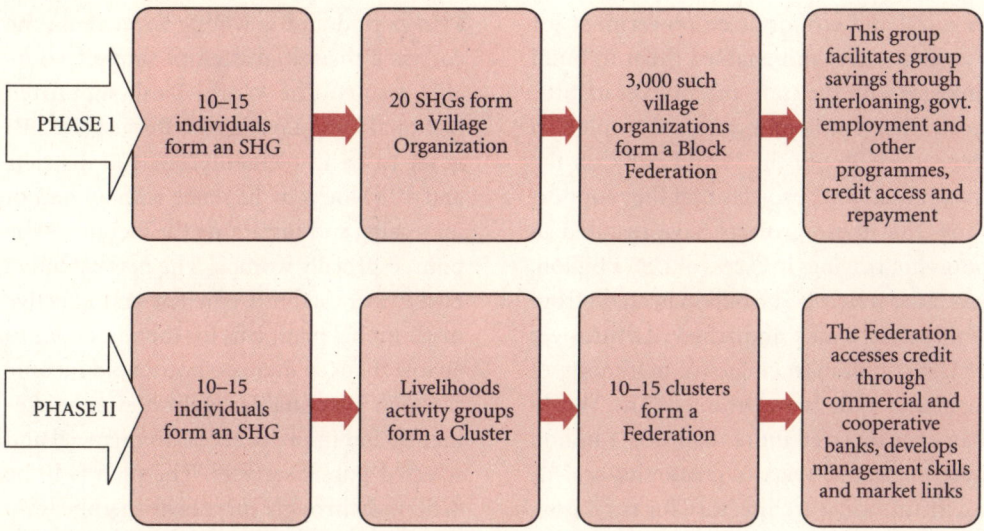

| PHASE 1 | 10–15 individuals form an SHG | 20 SHGs form a Village Organization | 3,000 such village organizations form a Block Federation | This group facilitates group savings through interloaning, govt. employment and other programmes, credit access and repayment |

| PHASE II | 10–15 individuals form an SHG | Livelihoods activity groups form a Cluster | 10–15 clusters form a Federation | The Federation accesses credit through commercial and cooperative banks, develops management skills and market links |

Source: Compiled from various documents of NRLM in public domain.

since 2000. The government is set to spend ₹225 billion for the scheme as an initial investment over the next plan period.

4.3.1. Key challenges in rolling out NRLM on a large scale

There are several challenges in implementing NRLM as the magnitude and nature of poverty are varied. Some of the major challenges are already being debated at this juncture. These are:

1. Feasibility of organizing 70 million BPL families into SHGs.
2. What will these SHGs do?
3. What skills are required by the SHGs and their members to get meaningful work?
4. What skill training and placement is envisioned?
5. What will be the consequence of the absence of a sustainable employment strategy?
6. This could be another flawed scheme which could turn the SHGs into a vehicle for routing other welfare programmes and highly corrupt subsidy-driven schemes.
7. At one level, such programmes are a silent acceptance of defeat in solving the problems of rural India, with no long-term solutions on the difficulty of endowing the rural masses, especially the rural youth with the requisite marketable vocational skills and career counselling to make them more employable.
8. It is not clear whether SHGs can move beyond the primary production level to the next level of high quality products, that is, services and value-added processed goods.
9. Political will at both the central and state government level to ensure fund entitlements and simple transfer of money sans the corrupt system so that this does not turn into another politically driven programme, leading to election slogans to win the votes.
10. Is it a short cut without a back-end support structure and committed investments in education and skills to help the rural poor out of poverty?

4.3.2. National rural livelihoods project in 12 states

In 2000, the World Bank extended its support to the state governments for the promotion of economic livelihoods, and mobilization and delivery of services, to the poor, in select districts of Andhra Pradesh, Madhya Pradesh and Rajasthan. Several studies indicate that these initiatives have resulted in social and economic empowerment for the rural poor, and enabled them to build linkages with the state and market institutions. The Implementation Completion Reports (ICRs) of the World bank on the three initial state projects that they support show that these projects have resulted in household savings in excess of US$ 1 billion, leveraged nearly US$ 6 billion in credit from commercial banks, and achieved a turnover of US$ 1 billion in collective marketing of farm and non-farm produce. The World Bank has invested more than US$ 1 billion over the last 10 years to create this scaled-up institutional architecture for rural poverty reduction, and mobilized 30 million rural poor into institutions of their own, which enables them to access livelihood opportunities, and build social, financial and economic capital. These programmes have resulted in social empowerment of the excluded castes and indigenous people, enabling them to build social and financial capital, and increase access to growth opportunities. They have also been taken up in areas affected by internal conflicts and in the poorest regions.

Based on the lessons learnt and with the kind of investment made by the World Bank (₹2,946 crore in livelihood missions in India), it is now committed to support scaling up of the scheme in 12 states, with an investment of about ₹5,000 crore. The government has committed to spend ₹22,500 crore on the scheme over the next Plan period and is willing to increase the corpus if the initial attempt shows favourable results. The World Bank-supported National Rural Livelihoods Project (NRLP) is set to be implemented in 100 districts and 400 blocks in 12 states with an aim of increasing and sustaining the income of the poor, especially women. The new extended NRLP will establish efficient and effective institutional platforms for the rural poor to enable them to increase household income through sustainable livelihood enhancements, and improve access to financial and selected public services. The plan is to be achieved through increased membership of the rural poor in inclusive, community-managed institutions, leveraging of financial services, increased productive assets and better access to public services.

Some of the 12 states have been chosen because of their past experience in implementing World Bank-supported livelihood projects, and where the implementation systems are already in place (Bihar, Madhya Pradesh, Orissa and Rajasthan). Other states have been identified on the basis of a high incidence of poverty and large number of rural poor (Uttar Pradesh), tribal population (Jharkhand and Chhattisgarh) and pockets of acute poverty at the sub-regional level combined with a pre-existing base of substantial social capital (Karnataka, Maharashtra, West Bengal, Gujarat and Assam) (see Box 4.4).

Box 4.4: *Doing it differently—Gujarat government's plan for poverty reduction through profits*

In the beginning of the year 2010, the Government of Gujarat set in motion a unique social sector scheme—'Mission Mangalam'—which brings in participation of the private sector, and involves corporate houses in livelihoods promotion and welfare of the rural poor in the state. The programme envisaged formation of SHGs in all areas of the state, linking them with banks, building their capacities for sustainable livelihoods and jobs using market mechanism and corporate houses. Thirty-two corporates, which include Reliance, Tata Motors, ITC, Fabindia, McCain Foods, Arvind Ltd. and Godrej Agrovet, agreed to share their expertise with SHGs for skill training. The idea was to involve the private sector in the ambitious task of poverty eradication and women's empowerment, and create profitable, scalable and sustainable win–win business models. Initiated in 2010, Mission Mangalam has succeeded in reaching out to more than 2.5 million women in rural areas, organized into 200,000 SHGs ('Sakhi Mandals'). A new company—Gujarat Livelihood Promotion Company (GLPC) has been promoted by the Government of Gujarat.

Recognizing the fact that there is a plethora of agencies that promote SHGs under numerous programmes, the Government of Gujarat took the bold step of bringing all of them together under one fold. In order to avoid duplication of efforts and fast track the progress, the Government of Gujarat has proposed a mechanism to centrally track all SHGs, create an online computerized database and real-time MIS, and give each of them a unique ID code, to eventually bring the rural poor out of poverty. This involves all stakeholders, including different government departments, bankers, SHGs, NGOs, MFIs, insurance companies and corporate houses.

For example, there was a tie-up with Jaipur Rugs Company which alone aims at benefiting 50,000 weavers in Gujarat, which was supported by the state government through reduction in the cost of looms. Similarly, corporates with international retail chains such as IKEA and TESCO facing disaggregated supply chain and production constraints in scale and speed are connected to producers at the bottom of the pyramid (BoP) in the interiors and backward regions. As a part of financial inclusion, GLPC has signed 10 MoUs with banks and financial institutions with a financial commitment of ₹18,000 crore covering more than 25 lakh beneficiaries. The State Bank alone has earmarked ₹5,000 crore, for livelihood projects over the next 3–5 years, making Mission Mangalam India's largest initiative in the field of financial inclusion.

State Level Bankers' Committee (SLBC) has made a commitment to provide a cash credit for a minimum of ₹50,000 to every SHG passing the grading process. This translates to a total of 25 lakh rural women members of the existing 2 lakh SHGs to be provided with cash credit amounting to more than ₹1,000 crore, accelerating financial inclusion for the marginalized communities. Mission Mangalam recruited 16 leading institutions, including IIM-Indore, Aga Khan Rural Support Program and NSDC as key knowledge partners.

Mission Mangalam has been endorsed by the who's who of India Inc., including Ratan Tata, Mukesh Ambani, Kishore Biyani and other top corporate leaders. Being first of its kind, Mission Mangalam is seen as a new approach and an innovative model in generating sustainable livelihoods.

Source: *India Weekly USA* (2011).

Uttar Pradesh has started the NRLM,[8] in a very modest way, with the launch of the UP State Rural Livelihoods Mission in four districts. The core team is to prepare a draft for the 'Poverty Reduction Action Plan' for the first phase. The state government has included experts from the Lucknow-based Bankers Institute of Rural Development (BIRD) as they were involved in the initial planning for the NRLM at the central level.

The Department of Rural Development, Government of Himachal Pradesh has finalized a poverty reduction framework under the NRLM for the coming seven years with annual plans and specific targets to create 25,000 livelihoods in the state in the next 12 months. The diagnostic study of poverty, backward and vulnerable groups and value-chain analysis will help determine the various sectors/sub-sectors, products and services for building linkages with the private sector.

While Orissa and Rajasthan are among the first to launch the NRLM, now Bihar, Gujarat, Andhra Pradesh and Madhya Pradesh too have got down to work (see Box 4.5).

It has a long way to go in making a shift from the process-oriented approach of SHG/Federation formation and institution building vis-à-vis the market development

---

[8] *Indian Express*, 2 April 2011.

Box 4.5: *From the level of subsistence to sustenance: Enterprise approach for economic empowerment in rural non-farm sector*

Over the years, the Government of Andhra Pradesh has supported SHG members, turning them into rural entrepreneurs. They have been supported with skill/trade and enterprise training including a package of financial loan and grants. These enterprises have come up in the major non-farm livelihood sectors—like textiles, handicrafts, jewellery, toys, chemical and minerals, forest based, leather, food products, agro/horticultural based, fisheries and electrical and electronics which are classified and clubbed under 100 different sub-sectors. There are around 30,000 enterprises in operation which provide employment to over 150,000 persons, and generate considerable wealth in the villages. The entrepreneurs have developed market linkage with the local and district level retail and whole sellers to sell their products. They have also developed links with raw material suppliers for their products.

The SHGs are formed by the Society for Elimination of Rural Poverty (SERP), a body under the Rural Development Department of the Government of Andhra Pradesh. Around 1 lakh SHGs exist in the state, consisting of 1.2 crore women members. These SHGs are federated at the village, sub-district and district level and carry out a number of livelihood and social activities. Employment Generation and Marketing Mission (EGMM) is another organization attached to the state government which creates employment for the families of the SHG member, and supports non-farm livelihoods of the poor.

The microenterprises' penetration of larger markets is limited and requires fine-tuning of their skills for better product development; improved quality of the product; better management of their units; better infrastructure, tools and machinery; access to credit as they are not legally registered; better packaging and branding and so on. The state government intends to make interventions in order to increase the sustainability of rural enterprises, and create local employment. At the same time, it aims at improving the profitability of the enterprise units by at least 50 per cent within a year. Average profitability of the units could be in the range of ₹2 lakh a year.

Source: Extracted by author from documents of SERP EGMM, Government of Andhra Pradesh.

approach as it seems, NRLM brings a paradigm shift towards the later by roping in the private sector as a major player and devising more of market based solutions in reducing poverty in India.

4.4. Skilling India: Vocational training

Seventeen million Indians reach employable age every year, but only 0.5 million find white collar jobs in the formal sector. Most of the other 16.5 million are school dropouts, while some are unable to secure steady jobs even after higher education. More than half—the less educated—get involved in agricultural and self-employment activities. But 7 million or so are the unemployed and underemployed youth: educated to standard VIII and above, poorly equipped to work in the agricultural sector, lacking capital and skills to launch their own business and disgruntled with the schooling system for failing to live up to their expectations (Gram Tarang 2010).

Unemployment is low in India because the majority cannot afford to remain unemployed. The unemployment that exists is disproportionately associated with the better educated youth. In 2004–05, NSSO data showed that on an average, an unemployed person has had 8.8 years of education, while an employed person only 4.4 years (Ghose 2010).

While India grapples with the employment related issues of its rapidly growing youth, the manufacturing and services industry is facing a growing shortage in the supply of workers. The NSDC's Skills Gap Reports (see Chapter 5) identified a demand for 244 million new workers across 21 key growth sectors by 2022. But only 120 million will be added to the workforce. India must ensure that at least this number gets hired fruitfully.

What is the skills base of the young employable population? The 2009–10 survey of the Ministry of Labour and Employment showed that 41 per cent of workers are illiterate (a figure which competes closely with the general population) and a further 14 per cent have only completed primary education (*Business India* 2011). NSSO 2008–09 data showed that only 1.5 per cent of urban literates and 0.2 per cent of rural literates have higher or technical education, and the figures are no different if we look at just the youth (15 to 29 years) or the full adult population. Currently, India has only 2.5 million vocational training seats (around 7,500 technical institutes for higher education and only 2,500 polytechnic institutes).[9] The current capacity of all India's skill development programmes stands at only 3 million (11th Five Year Plan).

Following the World Bank's 2006 report delineating critical gaps in India's skilling machinery, the Government of India (World Bank 2006) formulated the national skill development Policy that set out an ambitious target of skilling a workforce of 500 million by 2022. The task is clearly stated in the Policy as follows (NPSD 2009):

1. Increasing capacity and capability of the existing system to ensure equitable access to all.
2. Promoting lifelong learning, and maintaining quality and relevance, according to changing requirements, particularly of the emerging knowledge economy.
3. Creating effective convergence between school education, various skill development efforts of the government and government and private sector initiatives.
4. Capacity building of institutions for planning, quality assurance and involvement of stakeholders.
5. Creating institutional mechanisms for research development, quality assurance, examinations and certification and affiliations and accreditation.
6. Increasing participation of stakeholders, mobilizing adequate investment for financing skill development, and attaining sustainability by strengthening physical and intellectual resources.

In 2008–09, the government provided the first *tranche* of ₹1,000 crore towards National Skill Development Fund (NSDF) and established the NSDC. The Corporation has a mandate to train 150 million people, while the labour ministry is expected to train another 100 million by revamping and creating new Industrial Training Institutes (ITIs) with government and World Bank assistance.

The NSDC—established to address unemployment and underemployment among India's youth, thereby reversing the neglect and stigma of vocational training in India—has covered significant ground. By March 2011, it had completed skill-gap analysis of 21 sectors, approved funding for 26 private sector (mostly for profit but also NGOs) skills providers, which together target to skill about 45 million people in the next five years. It had also initiated the formation of 28 Sector Skill Councils with industry collaboration, of which six were either approved or incorporated by June 2011. The role of these councils is to identify sector skill needs, maintain skill inventory, develop standards, accreditation process, and criteria, plan and execute training of trainers, promote sector-specific training institutes and so on. In the context of the industry and developmental requirements, NSDC had also prioritized its targets to focus on training 30 to 35 million people each in automotive, construction and unorganized sectors in the short term (*Business Standard* 2011).

To meet its mandate of training 150 million people by 2022, NSDC's challenge is to train/re-skill 15 million workers, on an

---

[9] All India Council for Technical Education (AICTE).

average, every year. The projects funded by it are still in their nascent stages, and even the sector skill councils will take 3–4 years to become active and functional. So, it will be some years before the impact of NSDC's initiatives becomes visible.

NSDC entered a market in which several corporates are already active. Industrial corporates like L&T, the Mahindra Group and Ashok Leyland have been training their own and suppliers' workforce for some time. It is hoped that government money, and the expertise of career skills professionals, can overcome some of the problems that have been faced by these initiatives, in recruiting the trainees, finding and keeping good faculty, and deepening their learning beyond the 'gift wrap' which is being increasingly offered by temping agencies from whom they source the labour.

The annual budget allocation of ₹500 crore, during 2011–12, towards the NSDF is considered inadequate to meet the ambitious target of teaching skills to 500 million people by 2022. It would need at least a 10 times higher budget provision, that is, ₹4,000 to 5,000 crore annually to meet this target. The current pace of investment is not sufficient to train 40 million people each year to meet the target. Neither has the government made a budget provision for the 50,000 skill development centres that are planned to be set up directly by the government in 'unserviced', or low-opportunity, backward areas.

The pitiful state and small size of India's vocational training infrastructure, and the challenge of meeting the targets set, have led the government to make a shift towards integration of training in the schooling system, in addition to supporting post-school skills providers. At present, the coverage of formal vocational education (VE) at secondary school level is abysmally low. It is provided through 150 (approximately) vocational courses of two year duration, but is imparted only in 8 per cent schools. Even the National Institute of Open Schooling, which offers 80 vocational courses, has a total enrolment of about 600,000 students. The reasons for low enrolment to these courses are manyfold, ranging from obsolete syllabus, which is not linked to changing market requirements, to poor infrastructure, and absence of a qualified training staff.

The Ministry of Human Resource Development (HRD) is likely to unveil a new initiative in 2011, integrating vocational education with mainstream education.[10] This is intended to provide alternative avenues to reduce pressure on the universities that are unable to cope with the demand for undergraduate admissions and at the same time will also help create a pool of trained manpower for different industry verticals.

As a first step, the HRD Ministry has tied up with 10 state universities (in Madhya Pradesh, Andhra Pradesh and Maharashtra, among other states) to offer vocational courses at the graduation level with multi-entry and multi-exit facility for students. The Ministry aims to make these courses flexible for the students who can pursue vocational courses for six months, in a modular way, and be awarded a certificate which will help them get a job if they want to take a break from their studies in order to earn. But to make it a success, the fundamental requirement is a good quality vocational education with experienced faculty, and good curricula.

Whether offered in schools or other institutions, the success of vocational training initiatives are critically linked to educational levels among the participants, and low levels of schooling are a serious problem for the programmes' success. Two recent developments, however, hold promise to shift this educational profile. First, the Right to Education (RTE) Act, 2010, makes it mandatory for every child in the age group of 6–14 years to be provided with eight years of elementary education (with 25 per cent enrolment for children from weaker sections). Second, as discussed in Chapter 2, the NSSO 66th Round survey reveals a remarkable upward trend in spending on education.

---

[10] *Mint*, 4 July 2011.

In India and many developing countries, since only a tiny proportion of their workforce receives vocational training, it is interesting to consider to what extent does the general education act as a proxy for employability or the quality of human capital. Chadha (2004) takes formal education levels unquestioningly as a proxy, while Deshpande et al. (2007) report on the complexities of this debate, that is, the manner and extent to which formal schooling contribute to employability and productivity. They present the argument of Bowles and Gintis (2000), that schooling is profitable for employers, not because it produces direct productive skills, but due to 'its effects on individual's norms and preferences, making the prospective worker more attractive to the employer by attenuating problems of work incentives and labour discipline'. It is because of traits such as 'a predisposition to truth-telling, identification with the objectives of the firm's owners and managers as opposed to the objectives of co-workers or customers, a high marginal utility of income, a low disutility of effort and a low rate of time preference' (Bowles and Gintis 2000), that schooled workers are more profitable for firms.

In other words, formal education equips people to represent the management, to act as supervisors and to feel distanced from the workforce. This is a business advantage in some ways (trust, correct representation of management's interest) but is also a business cost, wherein formal education among junior management keeps them aloof from the majority of the workforce and positions them poorly to represent their concerns, or motivate them. Labour, even if it's skilled, is still regarded in India as a low-class, low-caste job. Dignity and inclusion of manual labour is not only at the level of employability alone, it's also about how labour is regarded in the firm and in the society.

While the NSDC's partner base (discussed subsequently) and the new thrust towards integration with schooling are the most significant initiatives offered by the government, there are others which must be noted. First, the Ministry of Labour and Employment's Modular Employable Skills (MES) Scheme; and second, the government's plan to revamp certificate-level training institutes, namely ITIs. The MES Scheme was launched in 2007 as a strategic framework for its Skill Development Initiative for early school dropouts, ITI/Industrial Training Centre (ITC) graduates and existing workers, especially in unorganized sector. The scheme carries full financial support through reimbursement for trainees, and a certificate issued by the National Council of Vocational Training (NCVT), which is recognized across India and internationally for employability of the imparted skills. The key features of the scheme are:

- Its open architecture, allowing for active participation from the industry/private sector in every stage of design and implementation. This facilitates updating the curriculum to industry requirements, and new skills can be easily added to the system.
- The delivery mechanism of the modules is flexible (part-time, weekends, full-time, onsite/offsite, etc.) to suit the needs of the various target groups.
- MES offers short duration modules with the 1–2 years skill acquisition process shortened to a span of three months.

Though an ongoing initiative, the MES scheme holds great promises for scaling up its impact. Since its inception, the MES Scheme has developed about 1,200 modules covering 52 sectors, registered more than 6,000 Vocational Training Provider (VTP) institutes and trained close to half a million people, of which roughly half also found employment.

Vocational training through ITIs and privately managed ITCs suffers from a number of structural deficiencies, such as lack of labour market relevance of the training, absence of industry–institute interaction, obsolete curricula and so on. In addition, the regional distribution of ITIs/ITCs is skewed towards certain states, resulting in regional imbalances in availability of vocational training.

To address these problems, the government has taken certain initiatives to improve the functioning of ITIs/ITCs. These include:

- A total of 8,039 ITIs and ITCs have been affiliated with the NCVT, and their capacity has been increased by 100,000.
- Of the 1,896 government ITIs, 400 have been selected for an upgradation.
- MES courses, discussed earlier, have been introduced in many ITIs.
- Five hundred ITIs have been selected to be upgraded into Centres of Excellence, 21 new sector-specific courses were introduced to ensure industry relevance of the certificate and so on.

The new private sector skills providers, funded by the NSDC, span a huge variety of sectors and operate in different ways, according to their origins and values. The majority have focused on service sectors over industry (retail, health care, banking and insurance, drivers, etc.) and several of the organizations have been founded by ex-corporate leaders, while others, by those with a more rural development background. States like Gujarat have entered into agreement with private sector companies like TeamLease, Enveronn and Core Projects and Technology to boost employability in the state (see Box 4.6). Discussions with these partners, however, reveal that they face similar challenges.

First, they are all struggling to mobilize trainees. The skills providers find their costs of mobilization rising as they go deeper into villages and urban settlements to source prospective trainees and workers. While young people may be persuaded to attend training for a stipend, they are reluctant to pay a fee and may not be sufficiently committed to reach the place of employment, or to get through the first difficult weeks of adjustment once they are there. Much of the feedback from neighbours who have made

the shift also does not give them confidence, so that getting a job in an organized firm is becoming a negative brand.

Second, the providers offer overwhelmingly short courses (1–3 months), filtering young rural people into low-grade jobs. Pushed on numbers rather than quality, they are struggling to demonstrate 'added value' to their trainees, vis-à-vis a worker who might get offered the same job off the street. The jobs are generally paid a minimum wage or very marginally above it with some, but not full, statutory benefits (PF, ESI, paid leave, bonus, etc). Critically, they often offer scant opportunity for career progression and are not necessarily good learning environments.[11]

Also, the providers are struggling to keep the trainees in their new jobs for more than a few months, and to stem the attrition rates. Providers explain that, a mismatch in expectations and reality, discomfort with a strange environment, unwillingness to work long hours in sedentary jobs and confusion or discontent due to communication gap with the supervisors and other seniors are some of the reasons why young people quickly leave their posts.

Providers are exploring a variety of approaches to address these constraints:

- Addressing the quality and impact of training, by:
  o Training for career employability and transferable skills (i.e., hitting at a deeper level, to train the youth to be better life learners).
  o Moving beyond text to non-text forms of teaching.
  o Better assessing, categorizing and building on existing capabilities of participants.
- Spending more time on induction and matching expectations to what trainees will find during the training period.
- Fostering closer engagement with industry in multiple ways, through the

[11] Interviews with four NSDC partners.

Box 4.6: *Training companies step up on skill upgradation centres*

The Government of Gujarat has estimated the skilled manpower requirement in the next five years at 500,000. Resultantly, private sector companies have been eyeing the skill development sector in Gujarat. TeamLease, Everonn and Core Projects and Technologies have been setting up training centres in Gujarat. TeamLease,[12] for example, has entered into an agreement with the Gujarat government to set up TeamLease University (TLU), comprising 22 community colleges across the state to improve accessibility, increase inclusiveness, lower costs and create vertical mobility. Each of TLU's 22 colleges has a plan to look at enrolling 300 to 700 students.

For its part, the Government of Gujarat, through the Centre for Entrepreneurship Development (CED) has been empanelling 22 national-level training expert institutes for boosting employability in the state, through skill development. CED has a target of 300 skill centres by 2013. Private players have also set their own respective targets for Gujarat. Core Projects and Technologies plans to start with 10 centres generating a skilled manpower of 300 to 400 each, at a total investment of ₹5 to 6 crore. Similarly, Everonn Systems has already started 12 skill development centres in hard skills like refrigeration, construction and carpentry. By March 2012, Everonn plans 21 centres in the state; each will impart training to around 90 to 100 students per month.

Source: *Business Standard*, 6 July 2011.

---

industry-lead (NSDC-promoted) Sector Skills Councils, as well as partners' own engagements. The purpose is not only to better shape training to industry needs but also to shift industry assumptions about vocational training versus formal education as a desirable requisite.

- Keep better track of the alumni and engage them in future recruitment and training.
- Also, improve mobilization of trainees directly, by explaining the value proposition better, in the villages and drawing on local opinion makers.

4.5. Conclusion

The flagship programmes of the Government of India, like, NRLM, NREGP and the skill initiatives are highly ambitious in achieving the scale of operation throughout the country. The central government only provides guidelines and resources and the success of the programmes are largely dependent on the readiness, political will and management capacity of the respective state governments. It is observed that the states in which the programmes have made a dent and proved

to be successful have continued their efforts, and put strong focus on reaching the target population, backed by requisite human resource capacity and appropriate qualitative and quantitative standards.

The role of the civil society organizations is not well established in the programme implementation and innovative approaches are needed to reach the unreached and ensure last mile connectivity. In some cases, civil society organizations are associated as either service providers or subsidiary players. The government system is also not aligned towards implementing such large-scale community-driven programmes like NRLM. The HR requirements of programmes such as NRLM may not match with the existing system wherein the dynamics between professionals and front line government officers may be difficult to handle.

In spite of weaknesses and enormous challenges, there is strong evidence of greater awareness in the public, innovative approaches to reach the poor making the system transparent and a growing sense of realization at various levels of government—central, state, district and panchayat—towards accountability in service delivery. Private sector is no longer seen as a

---

[12] *Mint*, 23 January 2011.

no-go and the voice of the civil society carries greater weight. All these contribute towards complementary efforts in PPP mode which are beginning to materialize in livelihoods promotion, skill development, agriculture, retailing, infrastructure and so on.

For example, in Bihar, SHGs in Sekhwara and Purnia had applied for licenses and took over the running of the PDS in their respective villages.[13] The Planning Commission has 11 cases of village SHGs taking over the PDS system and implementing it much more efficiently than the state government. Most of these villages are in Andhra Pradesh, Kerala, Bihar and Rajasthan. In these cases, villages with SHGs have been able to reduce leakages in PDS by an average of 5–10 per cent over the last 2–3 years. In some cases, community groups in the states have got roads built under PMGSY, housing benefits under IAY, marked out irregularities in NREGA, and got drainage systems built, among other things. The World Bank, which has been supporting state-level livelihood programmes in several states, also believes that the scheme has the potential to enhance the delivery system of the government.

References

Bowles, S., and H. Gintis. 2000. Does schooling raise earnings by making people smarter? In *Meritocracy and economic inequality*, ed. K. Arrow, S. Bowles and S. Durlauf. Princeton: Princeton University Press.

Business India. 2011. Building capacities. *Business India*, 3 April.

Chadha, G. 2004. Human capital base of the Indian labour market: Identifying worry spots. *The Indian Journal of Labour Economics* 47 (1).

Deshpande, L., A. Satpathy, and S. Deshpande. 2007. Personal income distribution and heterogeneity of labour markets in India. *The Indian Journal of Labour Economics* 50 (4).

Ghose, A. 2010. India's employment challenge. *The Indian Journal of Labour Economics* 53 (4).

Gram Tarang. 2010. *Gram tarang employability training services* (brochure). Bhubaneswar: Gram Tarang ETS.

India Weekly USA. 2011. League of India. *India Weekly USA*, 20 June.

Mehta Kapur, Aasha, A. Shepherd, S. Bhide, A. Shah, and A. Kumar. 2011. *Chronic Poverty Report—Towards Solutions and New Compacts in a Dynamic Context*. Report published by Indian Institute of Public Administration and Chronic Poverty research Centre.

Mehta Kapur, Aasha, and Sanjay Pratap. Forthcoming. *Policies and Programmes, Analysing NRHM and ICDS to Identify What Has Worked, What Has Not and Why?*

NREGA. 2010. Report of the Central Employment Guarantee Council's 'Working Group on Wages'.

NPSD (National Policy on Skill Development). 2009. Formulated by the Ministry of Labour and Employment, approved by the Cabinet in its meeting held on 23 February 2009.

World Bank. 2006. Skill Development in India, the Vocational Education and Training System.

———. 2011. Social protection for a changing India. Commissioned by the Planning Commission. *Financial Express*, 19 May.

---

[13] *The Economic Times*, 16 June 2011.

Private Industry and Services—What Is 'India Inc' Delivering in Employment to the Poor?

5.1. Introduction and summary

India is in the throws of its own growth story. Infrastructure and realty developments hit us anew every day; prices and wages increase by the month; new rugged crowds flock in to products and services which used to be for elites; workers no longer show for work because they're busy on their own growth trajectories. The changes are so conspicuous that it is easy to imagine they reach India's working heart: its villages of farmers and migrant workers, and its low-wage urban settlements. And yet, the story from the heartland—from statistics and small qualitative studies as we saw in Chapter 2—reminds us that the choices for most are as limited and as tough as ever.

This chapter addresses the topic of jobs for India's poor inside private-sector industry, services and their supply chains. The private sector's role in the livelihoods of the poor is of course not limited to one of an employer. Business and industry is foremost a purchaser and processor of primary sector goods from India's farmers. The private sector also helps to generate livelihoods in trade and logistics when its goods and services are channelled to the 'bottom of the pyramid'. But it is in its role of employer that the private sector has the deepest impact; first because such jobs are typically full-time, and second, because the poorest are most easily included in growth through the employment route, since they typically lack capital to trade or land to produce on a scale beyond subsistence.

While a previous SOIL Report looked at the role of corporate farms and handicraft supply chains in supporting poor people's livelihoods (Datta and Sharma 2008), this year, we focus on employment, to match the mood, towards better jobs, in the government and the press.

Section 5.2 examines the evidence that we are witnessing an upward trend in the creation of quality jobs in India. Section 5.3 takes a detailed look at those sectors and professions which appear to offer the best hope for growth in employment for less skilled groups, and discusses future projections. Section 5.4 discusses the regulatory climate for hiring, and the arguments for liberalizing the labour law to lower the bar for the organized sector. Section 5.5 looks at the prospects for quality jobs in high-growth sectors, and discusses in detail what is demanded by the employers of our less skilled youth entering the job market. Section 5.6 closes with some illustrations of how employers can themselves improve the 'job offer' to better attract the attentive and committed workforce they need.

5.2. An end to jobless growth?

According to the business press, the Ministry of Finance and a range of corporate-geared surveys, this year's outlook for growth and job creation across sectors is good. The Economic Survey reports that growth in the industrial sector will be 'moderate but sustainable' while it continues to remain stagnant as a percentage of GDP (now at 20.5 per cent). This is in marked contrast to the service sector which is now at 65 per cent of GDP (2009–10). The dominant information technology and ITES sector bounced back from the global crisis surprisingly rapidly and posted a growth of 19 per cent between 2009–10 and 2010–11. 'Even during the crisis year', concludes the Economic Survey:

> …annual services growth was around the 10 per cent mark, which it has maintained since 2005–6. This is in contrast to the overall GDP growth which fell to 6.8 per cent in 2008–9 from 9.3 per cent in 2007–8. Thus the resilience of the services sector has greatly contributed to the resilience of the economy. (Economic Survey 2011)

Bank and non-bank credit is now flowing well in spite of the RBI's rounds of monetary tightening and increased interest rates, while FDI is still affected by the global slowdown, hurting the industry more than the key services (financial, telecoms, ITES and real estate).

The Labour Bureau's quick quarterly surveys—tracking global recession-affected industries—show that employment, while it shrunk in all tracked sectors in the three quarters of the late 2008 to mid-2009, has recovered in most sectors since then. Textiles and apparel (especially handloom and power loom sectors), leather and gems and jewellery remain shaky and are still reporting negative employment. Meanwhile, high-growth service sectors are inching towards exports, and to less developed northern and eastern states. While GDP growth estimates for 2011–12 have been revised down, they still stand at just below 8 per cent.

Other than an upbeat forecast for corporate growth, and some evidence of recovery of labour-intensive sectors since 2009, what is the prognosis for creation of jobs? The question pertains not to subsistence level self-employment or poorly waged work in the unorganized sector, but to jobs with good wages and prospects in the organized sector.

Several recent articles (Gupta et al. 2009; Nagaraj 2011; Goldar 2011a, 2011b) debate the meaning of the evidence that employment in the organized manufacturing industry shows a sharp growth since 2003–04. Reversing a long-term trend of low growth, maybe even shrinking employment, the figures from the Annual Survey of Industries (ASI) show an astounding annual growth of 7.5 per cent between 2003–04 and 2008–09. Goldar compares this figure to trends since 1980, looking at annual growth in value-addition alongside employment (see Table 5.1).

Goldar remarks that the employment growth between 2003–04 and 2008–09 has been fastest in those industries that are incorporated as private limited companies, in which the rate of employment increased at 14 per cent a year.[1] He further argues that employment growth has been faster in the less labour-intensive industries, highlighting that the average or low 'labour intensity'

Table 5.1: Trends in employment and value-addition in organized manufacturing

	1980–81 to 1989–90	1992–2003 to 1996–2007	1995–2006 to 2003–04	2003–04 to 2008–09
Growth in employment (annual per cent)	0.3	2.8	−1.5	7.5
Growth in value-addition (annual per cent)	8.6	13	n.a.	10

Source: Goldar 2011a, from ASI figures.

[1] The proportion of companies registered as private limited also increased in the period, from 25 per cent of the ASI sample in 2003–04 to 33 per cent in 2008–09.

industries (auto and auto parts, fabricated metal products, basic metals and electrical machinery), increased their employment more than most labour intensive industries, many of which decreased their share (including textiles, tobacco and food processing). While this growth may be accompanied by some decline in 'labour intensity', Goldar nonetheless feels it is safe to hail the end of the long and persistent period of 'jobless growth' in India.

The Ma Foi Randstad Employment Trends Survey (MEtS) gives the projections on hiring trends in the 13 broad sectors used by the Central Statistical Organisation (CSO). MEtS's current figures are derived from the annual surveys of 600 or so firms,

across sectors, on direct hiring plans, while older figures are corroborated from CSO, ASI and NSSO data. The figures cover only workers who are hired as regular permanent employees, and therefore, exclude those hired casually, through contractors or subcontractors, and in the unorganized sector. It can help us to ascertain whether the upward trend of formal sector job creation is robust or not.

Figure 5.1 shows:

- Hiring is on the increase in all sectors following sharp dips between 2008 and 2009. Though some sectors (energy and organized retail) are still muted, in all cases the upward turn of the trend line is unmistakable.

Figure 5.1 Employment trends in organized corporate sector, 2005–11 (000s)[2]

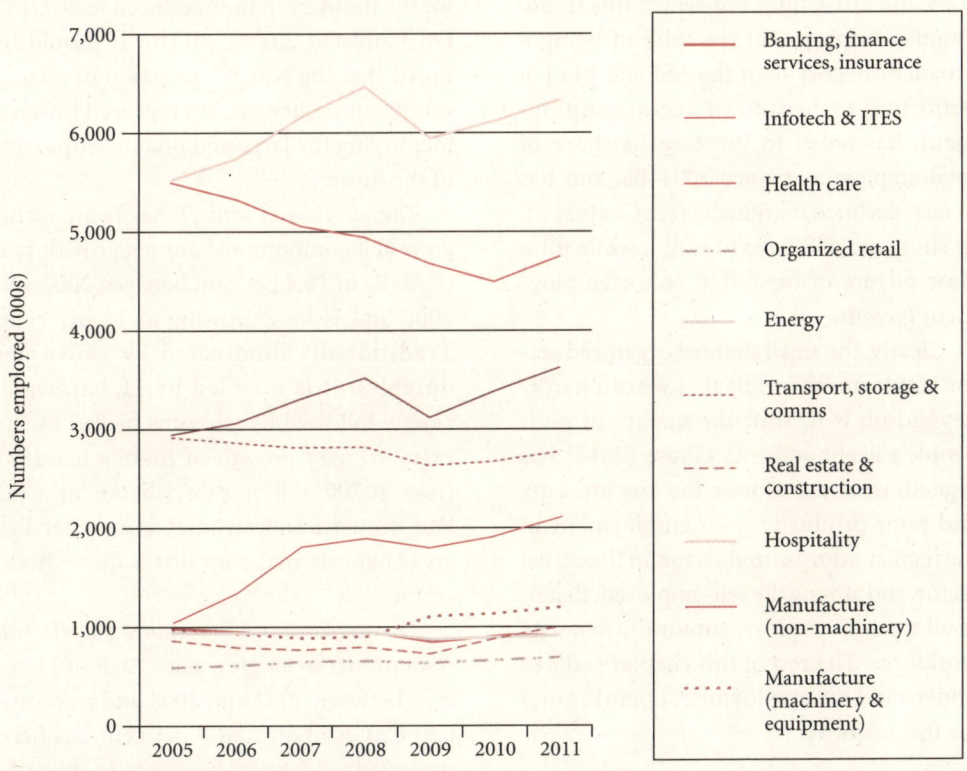

Source: Ma Foi Randstad Employment Trends Surveys (Wave 4, 2010; Wave 1, 2011).

---

[2] Three sub-sectors reported in the MEtS are excluded here since figures were not available or were unclear and/or they were less relevant to lower skilled groups. These are education, training and consultancy, pharma and media and entertainment.

- If the projections for non-machinery manufacturing are met, then this is the end of a long period of contraction where the sector reduced one-fifth (one million workers) of its permanent workforce between 2005 and 2010.
- Machinery and equipment manufacturing is a smaller employer but turned around earlier in 2008 and continues its steady upward trend.
- Other than the manufacturing sector, the increase in speed of hiring is greatest in the services of ITES, health care and hospitality sectors.

The MEtS therefore supports Goldar's analysis that the period of growth without decent jobs is over for the manufacturing and services sectors. But clearly, as yet the NSSO 66th Round data, collected between 2009 and 2010, does not reflect this trend. Regular employment, in spite of being a broader category than the ASI and Ma Foi definition of organized sector employment, has failed to increase its share of total employment since 2004–05, and has in fact, declined marginally (see Chapter 2). In short, we will have to wait a while for a clear picture of organized sector employment growth.

Clearly, the small share of organized sector employment means that we can hardly depend on it to shift the quality of poor people's livelihoods. As Ghose (2010) has argued, we must address the low intensity and poor productivity of employment in the regular unorganized sector, in the casual sector, and among the self-employed, that is, in all types of employment for the majority workforce. The rest of this chapter seeks to understand the employment opportunities for this majority.

5.3. The employment opportunity

This section will examine the opportunity for employment and livelihood for less skilled groups. It takes a closer look at the sectors

over time, since those industrial and service sectors which promise both high growth and employment should also be those which offer better quality jobs. The selected sectors are sourced from the National Skills Development Corporation's (NSDC) baseline surveys of 21 high employment sectors, produced by ICRA Management Consulting Services (IMaCS 2008) and their projections to 2022, the year when the NSDC hopes to achieve its contribution towards skilling 500 million Indians.

These 'skill gap' reports are a useful source as a summary of sectoral profiles and 14 of them (those most relevant to less educated workers) are selected and collated here for analysis. Other key sources used here are the Ministry of Finance's Economic Survey 2010–11 (2011) and the MEtS which summarizes the short-term hiring projections for the industry in the organized sector (Ma Foi Randstad 2011a, 2011b). It should be noted that the NSDC's selection of sectors is not comprehensive but is geared towards identifying the large and quality employers of the future.[3]

The electronics and IT hardware sector grew at a compounded annual growth rate (CAGR) of 16.4 per cent between 2002 and 2008 and is now growing at 13 per cent. Traditionally dominated by consumer durables, it is now led by IT hardware, closely followed by telecoms fuelled by the extraordinary growth of mobile handsets (now at 700 million subscribers). Strategic and industrial electronics is another key area. Exports make up just a third of the sector.

The tourism and hospitality (hotels and restaurants) sector grew at a CAGR of 11 per cent between 2002 and 2008 and a continued CAGR of around 9 per cent has been projected for the next five years. In spite of a

---

[3] Some key omissions from NSDC skills gap reports include: domestic service, the paper and printing industry, beauty industry, telecoms (running rather than constructing) and those parts of the capital goods sector which are excluded from construction equipment.

liberal FDI regime, poor transport and hotel infrastructure has hobbled India's foreign tourism, and the figure for foreign tourist arrivals (FTAs) hovers around 5.5 million annually, a paltry 0.58 per cent of the global FTAs. The number of Indians travelling abroad is double the number of foreigners coming to India. Domestic clientele make up a rapidly increasing share of the market and the domestic industry is growing at 15 per cent. Meetings, incentives, conferencing and exhibitions (known as MICE) are a key component and revenue stream.

The auto and auto components sector grew at a CAGR of 14 per cent between 2002 and 2008. This growth is due to the original equipment manufacturers (OEMs) assembling branded vehicles and Tiers I, II and III component suppliers. Two-wheelers still dominate sales in units (75 per cent) but not in value (32 per cent). Passenger vehicles make up only 16 per cent of sales units but represent 62 per cent in value. It is still a concentrated market with Maruti Suzuki retaining 45 per cent of sales for passenger vehicles, in 2009. New industry trends include: growing electronic vehicle content, stringent emissions requirements and an emerging export market in components (20 per cent of the total component sales in 2009).

The chemicals sector grew by 3 per cent CAGR between 2002 and 2008. The sector is dominated by fertilizers (nitrogen, phosphorous, potassium) which constitute nearly half of the total; petrochemicals (polymers used in production of plastic and textiles) amount to more than a quarter of the total and alkali chemicals (soda ash, caustic soda and chlorine; used in finishing, cleansing and manufacturing glass) which make up 17 per cent of the total. Current performance is uneven as dyes and dyestuffs and polymers are growing rapidly, while the production of pesticides and organic chemicals is slowing down. The sector is heavily concentrated in the western states of Gujarat, Maharashtra and Rajasthan.

The pharmaceutical sector grew at 13.4 per cent (CAGR) between 2002 and 2008 and according to the industry, is set to double in size over the next two years. India is the world leader in the production of generic drugs and its pharmaceutical sector is now third in the world in terms of volume. This is made up of the bulk manufacture of active ingredients (mostly exported to Russia, the United States, the United Kingdom, Germany, etc.), and production of formulations, that is, ready-to-consume drugs, mostly for domestic market. The sector is set to take a boost in exports as large clusters of drugs in the US and European markets are due to go off-patent in the coming years. The sector is heavily influenced by consumer health trends. The share of traditionally dominant anti-infectives (antibiotics, vaccines) is reducing while it is increasing for cardiovascular, anti-diabtetic and gastrointenstinal drugs. The size of the domestic drug market is rapidly attracting global pharma giants.

The textile sector grew at a CAGR of 6.9 per cent between 2002 and 2008. The sector consists of manmade fibre producing units (mostly polyester, where India has a 7 per cent share of the global market), spinning mills (predominantly in Tamil Nadu), hosiery and weaving units (both handloom and power loom) and fabric finishing units and ready-made garment (apparel) producing units, of which there are 13,000 in the country. There are also some composite mills combining spinning, weaving and finishing, though they are declining.

Handloom, power loom and garment units are the major employers, each with 5.5 to 6.5 million workers. The apparel sector has traditionally been export-geared, and India still has only 3.6 per cent of the global market share as against China's 30.7 per cent. Apparel took a severe hit in 2009 (shrinking by 5 per cent), but by late 2010 appears to have fully recovered to pre-global recession levels. The domestic apparel market is expanding rapidly alongside organized retail.

The health care services sector (i.e., health care delivery and medical equipment) grew at a CAGR of 12 per cent between 2002 and 2008. 75 per cent of all spending on Indian health is now in the private sector. India still has only a quarter of the doctors, and a fifteenth of the nurses required as per the population. India's need for hospital beds will increase rapidly with an aging population (180 million Indians will be over 60 years old in 2025) and the rise of critical diseases such as cardiovascular problems and cancer. Spending on private health care is expected to rise to 14 per cent annually, fuelled by the penetration of health insurance and rising income. Short-term growth is likely to be concentrated in Tier II and III cities, opening up new jobs for rural populations closer to home. The sector's rapid growth is assisted by the absence of regulations and relaxations on hi-tech imports.

The organized retail sector grew at an astounding CAGR of 36 per cent between 2002 and 2008, though its reach remains uneven across the goods sectors. Apparel, for example, dominates the sector with 38 per cent, while food constitutes another 11 per cent and footwear, 10 per cent. The focus of organized retail has shifted from the eight 'megacities' (the big six plus Ahmedabad and Pune) to the next level of boomtowns, a group which is rapidly growing in number and includes Kanpur, Lucknow, Nagpur, Bhopal, Jaipur, Coimbatore, Surat, Ludhiana and Jalandhar. Encouraged by the growth in consumer income, high growth and affordable land in Tier II and III cities and entry of global retail giants in India, its growth has been projected at 80 per cent by 2014.

The logistics sector is divided into warehousing and transport.[4] While warehousing grew at a CAGR of 20 per cent, the transport sector grew at 8.7 per cent, between 2002 and 2008. In the transport segment, road transport dominates with 65 per cent of all freight. The vast majority of operators are small, owning a fleet of less than five trucks. While 70 per cent of Indian Railway's revenues come from freight, the railway has only 13 per cent market share on internal freight, down from 50 per cent in 1960. Rail freight is dominated by the key commodities—coal, fertilizer, cement, petroleum products, foodgrains and iron ore. Air freight (domestic and international) is growing rapidly for high-value and easily spoiled goods, while sea freight's growth is slowly declining. The growth of logistics sector depends closely on infrastructure achievements, which, as discussed, is hobbled in ports and railways sector and especially in the roads sector. It also depends on lowering the transaction cost of the procedures.[5] Trends include: the growth of third-party logistics providers (3PL) who offer a combined package of services to supply chains, including multimode transport, freight forwarding, cold chain and express courier and track and trace services.

The gems and jewellery sector grew at a CAGR of 12 per cent between 2002 and 2008, divided into diamond cutting and polishing, and fabrication of jewellery. The cutting and polishing segment is still recovering from a global recession, while the jewellery fabrication segment is rapidly growing, bolstered by domestic sales. Emerging trends include: growing acceptance and affordability of diamonds in the domestic market and the growing role of technology in the cutting and polishing segment, which will lead to a substantial reduction in less skilled labour in this sector in the coming years.

---

[4] Includes transport of goods and services by air, sea, road and rail, but excludes passenger transport. There are also value-added services, such as packing, labelling, express services and cold chain, though we just mention these.

[5] For example, the average turnaround in major Indian ports was nearly 4.5 days in 2009–10, as against a single day in Singapore, and this is getting slower. The domestic warehousing sector is similarly hobbled by lack of procedures to deal with stock pledged to banks and delays due to 'no entry' zoning in cities (Economic Survey 2011).

Infrastructure construction consists of: construction for transportation (roads, bridges, ports, airports); power sector infrastructure; telecoms infrastructure and irrigation and urban services. Infrastructure construction has witnessed a rapid increase in public spending, doubling and trebling with each Plan period for power and transportation, respectively, with overall infrastructure spends raised by 2.5 per cent over the 11th Five Year Plan period, to hit 8.37 per cent of GDP in 2012. However, in spite of the provisions made, spending on power and roads has lagged behind target in 2010–11, with the road sector particularly hampered by land acquisition problems. Trends include: reduction in manual site time and the role of less skilled labour, due to modularized components, and increased investment in solar energy (an increase of 61 per cent in Budget 2011–12).

Building and real estate grew at a CAGR of 12 per cent between 2002 and 2008. It is dominated by residential building and real estate which makes up 82 per cent of the total business, with a current demand of nearly 5 million for new housing. The balance is made up of commercial building and real estate at 9 per cent and development of SEZs also at 9 per cent. Commercial demand is growing rapidly in Tier II and III cities, driven by growth in organized retail and affordable land prices. The sector is still muted after the severe impact of global recession, and the much hyped demand for residential properties has taken longer than expected to translate into actual purchases. Trends include: reduction in the role of less skilled labour and manual site time; entry of specialized facilities management services for infrastructure support—security, plumbing, gas pipe, TV cable, electrical services and building maintenance.

The construction materials sector is broadly divided into cement, steel and construction equipment segments.[6] Between 2002 and 2008, these three segments grew at 8.3 per cent, 7.8 per cent and 20 per cent CAGR, respectively. In spite of a construction boom, India's per capita cement and steel consumption still remains below global average, at 0.15 t and 0.04 t, respectively.[7] Steel production is heavily concentrated in Eastern India. Construction equipment consists of equipment for mixing and transporting concrete, earth-moving equipment, drilling and tunnelling equipment, road construction equipment and material handling equipment. Trends include: increasing automation of the manufacturing processes, consolidation of cement and steel sectors and outsourcing of support functions such as transport, storage, packaging and so on.

The leather and leather goods sector grew at a CAGR of 11.9 per cent between 2002 and 2008.[8] It divides into finished leather and leather products, and continues to be dominated by exports (70 per cent of the total size). The products sector is dominated by footwear, and also garments, harnesses and saddler. This sector is set to increase its share in exports with a small shift from finished leather to leather goods, even though the demand for finished leather continues to be dominant, and it will employ nearly half of the incremental workers by 2022. The leather industry faces a special manpower challenge due to its unattractiveness and the stigma attached to working in it.

The furniture sector grew at a CAGR of 17 per cent between 2002 and 2008, dividing into household (65 per cent total), and office and contract manufacturing (for hotels and restaurants) segments. Exports, at 30 per cent annually, are insignificant but growing rapidly. Domestic sales are fuelled by the real estate and the organized retail boom. The sector remains dominated by wood

---

[6] Other less significant segments include paints, aluminum, glass, plastics and timber segments.

[7] Per capita cement consumption is 0.4 t globally and 0.83 t in China, while per capita steel consumption is 180 kg globally and 320 kg for China.

[8] This is the figure for leather exports, which is 70 per cent of the total sector.

(60 per cent) and the manufacturing is concentrated in Maharashtra and Tamil Nadu.

The food processing sector grew at a CAGR of 9.8 per cent between 2002 and 2008. It includes the segments of grain processing (which still dominate at 34 per cent), dairy (16 per cent), bakery and sugar-based products (20 per cent), meat and poultry (14 per cent), fruit- and vegetable-based products, edible oils and beverages. The industry, generically, consists of inputs to produce farms, such as, seeds, fertilizers, extension services, procurement and crop insurance; trade and distribution like, purchase,

warehousing, trading in terminal markets and facilitation services; processing, which includes, grading, sorting, milling and value-addition and wholesale and retail trade. Demand for processed food goods responds to increase in incomes,[9] and in India, this is bolstered by an expansion in the number of households as both urban and rural people shift to nuclear arrangements.

Let us take a collective look at the projected growth and employment in these sectors. First, we take NSDC's IMaCS projections for sectoral growth and for employment growth (Figures 5.2 and 5.3). Then we compare these with alternative projections

Figure 5.2: NSDC skills gap reports: Projected growth in key employment sectors, 2008–22 (₹crore)[10]

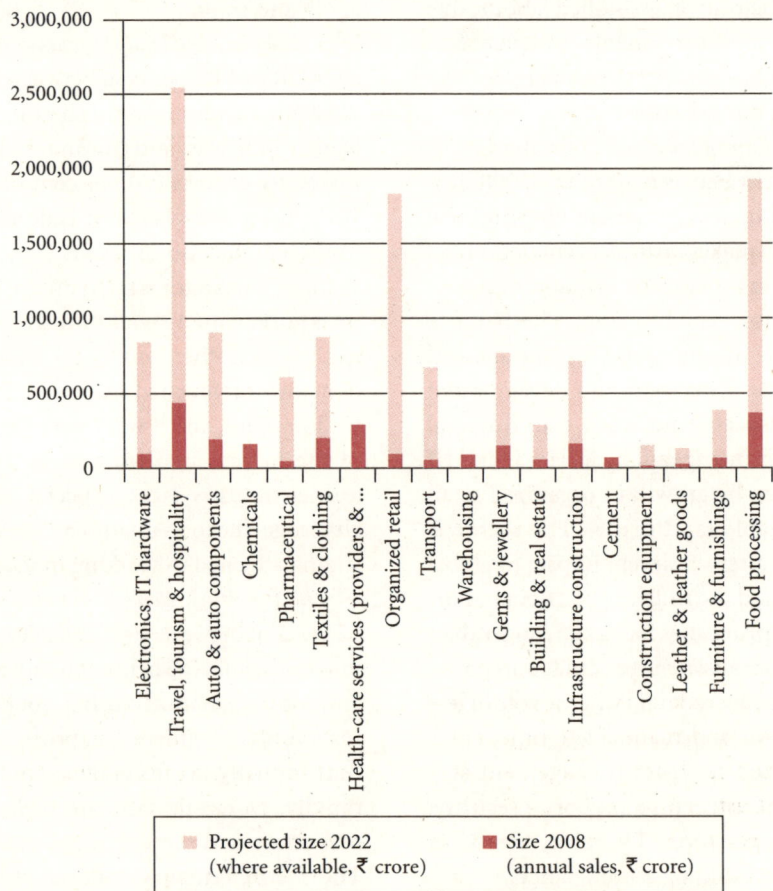

Source: NSDC skills gap reports.

---

[9] In a 2007 report, NCAER categorized 91 million Indians as 'consumers', that is, with income ranging between ₹3,800 and ₹18,000 per month, an increase in 37 million since 2001.

---

[10] The sector skills reports reviewed for this chapter differs slightly from the list in the graphs since some reports addressed two distinct sub-sectors.

Figure 5.3: NSDC skills gap reports: Projected incremental employment in key sectors, 2008–22

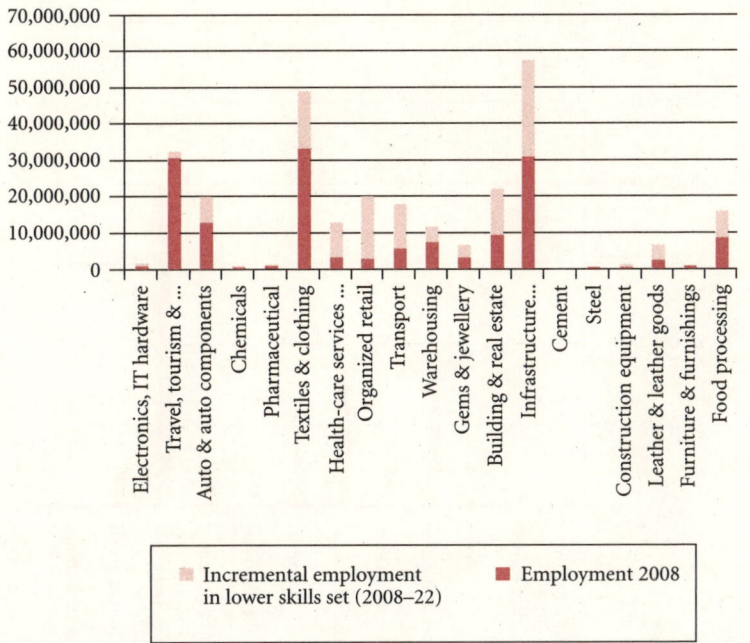

■ Incremental employment   ■ Employment 2008
in lower skills set (2008–22)

Source: NSDC skills gap reports.

developed by TeamLease in their Labour Report (TeamLease 2009) (Figure 5.4). We also reference the short-term projections from the MEtS (Ma Foi Randstad 2011a, 2011b).

Figures 5.2 and 5.3 show the following:

- Phenomenal growth rates have been projected for the sectors where the figures were available. By 2022, the sectors are set to grow to an average of a little over seven times their size in 2008, raising questions of sustainability.

- The sectors offering high growth are not necessarily the big employers. For example, sectors such as electronics, pharmaceuticals, cement and construction equipment appear to offer great investment opportunities but are not large job creators.

- The older sectors which are already well established as key employers, such as, travel and tourism, auto components and textiles, have more conservative projections for future employment, as compared to newer sectors which are not yet 'tried and tested'. Emerging sectors

such as health care services, organized retail, transport, warehousing and some food processing sub-sectors, are still so new that getting a clear idea of the job quality in these sectors is difficult, and so, it is hard to make projections.

- Large projections have been made for the lower skills set of sectors well known for low-quality jobs. The incremental employment numbers offered by textiles (nearly 16 million), organized retail (17.3 million), construction (13 million in real estate and 29 million in infrastructure) and transport (12.2 million) are enormous, but we already know a lot about the poor quality of these kinds of jobs (see Chapter 2). So the important question is—what opportunities will arise from continuous and rapid growth, to improve this quality?

The bigger question is whether it is even possible to forecast with any accuracy so far into the future. Such estimates are based on the enormous assumption that current growth rates will continue 14 years on. More robust estimates would have to be based on

Figure 5.4: Comparing NSDC and TeamLease projections for incremental employment

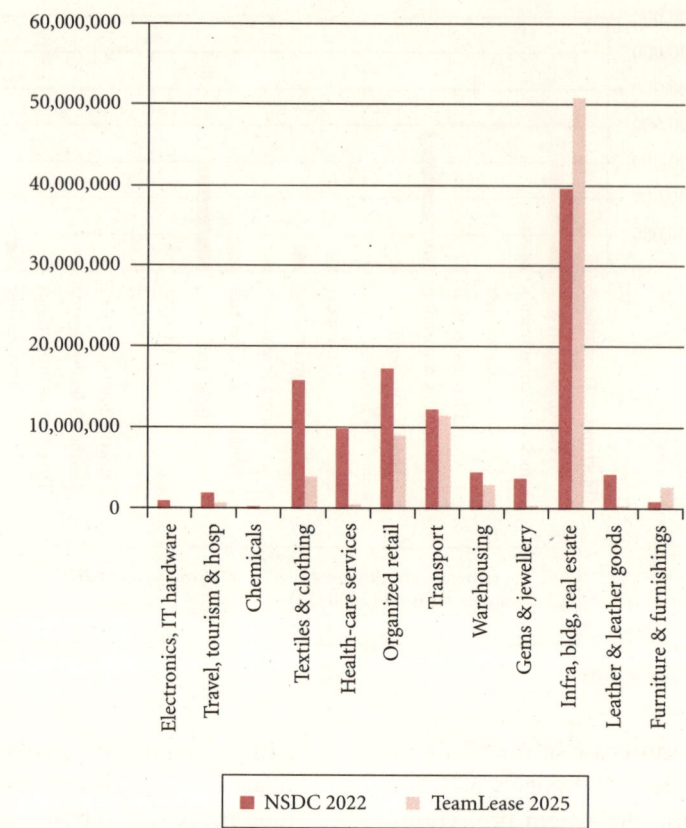

Source: NSDC skills gap report, TeamLease Labour Report 2009.

the investment and hiring plans of firms, which tend to be uncertain even for the next two years. Ma Foi Randstad, the manpower global, stated that it rarely makes forecasts beyond two years for its clients, and its MEtS report, widely accepted as the standard for job forecasts for India's corporate sector, makes projections for only a year ahead.

To check the validity of the NSDC figures, they can be compared to TeamLease's attempt at audacious forecasting for incremental employment from 2008 to 2025. Figure 5.4 compares the two projections, for those sectors where definitions were shared sufficiently to make them comparable.

Figure 5.4 shows some glaring differences, which might lead us to question the worth of such forecasts altogether:

- Textile and apparel, flagged by NSDC to continue as a huge incremental employer

(16 million) is seen by TeamLease as a growth slower (4 million).

- NSDC's bold projection of nearly 10 million nurses and health technicians is at odds with TeamLease's estimate of less than half a million.

- TeamLease's estimate for the retail sector, while still high at 9 million, is just a little over half of NSDC's projection of 17.5 million.

- TeamLease is conservative about the two traditional handcrafting-based sectors, mainly, gems and jewellery and leather (with projections of under 350,000 for each), while being inexplicably optimistic about another labour-intensive industry—furniture (at just under 3 million). NSDC is optimistic about the first two (3.5 million for gems and jewellery, 4.2 million for leather), but more conservative about furniture (just over 0.75 million).

But there are some striking overlaps in the two estimates for other sectors, which are worth noting:

- Both make similar forecasts for the transport and warehousing sectors, each projecting 12 million and 3 to 4 million incremental jobs, respectively.
- For infrastructure construction and building and real estate, both sources make enormous growth predictions of 40 million and 50 million, respectively, which are broadly comparable.

In general, it could be said that the TeamLease figures are less wildly optimistic than the IMaCS figures, and it is readier to imagine a decline in sectors and professions which are currently dominant and in traditional employment sectors such as, textiles, leather and so on. The TeamLease report lists several occupations whose workforce will actually shrink, notably, rubber and plastic workers (by 75,000), metal processors (by 0.1 million), tool-makers and machine tool operators (by over 50,000), clerks (by 0.6 million) and unskilled labourers across sectors (by 0.5 million).

We have focused on those sectors and professions that offer jobs requiring lower skills which provide the best chance for school dropouts and school leavers who lack the opportunity or resources to pursue higher education or vocational skills. But even within these categories, the quality of jobs varies. One indicator of a high-quality job is that the worker is given a regular status (just as we saw in Chapter 2 that casual status can be used as a proxy for low-quality job). Regular status can be defined as affording entitlements, not only to minimum wages and statutory social security (ESI and PF) but also to other benefits such as paid leave and annual bonus, and some modicum of job security (i.e., due process for dismissal).

As per this criteria, the growth in the Indian economy has so far failed to deliver on job quality (as shown in Chapter 2).

The proportion of workforce in 'regular' employment[11] has remained stagnant and has in fact showed a slight decline since 2004. So the employment growth which we have evidenced must be viewed critically in terms of its prospects to deliver not only in numbers, but also in the quality of jobs offered. We can get a glimpse of these prospects in quality by comparing sectors in terms of regular jobs in proportion to total jobs they create. Table 5.2 uses NSDC (total jobs) and Ma Foi (regular jobs only) figures for the year 2008, for selected sectors.

Table 5.2: Regular jobs as a proportion of total jobs for selected sectors, 2008

	Total jobs 2008	Regular jobs as per cent total
Organized retail	2,838,000	23
Transport, storage and communications	13,212,000	21
Real estate and construction	9,300,000	9
Hospitality	30,500,000	21

Source: NSDC skills gap reports 2008; Ma Foi Randstad 2011a.

While the concept of employment elasticity is well established as the measure of how employment increases with increase in the size of the economy, we need to move towards an idea of elasticity in employment quality: what patterns can be observed in the job-quality producing effects of growth?

The rest of this chapter discusses the nature of the job quality problem in detail. The next section (Section 5.4) examines

---

[11] The NSSO's definition of 'regular' is much wider than that being used here, encompassing

> …persons who worked in others' farm or non-farm enterprises (both household and non-household) and, in return, received salary or wages on a regular basis (i.e., not on the basis of daily or periodic renewal of work contract). This category included not only persons getting time wage but also persons receiving piece wage or salary and paid apprentices, both full time and part-time. (NSSO 2011)

Therefore the proportion of those with 'bargainable' jobs and job security is likely to be much smaller.

the legal and administrative environment for hiring and getting hired, and the role of governance in shaping and constraining the quality of jobs emerging from growth.

5.4. The climate for hiring

A popular explanation for the poor quality of jobs emerging with growth is that the existing government regulations discourage firms from offering regular employment. Instead, they hire casual labour through agencies or outsource work to smaller firms in the unorganized sector. It is argued that if labour laws were to be rationalized, its more punitive provisions removed and the administrative procedures reduced and smoothened, then better quality jobs would emerge in much greater numbers. Goldar, for example, has argued that an additional three million jobs can be created in the manufacturing sector simply by reforming and liberalizing the Industrial Disputes Act. A recent survey asserted that such reforms were a prerequisite for realizing the benefits of our huge young population (the 'demographic dividend'). 'In China, wages have been going up and it is losing its edge of having low cost labour. If we can fix our labour laws, there is a huge opportunity for us', says Manish Sabharwal, co-founder and chairman, TeamLease (*Business India* 2011, p. 44). The effect of such reforms, argues TeamLease, would be to erode the distinction between organized and unorganized employment. On the one hand, this would raise flexibility and reduce the cost of hiring for those in the organized sector; on the other hand, it would extend the number of workers who are covered by these lighter provisions.

Since 2005, TeamLease has published a labour law environmental index on which it tracks and ranks the performance of different Indian states with respect to how well their governments 'facilitate the smooth functioning of labour markets' (TeamLease 2009). The variables tracked (each given an equal rank) are as follows:

- The difference in the average wages paid to registered workers and the legal minimum wage (the bigger the gap the better)
- The number of lockouts and strikes relative to the number of units (the lower the better, since other processes should resolve the issues)
- Number of prosecutions launched after inspections under the Shops and Establishments Act (applicable to services firms—the higher the better to demonstrate enforcement)
- Cases disposed as a share of prosecutions launched (the higher the better to demonstrate commitment to expediting the process), under the above act
- Share of employee-instituted cases to total cases (the lower the better to demonstrate employees have other avenues to resolve disputes with employers)
- Share of cases to total organized workforce (the lower the better)
- Number of 'transaction-cost reducing' amendments to labour laws (the higher the better, since the transaction cost, rather than the a priori 'pro labour' or 'anti labour' spirit of the law, is seen as the key encumbrance)[12]

In the state rankings (2005–09), Maharashtra has been at the top since 2005, while Andhra Pradesh occupied the second position, an improvement from the eighth place in 2005. Karnataka and Madhya Pradesh have retained their strong positions at 3rd and 4th place, while Delhi, and particularly Punjab, have plummeted to the 8th and 12th place respectively, since 2005. At the root of TeamLease's index is a campaign to convert labour into a state

---

[12] In this respect, TeamLease (2006) distinguishes its view from that of other pro-liberalization commentators such as Besley and Burgess (2004) who index regulatory regimes in terms of being 'pro labour' and 'anti labour'. It is instead a matter of transaction costs, that is, the speed and smoothness with which judgements and amendments are made (TeamLease 2006).

subject—it is on the Concurrent List at present, for fear of encouraging a race to the bottom to attract investment. Meanwhile, various states have tweaked their business environment to attract investors by offering some exemptions in SEZs, ITES and so on.

Goldar (2011a, 2011b), in a similar vein as TeamLease, argued—that differences in job creation across states reflect differential degrees of de facto labour administrative reform—those states and sectors, where the labour laws and/or their application has been very relaxed, have contributed most to this employment growth. Reproducing the rankings from the labour reforms index of an Organization for Economic Cooperation and Development (OECD) working paper (Dougherty 2010), Goldar reports that the states contributing most to employment growth are Himachal Pradesh and Uttarakhand (where industry enjoys significant tax breaks), followed by Chhattisgarh, Haryana, Jammu and Kashmir and Orissa. It is notable that the list of top rankers is dissimilar to TeamLease's, and Goldar's argument is further weakened by the fact that these states contribute to employment at a rate which is only on par with, and not better than the national average.

Few would disagree with TeamLease's and Goldar's argument that labour laws need to be rationalized, harmonized and simplified to reduce government interference, paperwork and transaction costs. But if we were to liberalize the legal framework; for example, by keeping minimum wage clearly below the market-clearing wage, permitting unlimited use of contract workers, exempting employers and workers from the Provident Fund in favour of voluntary pensions and reducing the job security due to regular workers—would this improve the quality of jobs being created? And would it improve enforcement?

To date, the United Progressive Alliance (UPA) (I and II) has steered clear of addressing the labour reform agenda because of union lobbying and, perhaps a recognition

that overt labour policy reform would be more disruptive to growth than reform by stealth, that is, selective non-enforcement. Indeed, now the degree of selective non-enforcement is rampant in states like Haryana[13] and it can no longer be assumed that transaction or hiring costs are so high. And yet, better quality jobs do not appear to be emerging from this reduced employer burden. In Gurgaon's apparel sector, wages are on the minimum wage line and workers receive no premium for overtime, which has often been enforced (Labour Behind the Label 2010).

It is a popular perception, and one which TeamLease emphasizes in its 2008 report, that labour standards in the informal sector are a disgrace because effects of regulations do not reach these workers. The purpose of projecting this perception is to highlight how irrelevant labour regulations are to the vast majority, and, therefore, make the case for their reform and retraction. But if employers in the informal sector are not to be trusted with their workers when left to themselves, then why would formal sector employers behave any better if they were offered a more liberal framework?

Clearly, there are critical factors other than state regulation at play, which have prevented better quality jobs from emerging spontaneously (Anant et al. 2006) in the vast majority of firms which are either exempt from regulations or escape their enforcement. TeamLease (2006, 2008, 2009) and other studies (Gupta et al. 2009) have identified some of these as poor physical infrastructure, weak financial sector development and low human capital.

It cannot be taken for granted that there are only poor quality jobs in the informal sector. Informal firms, for example, often offer the freedom and opportunities for

---

[13] For example, Haryana's Labour Commissioner recently declared that there was no restriction on the hiring of contract workers and is turning an enormous blind eye to off-rolls workers not covered by statutory social security (PF and ESI) (personal communication with suppliers and global buyers).

learning to their workers which are scarce in organized firms.[14]

There is an urgent need to begin the rationalization and process-smoothening of labour regulation and administration, and there are plenty of non-controversial steps to start with.[15] With the selective non-enforcement, selective enforcement also needs to take place urgently. Workers interviewed by researchers and the compliance officers of global buyers are quite consistent in their priorities, which do not always overlap with those of the law and its administrators. Those parts of the existing legal framework, which contribute most directly to good-quality jobs, need to be recognized urgently and better enforced on a priority basis.

For example, workers interviewed by one of the authors of this report, across apparel and hard-goods sectors, are consistently enthusiastic about:

- A savings scheme to which the employer contributes
- Some form of affordable health insurance
- A wage package which permits not just subsistence but savings towards lumpy future costs and emergencies
- Provision of paid leave, especially during sickness
- Enough job security to raise issues with management without fear of being thrown out
- Career progression reflected in new learning and wage increments

Workers are less bothered about:

- Being contract workers: As long as the contractor is bona fide, meets the legal requirements and helps and supports workers in raising issues with the principal employer.
- Pensions: They prefer savings for lump sums during their working life.
- Job security: Above and beyond that required to raise issues, that is, they do not demand bargainable 'permanent' jobs.
- Collective bargaining: As long as management listens to their concerns.
- Limits on overtime hours: Most workers like the option of overtime above legal limits.

If selective enforcement could be launched to ensure that the first list is better addressed, then, this in itself would be an enormous achievement. Each list item relates to a provision in the law, which is either poorly enforced or poorly executed. For example, the Provident Fund is an employer-contributed savings scheme which has no merit for mobile and casual workers; in theory, contract workers do have the right to raise issues with the employer, but in practice, they do not because they can be easily replaced, unlike regular workers who qualify as 'workmen'. It is time to align labour law priorities to those of the vast majority of the workforce.

5.5. How good is the job offer?

What kinds of jobs are on offer and what kinds of futures are we pushing our young people into? This section continues the discussion on job quality with respect to demand from organized and corporate workplaces and their supply chains.

Back in 2004, G.K. Chadha wrote, 'In the changing economic regime, who is doing what, and how much a worker is capable of "seeing beyond himself," are clearly emerging as the real touchstones of production efficiency' (Chadha 2004). He argued that India's economy, far more open and competitive than in the 1980s and 1990s, would

---

[14] There is a growing literature on the ethics of work relationships in the informal sector. See, for example, Haynes (1999), Knorringa (1999), Harriss-White (2003) and Ruthven (forthcoming in 2012).

[15] As TeamLease (2006, 2009) suggests, we can park the contentious issues of closures, layoffs and hiring of contract workers in core activities, and begin with the huge tasks of rationalization and procedural and administrative reform.

require a workforce with a fundamentally different orientation beginning with a better educational base.

He wrote that there would be an equal impact, on both agriculture and industry:

> To be sure, a typical Indian worker of tomorrow has to be markedly different from his predecessor … The new agriculture is likely to become a more involved, cobweb of bio-tech and genetic complexities. Numerous soil-related and environmental issues … have to be resolved at the level of the farm household itself … Rigorous farm production and time management schedules are a must … Every farmer will have to be not only an efficient producer but also a well-informed market strategist … to be vigilant of numerous new issues which probably never touched his predecessor … An educated farmer would probably absorb all these obligations more intelligently. (Chadha 2004, p. 6)

Chadha made similar predictions for the industrial sector, listing the rise in exacting standards on consumer health and safety, fashion, quality, precision, aesthetic appeal, and to-the-millimetre product standardization. All these standards hang on nodes of deep supply chains, wherein 'technology of the tiny and small subcontracting industrial enterprises would essentially be a part of the technology of the large industry… Uneducated job aspirants would naturally engage low consideration of the prospective employers' (ibid., p. 6).

Krishnan (2010) discusses how skills and employability requirements have changed with technology. Taking the textile industry as an example, he shows how requirements shifted from direct involvement in production, to monitoring and troubleshooting of the production process as summarized in

Table 5.3. 'This is because with the introduction of new automated machinery, the technologies are no more separate from each other and detection of faults requires a thorough understanding of the production process and familiarity with different equipments used' (ibid., p. 371).

Such shifts are often accompanied by new ways of assessing workers, from time-based, to output-based. Once workers are accountable for the output, understanding of the production process and troubleshooting abilities become key requirements. On the other hand, worker discipline becomes more crucial as automated technology spreads and 'the viability of capital-intensive technology requires that they be run at high capacity levels' (Krishnan 2010, p. 378). Finally, the focus of worker negotiations is also shifting, from the 'hard' issues of wages (the traditional emphasis of unions) to 'softer issues like job satisfaction, job progression, work autonomy …' (ibid.).

The NSDC-commissioned skills gap studies (IMaCS 2008) examine the kinds of skills required by the industry and identify those said to be lacking most critically. The description of skills and tasks mirror that in the literature, as shown in Table 5.4.

It is striking that certain skills and capabilities are common across vastly different industries, and certain phrases repeat themselves: the ability to follow multiple types of standards (quality, health and safety, procedural); the ability to inspect, monitor and report aberrations; discipline of multiple forms (hygiene, shop floor, wastage minimization). However, employers demand more than this. They also ask for an ability to understand the context and what is behind the rules and procedures; good knowledge

Table 5.3: Skills requirements in old and new textile mills

	Old mills	New mills
Semi-skilled workers	Manual dexterity, physical strength in manual and repetitive tasks	Machine trouble shooting, process handling skills
Skilled, senior workers	Rigid, specific allocation of responsibility according to work category	Cross-departmental oversight and working

Source: Compiled by author from Krishnan (2010).

Table 5.4: Job content and skills requirements in the industry

Position	Description of tasks and skills	Industry comment on match with existing workforce
Supervisor	Follow machine maintenance schedule	
	Independent troubleshooting, problem solving	Their own lack of formal training limits ability to act as trainers
	Training, guiding and mentoring operators	
	Know and meet quality parameters	Ability to use machines efficiently, knowledge of efficiency metrics are lacking (e.g., systems for minimum downtime, line balancing)
	Adequate knowledge of productivity and efficiency to meet production targets	
	Manage and motivate large uneducated workforce, to ensure discipline, safety, delivery, sometimes in context of uneven workflow (flexibility)	Workforce management is weak
	Adequate 'domain' knowledge to get the big picture and issue appropriate instructions	
	Openness to new technologies, learn and implement with workforce	
	Communications to motivate suppliers (food processing)	
Operator/skilled worker	Ability to operate range of technical equipment, machines, materials	Technical knowledge is usually limited to 1–2 processes, needs to be broader, worker must be ready to learn new
	Inspection skills, can identify defects and report up technical problems	Poor problem-identification, lack of 'feedback orientation', lack of communication skills to report up
	Ensure minimum wastage in work processes	Generally ability to learn and adapt to new processes is limited
	Know and respect quality standards	
	Know health and safety standards, hygiene	Lacking where these are high and specialized, for example, chemical, pharma industries
	Have sense of 'big picture' knowledge, concepts behind technology and processes	Often lacking due to poor educational base
	Follow SOPs of firm	Need understanding of underlying logic of these procedures (e.g., chemical process)
	Accomplished in particular sub-trade (e.g., fitting, welding, plumbing)	ITI courses are generally inadequate
	Shop floor discipline, not motivated to unionize, not 'troublemakers'	Pool of mature workers in several industries are seen as 'political'. Punctuality and attendance is poor
	Basic maths literacy for measures, scales, calculations, for example, chemical production, food processing	
	Use of basic computers for CNC, control room, simulation	
	Continuous observation and alertness for defect spotting	
	Know environmental parameters (effluent, mines)	
	sharp presence of mind for fast machines	
	Understand and convert technical drawings	
	Hand–eye coordination, sensitivity and good sense for time-sensitive, manual and hand processes (jewellery, leather, furniture, poultry)	
	Physical attributes (physical fitness, stamina, eyes, lungs)	
	Team work, good relations with other sections (leather, dairy)	
	Visual examination skills, sizing, sorting, checking procurement (food processing)	

Source: NSDC skills gap reports.

of a particular trade as well as ability to work across equipments and processes, and above all, a capacity to accept and learn new processes and equipment.

Currently, these capabilities are demanded of workers working at or just above minimum wages. One cannot help feeling that industrialists demand a lot for their money. But they know better than anyone that these skills and capabilities are a 'wish list', and several are consistently lacking in the workforce they can access. In particular, managers complain that workers lack the initiative, rigour and communication skills to identify and report aberrations; their observance of standards is patchy and the mature workforce tends to lack discipline and get 'political'. Trained operators' skills are narrow and they are frequently slow and resistant towards accepting new equipment. Above all, they lack the background knowledge to see the logic behind the processes and procedures, and to be open to, and capable of, learning.

The NSDC's skills gap reports also cover requirements in the services sector and we can similarly observe how certain capabilities and tasks repeat themselves across industries, such as health care, travel and tourism, logistics and organized retail. A wide range of abilities are wrapped up in the phrase 'communication skills'—ability to listen, analyze, relate and speak—which come to the relief of workers delivering services on the frontline or smoothening processes in the back office. The challenge is increased with the need to respond appropriately and flexibly to a wide range of end customers, to persuade and overcome the resistance of customers in order to 'close' deals, all of which demand a very different self-perception than that of a factory operator. Detailed product knowledge, personal grooming and ability to follow procedures and a good level of literacy, are also important requirements.

Discussions with some of the skills provider start-ups supported by NSDC highlighted the minimum requirements of employers. The need for a 'positive attitude' or 'positive personality' is repeatedly emphasized. This implies, the worker is willing and able to receive and respond to feedback, is not discouraged too easily, accepts the learning period as a rough ride which will be got through and communicates clearly with seniors in case of a problem or if does not understand something. For most of us, such attributes are the bottom line of being a trainee, and yet, they cannot be taken for granted when the majority of the trainee force belongs to rural areas, is educated below standard XII and is from poor backgrounds. But the rising demand for workers by industry and services, and the government's commitment to lick its ill-fitting rural youth into an employable shape means that for an increasing number of young people, the workplace is their first exposure to industrial, organized and cosmopolitan space.

Un-habituated to long hours seated at desks or machines and confused by the communications around them, trainees can be additionally required to relocate to provincial towns, state capitals and even to distant states to take up placements. So even though their earnings are at times much higher than what they were getting previously, it may still seem like a poor trade-off. All the skill providers who were interviewed agreed that trainees' resistance to travel was a key hindrance to their work. While some providers have responded by ensuring placements within a narrow geographical radius, others send trainees in groups with their own warden and cook so that they feel more at home on arrival. But the rate of attrition remains high, ranging between 20 and 50 per cent of the placements made.

In spite of the offer of a secure minimum wage in the organized (or semi organized) sector, many youths are apparently unwilling to knuckle down to the job. Part of the problem is that the placements offered through the new skills sector routes are generally no better than the standard ones offered to freshers 'off the street', with minimum wages, some (usually not full) statutory benefits and poor progression prospects.[16] But the greater gap in expectations—between an employer and a trainee—is perhaps not about wages but about what is felt to be an acceptable and meaningful way to learn and to spend one's day.

In the skills debate, we have become so wrapped up in the race to skill 500 million that we are losing our common sense for lack of reflection.

First, the cultural gap between our poorly schooled youth and their work environment can be enormous. In making the leap, the young arrive in a space where their person and attributes are viewed as deficient in multiple ways. As they are asked to channel all they can into new and narrow productive activities, they must 'shelve' most of who they are and what they know. Unless the job milieu can become a sphere of meaningful and moral relationships, the youths are unlikely to make more than a physical leap. Intellectually, psychologically and emotionally, they will remain unassimilated. As Helena Lopes has argued, work is not simply a matter of earning wages to live or to spend at leisure; it also satisfies the needs essential for a person's well-being (Lopes 2011).

Second, the job offer is not competing with the alternative of being unemployed (as would be the case in Europe), but with that of being employed in informal trades and activities which may have positive as well as negative attributes. That the young people are undoubtedly poor does not diminish this point. Deeming a person poor is not only a relative judgment (felt all the more acutely in the city than the village) but one which reflects the dominant way in which we value some resources (cash income, education) over others (nature, free time).[17]

Also, we must recall how we ourselves learn and how we watch our children learn—more from exposure and less in the class room; less by doing what we're told and more from exploring routes which are not sanctioned; less by conforming to the grinding discipline demanded by a blinkered job, and more by taking detours, listening on the sidelines and grasping opportunities which nobody offered us. We learn, in short, by asserting our agency, often through small acts of resistance.

5.6. Going forward: Improving the job offer

The need for qualified workers in high-growth industry and services is reaching critical levels. Managers are reporting ever greater shortages of workers, in textiles, construction, auto manufacture, leather, road transport and so on and they are often at a loss as to how to address it. Here we argue that addressing the quality of the labour force—the usual response of employers, government and NGOs, discussed in Chapters 4 and 6—is only half the solution. The other is addressing the quality of the offer—the job, the terms and conditions, the work environment, the value—which the employers can give. This can be done in multiple ways.

New forms of collective bargaining and representation of workers in a workplace: Traditional, wage-based bargaining is fundamentally challenged in open global economies, but the principle of workers pushing for standards and their representation and role in shaping workplace conditions is not. Workers' and human resource

---

[16] This point is discussed in more detail in Chapter 4 under vocational training.

[17] In his visionary book, William Bissell imagines an India where such valuations might be overturned, revealing the invisible subsidies to wealthy urban colonies and the hidden assets to poor villages. 'A poor village can now trade its huge surplus of drinking water,

biodiversity and potential for forest cover, whereas a wealthy urban colony … will be forced to buy basic services' (Bissell 2009, p. 23). Aman Sethi, on the other hand, highlights the value of freedom in his wonderful new book. 'The ideal job … has the perfect balance of *kamai* and *azadi*', says Ashraf *Bhai*, a whitewasher in Delhi's Sadar Bazaar. '*Azadi* is the freedom to tell the *maalik* to f*** off when you want to. The *maalik* owns our work. He does not own us' (Sethi 2011).

organizations must find new ways to develop management–worker (and customer–supplier) relationships to ensure a constructive and meaningful pressure is brought to bear on the management by the workers who understand the business realities.

Industry must address productivity issues to justify better jobs: We have shown how the majority of India's wages—across industry and services—remains shockingly low. But productivity is frequently extremely low too. India's garment sector, for example, is about half as efficient as China's and a one-third of the USA's. It is standard for managers to blame workers (and perhaps their machines) for low productivity, but productivity experts know that in most cases the solution is in the hands of the management. 'Indian factories are typically disorganized, with inventories and spare parts chaotically organized, inadequate performance tracking, and extremely poor quality control' (Bloom et al. 2010). With increased attention to building second-tier managers, systems and communications throughout the factory, there will be gains in productivity which will justify higher wages.

New management thinking to build a better psychological environment for job satisfaction: Work is increasingly being done in the field of HR on the contribution of non-financial factors to job satisfaction (Ghosh 2010; Biswas 2011; Lopes 2011). The role of line and peer relationships in harnessing a worker's commitment and loyalty is highlighted as crucial. Ghosh (2010) explores the different values sets which drive organizations and demonstrates how such value sets influence the type and level of worker commitment. A worker can be motivated to work hard and stay with:

1. Affective or emotional commitment
2. Normative commitment that is a sense of duty and obligation
3. The view that the cost of leaving the organization would be too high

Each of these commitment forms is more suitable for some organizational values than for others. For example, affective or emotional commitment is more important for an organization perceived to be driven by 'humane' values (consideration, cooperation, fairness and moral integrity), while normative commitment is a more important response for an organization driven by vision (initiative, creativity, innovation). So, organizations which come across as being driven by certain kind of values motivate a commitment in keeping with those.

Another key aspect of improvement in the psychological environment is a more sincere and better dialogue between supervisors and workers. This has repeatedly been shown to be a key factor in job satisfaction (Biswas 2011). Also, it is important to know how to improve peer relationships for mutual learning, cooperation and creative suggestions, while laying the management's fear of a workers' association.

References

Anant, T., R. Hasan, P. Mohapatra, R. Nagaraj, and S.K. Sasikumar. 2006. Labour markets in India: Issues and perspectives. In *Labour markets in Asia: Issues and perspectives*, ed. J. Felip and R. Hasan. New York: Palgrave-Macmillan.

Besley, T., and R. Burgess. 2004. Can labour regulation hinder economic performance? Evidence from India. *Quarterly Journal of Economics* 119 (1).

Bissell, W. 2009. *Making India work*. New Delhi: Penguin Viking.

Biswas, S. 2011. Psychological climate as an antecedent of job satisfaction & job involvement. *The Indian Journal of Industrial Relations* 46 (3).

Bloom, N., B. Eifert, A. Mahajan, D. McKenzie, and J. Roberts. 2010. Does management matter? Evidence from India. International Growth Centre Working Papers Series, 10/0873.

Business India. 2011. A time for labour reforms. *Business India*, 1 May, pp. 42–48.

Chadha, G. 2004. Human capital base of the Indian labour market: Identifying worry spots. *The Indian Journal of Labour Economics* 47 (1).

Datta, S., and V. Sharma, eds. 2008. *State of India's livelihoods: The 4P report*. New Delhi: Access Development Services.

Dougherty, S. 2010. *Labour regulations and employment dynamics at the state level in India*. Paris: OECD.

Economic Survey. 2011. *Economic Survey*. Ministry of Finance. New Delhi: Government of India,.

Ghose, A. 2010. India's employment challenge. *The Indian Journal of Labour Economics* 53 (4).

Ghosh, S. 2010. Perceived organisational values & commitment to organisation. *The Indian Journal of Industrial Relations* 45 (3).

Goldar, B. 2011a. Growth in organised manufacturing employment in recent years. *Economic & Political Weekly* 12 February, XLVI (7).

———. 2011b. Organised manufacturing employment: continuing the debate. *Economic & Political Weekly* 2 April, XLVI (14).

Gupta, P., R. Hasan, and U. Kumar. 2009. Big reforms but small payoffs: Explaining the weak record of growth in Indian manufacturing. *India Policy Forum 2008–9*, 2008–09.

Harriss-White, B. 2003. *India working: Essays on society & economy*. Cambridge: Cambridge University Press.

Haynes, D. 1999. Just like a family? Recalling relations of production in the textile industries of Surat & Bhiwandi 1940–1960. In *The worlds of Indian industrial labour*, ed. J. Parry, J. Breman and K. Kapadia. New Delhi: SAGE Publications.

IMaCS. 2008. *The skill gap reports*. New Delhi: ICRA Management Consulting Services.

Knorringa, P. 1999. Agra: An old cluster facing new competition. *World Development* 27 (9).

Krishnan, T. 2010. Technological change & employment relations in India. *The Indian Journal of Industrial Relations* 45 (3).

Labour Behind the Label. 2010. Taking Liberties: The Story behind the UK High Street. London: Labour Behind the Label, War on Want.

Lopes, H. 2011. Why do people work? Individual wants versus common goods. *Journal of Economic Issues* March, XLV (1).

Ma Foi Randstad. 2011a. *Employment trends survey, Wave 4, 2010*. Chennai: MEtS..

———. 2011b. *Employment trends survey, Wave 1, 2011*. Chennai: MEtS.

Nagaraj, R. 2011. Growth in organised manufacturing employment: A comment. *Economic & Political Weekly* 19 March, XLVI (12).

NSSO. 2011. Key *indicators of employment and unemployment in India*. NSS 66th Round, July 2009–June 2010. NSSO, Government of India.

Ruthven, O. Forthcoming in 2012. The Regulation of informality: working metal for global homeware markets in Moradabad. In *Markets for peace: Informal economic networks and political agency*, ed. L. Buur and D. Rogers. Copenhagen: DIIS.

Sethi, A. 2011. *A free man*. Delhi: Random House.

TeamLease. 2006. *The India labour report 2006: A ranking of Indian states by their labour ecosystem*. Bangalore: TeamLease.

———. 2008. *The India labour report 2008: The right to rise: Making India's labour markets inclusive*. Bangalore: TeamLease.

———. 2009. *The India labour report 2009: The geographic mismatch and a ranking of Indian states*. Bangalore: TeamLease, IIJT.

Potential and Possibilities

Chapter **6**

6.1. Introduction

This chapter looks at some of the key emerging and ongoing developments in government policies and practices. While the government has reiterated its commitment to the inclusive growth agenda, the emerging trends suggest a qualitative shift in the manner in which services and subsidies will be provided to the poor. The first section discusses the four key livelihood initiatives (skilling and employment, market inclusion, decentralization and revival of agri-rural economy) which are likely to be included in the 12th Five Year Plan, and which will provide the overall direction of resource deployment and policy framework. The next two sections focus on newly introduced Unique ID (Aadhaar) Project and the proposed Direct Cash Transfer scheme, and discuss their implications for the poor as well as livelihood professionals.

6.2. 12th Five Year Plan: Livelihood focus

The Planning Commission started the discussions for developing the Approach Paper for the 12th Five Year Plan (2012–17) in July 2010. In a remarkable break from the past practices, the Planning Commission adopted an 'interactive and participative planning' approach (Shrivastava 2011), seeking suggestions and ideas from a diverse set of stakeholders through innovative channels. A conscious decision

was taken while designing the planning process, to take it into the public domain. Besides seeking inputs from industry and professional bodies (e.g., Confederation of Indian Industry [CII], Federation of Indian Chambers of Commerce and Industry [FICCI], Federation of Indian Micro and Small and Medium Enterprises [FISME], National Association of Software and Services Companies [NASSCOM] and National Bank for Agriculture and Rural Development [NABARD]), the consultation process also used other innovative non-conventional channels (such as, an essay competition in schools, a Facebook page, online discussion forums, etc.) to seek inputs from experts, civil society representatives and ordinary citizens.[1]

At the time of writing this section, the 12th Five Year Plan was still being formulated. However, the government has identified 'Faster, More Inclusive and Sustainable Growth' as the main objective of the 12th Five Year Plan (Planning Commission 2011).

An inclusive and sustainable growth presupposes enhancement of livelihood opportunities and options for the poor. It is also noteworthy that among the '12 strategic challenges' identified by the Planning Commission, four have direct and wide-ranging

[1] The documents summarizing the inputs from different stakeholders are available at the 12th Five Year Plan website: http://www.12thplan.gov.in/stakeholder_sugg.php

implications for the livelihoods of the poor (see Box 6.1). Based on a review of the inputs from diverse stakeholders, this section discusses the options which the government can exercise to meet these strategic challenges, and to enhance the livelihoods of the poor.

Other thrust areas listed in the Plan—such as improving effectiveness of programmes for the poor, special programmes for vulnerable groups and support to backward regions being put into practice—are yet to be rendered into clear-cut action plans, while there is a commitment to reduce the number of centrally sponsored schemes (CSSs) from the current 150 to about 10. In particular, the emphasis on instituting better governance and accountability standards will be of critical importance if these livelihood thrusts are to be achieved. While devolution is one way forward, strengthening proactive, citizen participation in governance will be of key significance.

The rest of this section looks at the four livelihood-related thrusts outlined above, in more detail.

6.2.1. Enhancing skills and faster generation of employment

To achieve the objective of 'inclusive and sustainable' growth, the skills of this vast reservoir of potential human resources need to be upgraded. The investments made by the government, the demand pull from the industry and the improving economic growth opens up huge opportunities for mainstreaming India's unorganized workforce. The initiatives currently in place fall far short of the vision of creating a 500 million strong skilled workforce by 2022. To achieve this target, the country needs to add 40 to 50 million trained, skilled and industry-ready people to the workforce every year. The issues which need to be addressed to meet this challenge include:

1. *Administrative infrastructure for deployment of vocational training/skill development*: At present, there is no centralized agency to lead and coordinate the various skill development initiatives—a total of 17 different ministries/departments are involved in the skills sector

---

Box 6.1: *The livelihood challenges in the 12th Five Year Plan*

1. *Enhancing skills and faster generation of employment*:
   It is believed that India's economic growth is not generating enough jobs or livelihood opportunities. At the same time, many sectors face manpower shortages. To address both these problems, we need to improve our education and training systems; create efficient and accessible labour markets for all skill categories and encourage faster growth of small and micro-enterprises.

2. *Markets for efficiency and inclusion*:
   Open, integrated and well-regulated markets for land, labour and capital and for goods and services are essential for growth, inclusion and sustainability. We have many sectors where markets are non-existent or incomplete, especially those which are dominated by public provisioning. How do we create or improve markets in all sectors?

3. *Decentralization, empowerment and information*:
   Greater and more informed participation of all citizens in decision-making, enforcing accountability, exercising their rights and entitlements; and determining the course of their lives is central to faster growth, inclusion and sustainability. How can we best promote the capabilities of all Indians, especially the most disadvantaged, to achieve this end?

4. *Rural transformation and sustained growth of agriculture*:
   Rural India suffers from poor infrastructure and inadequate amenities. Low agricultural growth perpetuates food and nutritional insecurities, which also reduces rural incomes. How can we encourage and support our villages in improving their living and livelihood conditions in innovative ways?

Source: 12th Five Year Plan website: http://12thplan.gov.in/

and the National Skill Development Corporation (NSDC), though dominant, has a limited mandate. While their different experiences can be a great source of mutual learning, at present they have poor coordination and focus.

The renewed focus on skill development provides the opportunity for the creation of a nodal administrative infrastructure, such as a separate ministry for skill development/vocational training, which can undertake a focused deployment of this initiative.

2. *Vocational education (VE) at secondary level*: To create a pipeline of skilled workforce, VE at secondary school level is essential, and this fact is recognized by the government (see Chapter 4). The high dropout rate between primary and secondary education is often due to the perceived low utility of secondary education for employment purposes. However, even among the rare secondary schools which offer VE, few students opt for them due to a lack of adequate quality and applicability of the courses, and a bias towards academic qualifications. To meet the target of 25 per cent students within the ambit of VE, there is a need to make the courses more relevant, and to establish industry/employment linkages as an incentive for more youths to join VE.

3. *Diverse and decentralized delivery channels for skill training*: The sheer size, heterogeneity, broad age range, wide geographical coverage, poor educational and income status and gender and social disparity poses a huge challenge to skill development initiatives. More decentralized approaches to delivery (e.g., mobile training, distance learning, involvement of panchayats, municipalities and local bodies) will be required to meet the diverse needs and constraints of these segments.

4. *More support to quality*: As shown in Chapter 4, skills providers offer overly short courses which struggle to add value to the kind of job an unskilled worker might be offered off the street. The government has been putting excessive emphasis on numbers, not quality. Yet it is the young people with quality training who will ensure lifelong employability, sustainability of the jobs they access and the capacity of the industry and services to grow in the longer term. Along with support in curriculum content and training skills, the government must balance the emphasis on short-term courses with long-term and in-depth courses (i.e., courses with a duration of more than six months) which even the poorest can afford.

5. *Addressing the management environment for trainees*: Chapters 4 and 5 showed that there are problems in the employers' perception and expectations from young trainees which reduces their chances of staying in employment, learning on the job and achieving success. Indian firms are well known for their weak second-tier management and this reflects in the poor ability of supervisors to guide, mentor, counsel and persuade young trainees to stay on and become productive. Furthermore, the low-quality jobs which prevail in the market (see Chapter 5) are the result of the managers' inability to organize work and guide and motivate workers towards improved efficiency. In spite of the shortage of good junior managers faced by the Indian firms, the government's vocational skills programme has so far ignored this challenge. This gives rise to the question whether the government can extend the same support towards an environment for training junior managers, as it has for manual and low-end skills.

6.2.2. Market efficiency and inclusion

Market inefficiencies are one of the main bottlenecks that keep the poor excluded from gainfully participating in and benefiting from socioeconomic growth. Various factors, ranging from government policies to information asymmetries contribute to these inefficiencies. Three specific markets which hold opportunities for reforms, and will have direct impact on the livelihood options of the poor are the markets for rural produce, for financial services and labour market. The following paragraphs discuss the potential improvements suggested for the 12th Five Year Plan:

1. *Market for rural produce*: Rural producers (farmers, artisans, weavers, vegetable growers, self help groups [SHGs], etc.) typically fail to realize the value of their produce due to poor market-linkages. Besides loss of value of the produce due to intermediaries in the long supply chain, the producers are also handicapped by their lack of knowledge of the market trends. Additionally, often the government's own policies and mechanisms (e.g., interstate octroi which hampers the free movement of agricultural produce to high-value markets, procurement portfolio of grains for public distribution systems [PDS] and Agricultural Produce Marketing Committee [APMC] Act) also result in de-linking the producers from the markets.

   Inputs by the stakeholders for the 12th Five Year Plan offer many options to the government to smoothen these market linkages; for example:

   • *Decentralized procurement*: While the government provides a ready market through procurement of PDS grains from the farmer at Minimum Support Price (MSP), the procurement through Food Corporation of India (FCI) is predisposed towards certain regions and states, and a limited variety of grains. As a result, farmers from the other states, and those producing other grains, are not able to get a fair price for their produce. A more decentralized approach for procurement and involvement of licensed private entities in procurement (to avoid putting pressure on an already stretched FCI) is one possibility which can augment the farmers' reach to the market.

   • *Modification in APMC Act*: Though there is no MSP for the perishable horticultural produce (vegetables, fruits), these products come under the APMC Act, and the producers can sell them only through the APMC *mandis*, and often only in designated regions. The collusion among the *mandi* operators denies the producer a fair remuneration for their produce. To take care of these anomalies, the 12th Five Year Plan is likely to suggest modifications in the APMC Act to exclude horticultural and perishable produce entirely from its ambit, and encourage the producers to sell directly to private entities.

   • *Investment in market creation*: The 'Issues to Approach Paper' of the Planning Commission (2011) suggests that creation of functioning markets for both inputs and outputs and investments in better rural infrastructure for storage and food processing are an important focus of the 12th Five Year Plan. Facilities for post-harvest handling, storage, processing and so on for perishable items, and reliable market extension services for items produced from inherited skills, such as handicrafts and so on will greatly enhance linkages of rural economy with external markets, and allow the small rural producers to realize a better price for their produce.

2. *Market for labour*: As discussed in Chapter 2, India's labour market is characterized by a large unorganized workforce, which lacks regulatory protection, and poor quality jobs. The 12th Five Year Plan will address these issues,

through skills development and with a thrust on creating greater efficiency and responsiveness in the labour market.

- *Flexibility of labour laws*: Chapter 5 outlined the arguments that labour laws and their administration do not allow sufficient flexibility to industries to manage their manpower in a manner that lets them cope with the vagaries of the market, thereby leading to casual hiring and outsourcing. It has been proposed that reforms should be made to key acts, such as, the Industrial Dispute Act and Contract Labour Act, to offer greater flexibility. At the same time, the core entitlements of workers—offered through organized sector schemes (Rajiv Gandhi Shramik Kalyan Yojana, Employee State Insurance Scheme, Employee Provident Fund, etc.)—need to be expanded to cover retrenchment compensation, unemployment allowance, retraining, redeployment and so on. Also, the social security schemes for the unorganized workforce (Rashtriya Swasthya Bima Yojana [RSBY], Swavalamban Pension Scheme, etc.) should be fully implemented.

- *Labour market information system*: The informal sector workers lack market information for high-value employment, and a large part of their effort goes into finding work. Conversely, employers too lack information about the availability of specific skill-sets. An on-time Labour Market Information System, which tracks the skill-sets by locations, volumes, demand trends and so on would be a high-impact opportunity to create an efficient and inclusive labour market.

3. *Market for financial services*: Only half of the Indian population has access to institutional financial services, which is even lower among the poor. Tenant farmers, migrant workers, rural artisans, weavers and so on find it difficult to get investment credit from banks, and have to borrow money from non-institutional lenders at exorbitant rates. Many of the proposals to provide easy financial access, some of which the government has already started implementing, are likely to receive further impetus in the prospective Plan. Following are some examples of the proposals made:

- Using banking channels to make payments under various public welfare programmes (as is happening with the MGNREGA) to provide incentives for the banks to provide financial inclusion.
- Promoting setting up shared common facilities to host low-value accounts which will lower the costs of providing financial access for the providers.
- Ensuring interoperability of business correspondent networks to enhance the viability of distribution channels in remote areas.
- Expediting computerization of land records since land can be a valuable asset for drawing loans.

6.2.3. Decentralization, empowerment and information

The 73rd and 74th Constitutional Amendments during the 1990s had laid the foundation for an empowered but accountable grass-roots level governance framework. Though the Amendment had lead to establishment of the Panchayati Raj Institutions (PRIs), in practice, the devolution of powers for local self-governance is still in a nascent stage, and a decentralized governance structure has yet to be translated into the state policies. The stakeholders have proffered suggestions for a number of possible initiatives for the 12th Five Year Plan, which will expedite the process of decentralization and ownership of governance at the local level. Three key areas where government intervention would make decentralization effective are:

1. *Implementation of Second Administrative Reforms Commission (ARC) recommendations*: The government could make a further push towards the implementation of the recommendations of the Second ARC, and give recognition to the local elected bodies at the panchayat and municipality levels as 'an institution of self government', who would collectively form the district planning committee (DPC) or district government. At present, the panchayats and DPCs (wherever they exist) have been given more of a status of agencies for the implementation of the government schemes and programmes, rather than as local governments themselves. Not only would this ensure that the development schemes and resources are aligned to the local needs, but also a greater and direct accountability of their proper implementation.

2. *Capacity building of local functionaries and elected representatives*: Decentralization of power and consequent expansion of the roles of the local elected representatives and functionaries would also require capacity building to handle new responsibilities. This would be even more important for women and people from disadvantaged classes. Moreover, the capacity building would need to go beyond just the training on government programmes, rules and regulations, as is the present case. So, it would also need to focus on skills/capabilities for local self-governance, issues of social justice, planning and monitoring, project management and so on, and would require involvement of civil society organizations and academic institutions.

3. *Democratization of information*: To empower the citizens to take advantage of local self-governance, simplification

of rules, regulations and procedures, and dissemination of such information to people would be an essential prerequisite. The government may also consider creation of a National Data Bank which will collect, disseminate and share useful information (especially the best practices in the field of planning and developmental initiatives) from the local communities and self-governing institutions.

However, a major challenge would be the implementation of an effective e-governance system at the panchayat level. At present, out of the 245,525 panchayat offices (582 zila panchayats, 6,299 block panchayats and 238,644 gram panchayats), barely 24 per cent (58,291 panchayats) have computers (Mybangalore.com 2011). Even among these, most are non-functional or they lack personnel who possess the required skills to handle the computers. To re-enable panchayats and local bodies, investment is required for upgrading both technology infrastructure and capabilities.

6.2.4. Rural transformation and sustained growth of agriculture

During the last few years, the share of agriculture to GDP has shrunk to 14.6 per cent. Also, the growth of agriculture during the 11th Five Year Plan was a mere 2.8 per cent. With more than 70 per cent of the population living in the villages, and about 58 per cent depending directly or indirectly on agriculture for their subsistence, low agricultural growth is a growing threat to rural incomes, and perpetuates food insecurity. Appreciating that the revival of rural farm-sector economy is critical to the inclusive growth agenda, the Planning Commission has fixed 4 per cent agricultural growth as the target for the 12th Five Year Plan. Budget 2011–12 provides some indications of the measures which the 12th Five Year Plan is likely to take to achieve this target. They are:

- *Increase in agricultural credit*: Many recent changes, as seen in the Budget 2011–12, indicate that the 12th Five Year Plan will target an increase in the access to agricultural credit by the farmers. For instance, the target for credit flow to farmers was increased by ₹100,000 crore, and set as ₹475,000 crore during 2011–12. Also in view of the enhanced credit targets, ₹10,000 crore was added to NABARD's Short-Term Rural Credit Fund, and a commitment was made to strengthen NABARD's capital base by ₹3,000 crore. The government has also provided incentives by lowering the interest rates for short-term loans from 7 per cent to 3 per cent for farmers who pay their crop loans on time.

- *Investments in post-harvest and processing infrastructure*: The Planning Commission anticipates that a significant growth can be achieved in the agricultural sector not just from grains alone, but also from produce, such as dairy, fishery and poultry (Ahluwalia 2011). As these are perishable items, the Plan is likely to see major investments in cold chain, post-harvest storage, warehousing and so on. NABARD's Rural Infrastructure Development Fund (RIDF) may play a larger role in these infrastructure development projects. In fact, Budget 2011–12 has already increased the corpus for RIDF from ₹16,000 crore to ₹18,000 crore with additional allocations for warehouse development.

Since, the payback period for pure agri-produce warehouses and cold-chains is about 12 to 15 years, fiscal incentives are being put in place to make private sector investments in rural infrastructure lucrative. For instance, cold chains and post-harvest storage are now considered as a sub-sector of infrastructure, enabling the private entrepreneur to avail a 10-year tax holiday. Lending for such projects will also be considered as priority sector lending. These initiatives, along with mega food parks for food processing will help the farmers reduce wastages, get a better price for their produce and increase their income.

- *Enabling regulatory environment for agriculture*: The 12th Five Year Plan is likely to give further boost to the regulatory changes being made by the government to support both easy access to the input factor for more productive agriculture as well as facilitation of smooth linkages to markets. For instance, changes such as the issuance of warehouse receipts would give the farmers the option to hold their produce if the current prices are unfavourable, besides being able to discount the receipts to raise money for the next crop cycle. Likewise, to promote modern farming methods, the government has reduced the customs duty on farm machineries and micro-irrigation equipments from 5 per cent to 2.5 per cent and 7.5 per cent to 5 per cent respectively. Such changes in the rules and regulations facilitate qualitative improvements in the farming practices and marketing of the produce.

6.3. Aadhaar: Unique identification (UID) project

The UID project is an ambitious initiative, launched by the Government of India in September 2010, to provide a permanent 12-digit UID number, called Aadhaar, to all citizens (and also to NRIs and foreign visitors, who will be provided with a different card), which will be linked to the basic demographic and biometric information. To execute this mammoth task, the Unique Identification Authority of India (UIDAI) was established in February 2009 as an attached office under the Planning Commission. Its mandate is to develop and implement the necessary institutional, technical, and legal infrastructure to issue the UID to all residents. To roll-out this exercise, UIDAI has signed MOUs with all the state and UT governments, certain union ministries, banks and other large institutions, who will act as the 'registrars' for enrolling and issuing UIDs. At the time of writing this report, the UIDAI had issued close to 10 million UID numbers, and planned to issue 1 million UIDs every day from October 2011. The UIDAI plans to issue 600 million UIDs over the next 5 years, and to cover the entire population within a period of 10 years.

Though the charter of UIDAI described UID as a non-mandatory voluntary 'facility', it allows access to certain services and benefits offered by the government and other institutions (see Box 6.2), so, the strategy which UIDAI has followed for enrolling and issuing UID also facilitates making it a de facto mandatory requirement for availing these services and benefits. In fact, many of its 'registrars' and partners (government agencies, banks, telecom service partners, etc.) have already started linking UID to a wide variety of services and benefits provided by them. Once this project scales up, UID will have a wide-ranging impact on the delivery of welfare benefits and livelihood opportunities for the poor. This section covers the rationale, potential benefits, opportunities and challenges of UID in making a difference in the lives of the poor.

6.3.1. Promises of Aadhaar

The delivery of government subsidies and services to their intended beneficiaries has remained one of the key challenges in promotion of 'inclusive growth'. Given the vast size and diversity of the country, the wide variety and needs of the marginalized poor and the human and administrative errors and corruption and inefficiencies across the supply chain, a very small percentage of resources intended for the poor actually reach them. UID/Aadhaar aims to tackle these lapses in three ways:

1. *Providing a proof of identity*: While different ministries and government departments offer a wide range of programmes and schemes for the poor and marginalized, often the intended beneficiaries do not possess the required documents (birth certificate, recorded rights to land, BPL card, etc.) to prove their identity and entitlement. UID/Aadhaar will provide an easy proof of one's identity across different schemes and services.

2. *Accurate identification of beneficiary*: Many marginalized segments of poor do not get enumerated, and therefore fail to access schemes and benefits which they are entitled to. On the other hand, resources for government schemes also

---

Box 6.2: *Aadhaar-enabled applications*

Aadhaar can be used by any system which needs to establish the identity of a resident and/or provide secure access for the resident to services/benefits offered by the system. It can be used in the delivery of the following programmes:

- *Food and nutrition*—PDS, Food Security, Mid Day Meals (MDMs), Integrated Child Development Services (ICDS) Scheme
- *Employment*—Mahatma Gandhi National Rural Employment Guarantee Scheme (MGNREGS), Swarnajayanti Gram Swarozgar Yojana (SGSY), Indira Awaas Yojana (IAY), Prime Minister's Employment Guarantee Programme

- *Education*—Sarva Shiksha Abhiyan (SSA), Right to Education
- *Inclusion and social security*—Janani Suraksha Yojana, Development of Primitive Tribe Groups, Indira Gandhi National Old Age Pension Scheme (IGNOAPS)
- *Health care*—RSBY, Janashri Bima Yojana, Aam Aadmi Bima Yojana
- Other miscellaneous purposes including Property Transactions, Voter ID, PAN Card and so on

Source: UIDAI (2010).

get siphoned off through fake identities and ghost beneficiaries. A unique identity number will help in identifying the legitimate recipients for government's welfare policies and programmes.

3. *Plugging leaks in the delivery mechanisms*: The delivery of government's subsidies and services relies on a long, complicated and largely unmonitored supply chain. Since the supply chain involves layers of unidentified intermediaries, keeping track to ensure accurate delivery becomes virtually impossible. By offering a real-time authentication of identity, UID/Aadhaar will enable keeping track of the subsidies across the numerous intermediaries in the supply chain—and thus, eliminating the diversion and leakage of the resources.

6.3.2. Aadhaar and inclusion

Clearly, lack of proper and accurate identification is not only a major barrier for the poor to avail government welfare programmes and services/subsidies, it is also one of the major causes of leakages and diversion of resources and services meant for the poor. By addressing these issues, UID/Aadhaar holds immense potential to transform the nature and quality of delivery of services and subsidies to the poor. Among the variety of potential applications, three have significant implications for the poor and their livelihoods. These are discussed below:

1. *Improving financial inclusion*: Despite its vast network of about 70,000 bank branches, of which 32,000 are in rural India, access to finance and banking services remains a challenge for the poor. For instance, a report by Skoch Development Foundation (Kocher 2009) found that among the rural population, only 17 per cent have access to formal institutional credit (13 per cent in case of lower income groups). Out of the 89.3 million farmer households, 45.9 million do not have access to any credit,

and only 54 per cent of the population is estimated to have a savings account.

One of the primary reasons for this state of affairs can be traced to the problems poor face in providing an authentic identification. The normal know your customer (KYC) norms require the applicant to furnish proof of both his/her identity (either Passport, PAN card, voter's card, driving license, identity card, or letter from a recognized public authority/public servant) and of residence (either telephone or electricity bill, ration card, bank account statement, or letter from employer/recognized public authority). These options are often not available to the poor, or are not valid (e.g., the ration card is no longer a valid proof of residence for the migrant labour once they move out of their village). In 2009, RBI relaxed the KYC norms for the no-frills accounts to allow the poor to open an account if the applicant is introduced by another account holder. However, for many marginalized poor (e.g., migrant rural labour), not only is it difficult to find an introducer, but at times it is even impossible to provide a local address to fulfil the know your resident (KYR) norms.

Within less than a year of its launch, the emerging trends have already started showing the huge implication of UID/Aadhaar on financial inclusion. For instance, in December 2010, Finance Ministry recognized UID/Aadhaar number as 'an officially valid document' under the amendments to the Prevention of Money Laundering Act (PMLA) to satisfy the KYC norms (*The Hindu* 2010), and RBI has also recognized UID/Aadhaar as acceptable for KYC norms for the no-frills accounts[2] (Tiwari 2011). UIDAI also worked with

---

[2] A 'no-frills' account can be opened with a limited or no cash balance, and provides only basic banking services (cash deposit, cash withdrawal, etc.) to the poor.

the National Payment Corporation of India (NPCI) to develop the Aadhaar-enabled payment system (AEPS), and tested its feasibility in Jharkhand during January–April 2011 with remarkable success (see Box 6.3 for details of the pilot project). An Aadhaar-compliant electronic payment infrastructure is being developed by the Visa Card, which will enable the un-banked and under-banked UID number holders to integrate into the financial mainstream (*India Infoline* 2010).

Since the UID number will provide an easy and reliable way of establishing one's identity, it would address many existing limitations in financial inclusion both for the poor, as well as for the banks; for example:

- It will provide a trouble-free way for the poor to establish their identity, without having to go through the complicated process of meeting the KYC norms. Then too, it will significantly bring down the customer acquisition costs for the banks by reducing the documentation required for the verification process.

- The UID's clear authentication and verification processes opens up the opportunities for the banks to network with the village-based BCs (such as, SHGs, local *kirana* stores and retailers), which will allow the customers to avail basic banking services locally. Moreover, the presence of multiple BCs at the local level will also give customers a choice—and therefore, make them less vulnerable to the local power structures.

- With rudimentary technology application, UID can provide a platform for building a micro-payment system, which will provide low-cost access to a variety of financial services (e.g., micro-credit, micro-insurance and micro-pension) to everyone.

2. *Efficiency through streamlining different welfare schemes*: The technology-enabled open source platform for UID allows for development of a wide range of applications, many of which hold the promise of bringing in greater efficiency in the delivery of the government's

---

Box 6.3:   *Jharkhand pilot project on UID-enabled financial inclusion*

During January 2011, UIDAI conducted a pilot project in Ranchi and Hazaribagh, which was an important milestone in demonstrating the viability of UDI-enabled financial inclusion.

UIDAI, along with three partnering banks—ICICI Bank, Bank of India and Union Bank of India—identified 30–35 villages, which were in the remote hinterland, and had little banking access. The banks appointed their own BCs (Business Correspondents) to enrol people and open bank accounts.

The team also worked with the Rural Development Department on the MGNREGA muster rolls, to test if the job card number could be mapped and linked to the UID number. This enabled the MGNREGA wages to be disbursed through these bank accounts. The UIDAI also partnered with NPCI,

which acted as the inter-bank switch and the authentication agency through which all authentication requests were routed.

People were told that when they enrol for Aadhaar/UID, they also had the option of opening a bank account. While the team had expected that each family/household would require one account, they found that women in the family were very clear that they wanted a separate bank account. As a result, within a period of just about three months, 60,000 new rural accounts were opened. The BCs were provided with devices made to micro-ATM specifications, and this enabled the villagers to collect their wages, and perform other banking transactions, at their door steps.

Source: Balajee, IFMR Blog, comment posted on 25 April 2011.

welfare programmes and services. Two programmes on which it will have a significant impact are discussed below:

- *PDS*: India's PDS provides subsidized foodgrains and kerosene to the poor through a network of about 478,000 Fair Price Shops (FPSs) or Ration Shops, which caters to the needs of about 62.5 million families. However, the delivery of these subsidies is far from efficient and is marred by errors of inclusion/exclusion in identification of beneficiaries (omission of poor, fake or duplicate ration cards, etc.), diversion and leakages of subsidies en route to FPS, non-availability of subsidies due to faulty Management Information System (MIS) foodgrain storage and so on. Only about 42 per cent of the foodgrains reach the targeted poor, and about 36 per cent of the budgetary subsidies get diverted to the black market (Planning Commission 2005).

  By enabling a real time authentication of identity, UID/Aadhaar will not only eliminate the fake and duplicate ration cards, but will also enable the tracking of subsidies across the numerous intermediaries in the supply chain—thus eliminating the diversion and leakage of the resources (see Box 6.4, for a similar use of technology to manage the PDS supply chain, which has been successfully implemented in Chhattisgarh).

- *MGNREGA*: MGNREGA is one of the largest interventions in the Indian labour market. During 2009–10, this programme spent ₹39,100 crore, covering 100 million job card holders, and 52 million rural households across 619 districts (Rajshekhar 2011). Since its launch in 2006–07, the rural household incomes have increased from ₹2,795 to about ₹3,500 in 2009–10, reducing distress migration (in fact, promoting reverse migration) in many parts of the country (Ranjan 2010).

  In spite of such positive fallouts, studies and evaluations indicate that MGNREGA too is beset with corruption and diversion of funds through fake and multiple job cards, irregular maintenance of muster roll, misreporting of job completed and so on (*Business Standard* 2010).

Box 6.4: *Computerization of PDS in Chhattisgarh*

In 2007, the Chhattisgarh government implemented an end-to-end technology solution—from procurement of produce, to storage and transportation to state warehouses and FPSs—to manage the long and leaky supply chain of the PDS.

This involved an online registration system for millers of PDS rice, as well as procurement and movement orders that are issued electronically. The government carried out allocations to FPS shops using the ration cards database. The online platform provides an account of commodity stocks which helped in efficient inventory management, reducing the transmission time for allocations from three weeks to two hours. Continuous monitoring of sales and stock levels at FPS outlets also ensured in-time stocking of the shops, so that outlets could meet the demand from beneficiaries at all times.

A unique feature of PDS in Chhattisgarh is the innovative citizen interface portal through which citizens can track the movement of PDS commodities and also register their grievances. In a 2009 survey, 92 per cent of respondents in Chhattisgarh reported receiving their full rations without problems.

Source: Computerization of Paddy Procurement under PDS in Chhattisgarh. http://indiagovernance.gov.in/bestpractices.php?id=663

To curb the corruption, the government is already in the process of integrating UID with MGNREGA job cards and muster roll (Eluvangal 2010).

UID-enabled MGNERGA will impact the functioning of the scheme in three ways:

○ By authenticating the actual work done by the beneficiary, siphoning the due wages from the beneficiary will be avoided.

○ It will enable a direct transfer of wages to the beneficiary account, thus reducing the risks attached with handling cash transaction.

○ It will also help eliminate 'ghost beneficiarie', by matching the wages paid and the project work completed.

3. *Outreach to migrant invisible population*: One of the key challenges in the agenda for inclusive growth is to ensure the reach of the social benefits and services to citizens whose identity does not feature in any of the official databases. Since these population segments are typically made up of homeless and/or migrants—consisting of street kids, destitute, beggars, head-loaders, casual street sex workers, trolley-pushers, snake charmers, rag pickers and so on—they remain invisible and undefined. They also do not possess conventional proofs of identity (ration card, high school certificate, voter ID, etc.), or even if they do, these proofs are invalid for accessing services and benefits at locations beyond their local region (panchayat, district, state, etc.). This lack of identification deprives them of access to public services, such as, PDS, health care, ICDS, legal rights and so on. Following are the examples of some such segments:

• *Nomadic and de-notified tribes*: There are 313 nomadic tribes and 198 de-notified tribes in India, constituting an estimated population of about 100 to 120 million. A majority of them still maintain their traditional cultural traits, and wander from place to place in search of livelihoods. According to the National Commission for De-Notified and Nomadic Tribes, 98 per cent of them are landless, and 54 per cent are not on the voters' list.

• *Migrant labour*: During the last couple of decades, rural to urban migration of labour has emerged as a regular and integral part of livelihood strategies for the poor. It is estimated that there are about 120 million migrant workers in India. However, most of them lack legal identification, permanent residence and other formal documents, and therefore, have no recourse to legal protection, and are frequent victims of exploitation. Since they lack an identity, they are also unable to access banking facilities, health care, ration through PDS or education for their children. A study by Centre for Micro Finance, for instance, found that only 22 per cent of migrant workers have a bank account. Moreover, 77 per cent of them reported that not having an official proof of identity and residency was the biggest reason for not having a bank account (Politzer 2011).

• *Urban homeless*: According to Census 2001, there are only 1.94 million homeless people living in India (and only 40 per cent, that is, 0.78 million, living in cities). However, given the very invisible nature of this segment, this figure appears to be a gross underestimation. Estimates indicate that beggars and street children alone account for 6 million and 18 million homeless, respectively (Saxena and Mander 2008). Surveys also indicate that contrary to popular belief, a majority of urban homeless are not seasonal migrants, they are the indigenous population of the cities, but are unable to access the welfare schemes.

Among all the population segments, this migrating populace would benefit most from getting an 'identity' through UID/Aadhaar. On the other hand, the very nature of their floating invisible profile presents a daunting challenge in enumerating and providing them with an identity. UIDAI is however cognizant of this challenge, and has made special provisions to achieve this task in its planning. According to *Aadhaar Handbook for Registrars* (UIDAI 2010):

It is part of the UIDAI mandate to make special efforts to enable the inclusion of marginalized communities (e.g., the homeless, migrant workers, nomadic/ denotified tribes, street children, etc.) in AADHAAR. UIDAI recognizes the important role of Civil Society Organizations in reaching out to such communities and has been having a series of consultations with CSOs across the country.

Recognizing that these marginalized groups cannot provide any proof of their identity or residence, UIDAI has made special provisions for their registration; for example:

- NGOs and CSOs who work with these segments can act as introducers for them without needing such documentary proofs.
- It has signed an MOU with the National Coalition of Organizations for Security of Migrant Workers, a consortium of 23 NGOs, to ensure that migrant labour is included in the UID project (Politzer 2010).

- It partnered with the Registrar General and Census Commissioner of India to make special efforts to include the 'not counted' population in Census 2011 by doing their enumeration at night (Census of India 2011).

Since one of the key benefits of the UID number is the portability of identity (i.e., agencies and services can contact the central UID database from anywhere in the country, and confirm the beneficiary's identity), it has the potential to transform the lives of these floating segments of the population.

6.3.3. Issues and Challenges

While the potential benefits of UID/Aadhaar are immense, it will need to meet two sets of challenges for its successful implementation and scaling up. The critics and experts (Dass 2011; Dreze 2010; Moss 2011) have pointed out the first as techno-legal challenges (cost of the project, processing capacity requirements, concerns about privacy, and identity theft, etc.), and the other set of challenges are whether UID can deliver what it promises. Many (such as, Khera 2011) have debated that UID has been proposed as a technological quick-fix for what are essentially problems of governance, and which are sociopolitical in nature; for example:

1. UID proposes to minimize—even eliminate—the siphoning off of welfare resources through accurate authentication of the beneficiary's identity. However, a significant amount of corruption also happens due to extortion and collusion between the beneficiary and the middlemen. Mere authentication of identity will not be able to eliminate such corruption, which happens due to weaknesses in the governance structures.

2. Though UID/Aadhaar promised to promote financial inclusion by smoothening the hurdles of KYC norms, authentication of identity is only one aspect

of financial inclusion. Kocher (2009), for instance, reports that out of 33 million 'no-frills' accounts opened during 2006–09, only 11 per cent were found to be operational and barely 2 per cent of these were opened in urban areas, painting an even more dismal picture for the urban poor. Poor are also unable to open a bank account due to a lack of sufficient networks of banks and post offices in remote areas. Thus, the success of UID/Aadhaar in promoting financial inclusion will depend very much on a large network of BCs.

3. While UIDAI has used an innovative and collaborative approach to capture the biometric and demographic information through a large network of 'registrars', the information captured will still carry the same risks of human error, corruption and local-level sociopolitical dynamics, which exist now.

4. Similarly, UID/Aadhaar would require an information update every 10 years for all adult citizens (every five years for children). Since this information will have to be provided/verified by the gram pradhan, tahsildar and other subordinate officers at the grass-roots level, good governance structures will be needed to avoid fake entries, corruption and irregularities.

5. Lastly, the purpose of UID/Aadhaar is to solve the 'last mile' problem in delivering welfare benefits and subsidies to the intended beneficiary. However, the enrolment and issuance of UID/Aadhaar numbers too faces the same hurdles. Thus, it is a danger that in spite of the best efforts, some citizens may fail to get a UID number. Since government services and benefits are increasingly likely to become Aadhaar-enabled, such a possibility can also permanently exclude those without a UID number from welfare programmes and other services.

6.4. Direct cash transfer

At present, the central government spends ₹160,000 crore annually on subsidies, of which ₹60,600 crore were spent on providing food subsidy through the PDS during 2010–11. The subsidy bill on fuel and fertilizer was ₹99,500 crore, before it was slashed down in the 2010–11 Budget. In the 2011–12 Budget, the finance minister announced that the government plans a step-by-step approach to shift subsidy to direct or indirect cash transfer to the poor. A system for cash transfer for cooking fuel (kerosene and LPG) will be operative by March 2012, to be followed by a cash-for-grains programme. GOI will use UID/Aadhaar (discussed in the previous section) for evolving a targeted cash transfer mechanism for the BPL families.

Implementation of this major policy change will have wide-ranging impact on the lives and livelihood options and opportunities for the poor. This section discusses the rationale and implications of this shift. It also reviews the performance of international and Indian experiences of cash transfer to identify the critical success factors, and the challenges to successful execution of the cash transfer policy.

6.4.1. Cash transfers: Rationale and anticipated advantages

Though India has elaborate administrative mechanisms for delivering subsidies on essential items to the poor, these channels, as mentioned earlier, are plagued by leakages and inefficiencies. For instance, for the direct subsidies (on foodgrains and kerosene), the Planning Commission (2005) found that only 42 per cent of the subsidized grains actually reach the poor. Similarly, another government of India report (Parikh 2010) estimated that as much as 35 per cent of subsidized kerosene gets diverted to the black market.

Similarly, the indirect subsidies for fuel and fertilizers appear to be availed more by the non-poor than by the intended beneficiaries. For instance, Sharma and Thaker (2009) found that a large part of the fertilizer subsidies benefited the large and medium farmers, instead of the small and marginal farmers though they account for 82 per cent of the cropped land. Similarly, even though LPG cylinders are heavily subsidized, only 9 per cent of the rural population uses LPG due to its lack of availability as well as the price (D'Monte 2011). Subsidies on diesel too have benefited the automobile industry more than the agriculture sector, with diesel-driven cars accounting for 15 per cent of the diesel consumption (more than the combined usage by the railways and for power generation), while the share of the agriculture sector is a mere 12 per cent.

Given these realities, there are valid reasons for the government, to not only review the viability of the current subsidy regime, but also to look for alternative mechanisms to provide the poor with access to basic services and benefits. The idea that instead of providing subsidies, directly giving cash to the poor is a more effective way of reducing poverty has gained increasing support during recent years. It is estimated that about 45 developing nations now provide cash to about 110 million impoverished families (Hanlon et al. 2010)—with positive results. Cash transfers have been implemented in two forms:

1. *Unconditional cash transfers*: These schemes come without any strings attached, and are grants (pensions to elderly, destitute, physically challenged, orphan children, etc.) which are provided as a protective social security measure to vulnerable people/communities. These are unconditional programmes which recognize the vulnerability of the beneficiaries and provide cash to enable them to cope with their circumstances.
2. *Conditional cash transfers (CCT)*: CCTs have become popular as a policy measure to address the issues of poverty and inequalities, after their success in Latin American countries (UNDP 2009). CCTs are given on the condition that the benefiting households demonstrate behaviours which improve their overall consumption of social services (education, health care, etc.), and thus, impact the well-being of the beneficiaries in the long term, promote formation of human capital/capabilities and help reduce inequalities in the society.

Cash transfer schemes are based on the premise that the poor themselves are best equipped to eradicate poverty. Hard cash in hand not only provides social security but also empowers them to use the money to meet their specific livelihood needs. Above all, direct cash transfers, whether unconditional or conditional, not only address the lacunae of the subsidies but also lead to other social benefits:

1. *Targeted reach to the beneficiary*: The money from the direct cash transfers reaches the targeted beneficiaries either through deposits in their bank/post office account or it is handed over in cash. By ensuring the targeted reach to the beneficiaries, cash transfers minimize/eliminate leakages.
2. *Reduction in administrative cost of delivery*: A large part of subsidies actually get spent as administrative costs of the delivery mechanisms. Cash transfers reduce the government expenditure in procuring, storing, transporting and distributing commodities.
3. *Empowering the beneficiary with choices*: By giving cash to the poor, cash transfers place spending power in the hands of the poor, and provide them with diversified choices.
4. *Developing local economy*: Lastly, cash transfers infuse cash in the local economy, and thus have multiplier effect in developing local markets.

6.4.2. A proposal for CCTs in India

In view of the widespread leakages and inefficiencies in the prevailing subsidy regime, and an increasing recognition of the efficacy of CCTs, there is a growing acceptance among the policy makers to shift from subsidies to CCTs as a measure for poverty alleviation. Kapur et al. (2008) made a case for cash transfers in an article, by pointing out that if the government were to distribute the ₹180,000 crore which it spends on centrally sponsored subsidies for food, fertilizer and fuel, equally among the 70 million BPL families, each family would receive ₹2,140—which is more than the poverty line income for rural households, and more than 70 per cent of the urban poverty line income.

The Institute of Manpower Research, Planning Commission has proposed five different CCT schemes targeting different community segments (Mehrotra 2010), which will have widespread implications for the poor:

1. *CCT 1—A Minimum Guaranteed Income*: A large proportion of the poor are unable to break out of the glass ceiling of poverty line, because they get caught in the cycles of indebtedness. For instance, the average outstanding debt per farmer household is around ₹12,600, and the small and marginal farmers account for 80 per cent of the indebted households. Poor often have to take consumption credit during days without wage income, or to take care of health or family contingencies. Since they are rarely able to save and accumulate income-enhancing assets, their future income goes into consumption and into servicing the debts.

   The Planning Commission proposes to launch a minimum guarantee scheme, which will help them to emerge out of debt, accumulate savings and thus build assets. The scheme envisages a monthly cash transfer of ₹250 into the post office/bank account of the poor over 2–5 years, depending on the income level of the BPL family. The money will be transferred on the condition that only half of the amount can be withdrawn at any point of time, which can be used for paying back old loans, medical expenses or school fee or to support any subsistence activity. This will ensure minimum savings which can then be leveraged by the poor to invest in income-generating assets and, thus, break out of the cycle of indebtedness.

2. *CCT 2—Conditional Maternity Entitlement*: Conditional Maternity Entitlement was already proposed in the 11th Five Year Plan, in view of the high incidence of anaemia among women and malnutrition among children. The scheme recommended a phased cash transfer of ₹4,500 to pregnant women and nursing mothers for the first two children to ensure wage compensation during and after pregnancy, and to provide additional income for nutritional needs.

   The cash transfer will be subject to the woman meeting certain conditions, such as registration and regular pre and post-delivery check-ups at the nearest ICDS Centre, taking necessary vaccinations to reduce the risks of maternal and child mortality and taking counselling for breastfeeding at the ICDS Centre.

3. *CCT 3—Converting Supplementary Nutrition (SN) Component of ICDS Scheme to Cash Transfer*: Despite having one of the largest programme (ICDS) for child development in the world, the child malnutrition rates in India are one of the highest, with about 47 per cent of children showing signs of malnutrition, and one in three malnourished children living in India. Looking at the severity of the situation, 11th Five Year Plan had recommended a review of the ICDS programme, with specific focus on its

SN Component.[3] The CCT scheme being considered by the Planning Commission aims to address this issue.

Under this initiative, instead of providing take-home ration for pregnant and nursing mothers and for 6 to 36 months old children, mothers will be provided cash. They will be counselled by the auxiliary nurse midwives (ANMs) and Accredited Social Health Activists (ASHA) about appropriate diet that is rich in protein content, and also about preparing/purchasing appropriate weaning food for their 0–36-month-old children.

4. *CCT 4—CCT to Replace Food Subsidies under Targeted Public Distribution System (TPDS)*: As discussed earlier, a large amount of food subsidy provided through PDS does not reach the intended beneficiaries due to leakages and diversion. Moreover, almost 50 per cent of economic costs of subsidies are spent in procurement, storage, distribution and delivery of the grains. It is proposed that instead of providing grains through the FPS, the poor may be directly given cash, which they can then use to buy foodgrains and other items of their choice from the open market.

The proposal recommends that replacement of subsidized grains with cash transfers should be first piloted in the cities, where there are enough private traders, and a choice exists for the customer. However, the PDS network would still be required in other regions (rural areas, northern and eastern states), where there are not enough private shops to handle the purchase requirements of the poor.

5. *CCT 5—Cash Transfer to Youth to Promote Skill Development*: The 11th Five Year Plan had renewed emphasis on skill development through formation of the National Skill Development Mission with a target of creating 500 million skilled personnel by 2022 (discussed in detail in Section 6.4 of this chapter). One of the strategies of the skill development mission is to link the funding of the training institutes with successful certification of the candidates.

The Planning Commission proposal envisions CCT to fund candidates from socially disadvantaged backgrounds (such as, SC, ST, OBC and minority communities) through a monthly stipend during training, and a subsidy given to the training institute at the end of the programme after placement of the candidate.

6.4.3. Issues and challenges

Needless to say, cash transfers would be a qualitative shift in the policy framework of providing social services and goods to the poor. They also offer a viable alternative to utilize public resources with greater efficiency and accuracy. Their successful implementation, however, will greatly depend on meeting four critical prerequisites:

1. *Accurate classification of the BPL households*: Given the complexity of poverty as a phenomenon, estimations of poverty and poor and vulnerable households have always remained a contentious issue in India. During the last decade or so, estimates of BPL households have varied widely from 37 per cent to 77 per cent across different surveys. While the Planning Commission has accepted the poverty estimates of 37 per cent BPL population, arrived at by the Tendulkar Committee (Planning Commission 2009), these estimates and the cut-offs for arriving at them (₹17 per day for rural poor, and ₹19 per day for urban poor) not only differ from

---

[3] Besides the service component of ICDS (immunization, health check-up, pre-school education, growth monitoring, etc.), its SN Component is structured to provide nourishment to the growing child in two forms: hot cooked meal is provided to 3–6-year-old children, and take-home ration is given to pregnant and nursing mothers and to 6–36-month-old children.

other estimates (see Table 6.1), but have also been questioned by the Supreme Court (Kanekal and Mathew 2011). In the cash transfer regime, these large variations across various surveys and estimates acquire a more than statistical significance, since they link and limit the access of the poor to a whole range of public services.

It is significant that among all the poverty estimates, the Planning Commission accepted the lowest estimates of BPL population. These comparisons also open up the possibilities of errors of exclusion in the implementation of cash transfer programmes. In fact, such possibilities are even more imminent now, since the government plans to use UID as a means of identification of the poor.

2. *Accurate targeting of the beneficiaries*: Accurate identification is a prerequisite for the cash to reach the intended beneficiary. As discussed earlier, there are significant errors of inclusion and exclusion in the government database. While the government has launched the UID project, which will help through biometric identification, the project itself is in the nascent stage. By the government's own optimistic estimates/targets, universal coverage of the population will take some years—about 600 million UIDs will be issued by 2016, and the entire population will be covered over a decade. While the government has announced that it will start piloting/launching cash transfer projects enabled by UID in the coming year,

it is not clear how these schemes will impact those who have still not received their UID. Moreover, the challenges in the implementation of the UID project (as discussed in Section 6.3.3) would be equally valid in its use in implementation of cash transfer schemes.

3. *Availability of social infrastructure*: Transferring cash to the poor in a targeted manner, and its proper use by the beneficiaries presupposes existence of supporting social infrastructure, which can provide avenues to spend the money gainfully. For instance, cash transfer presupposes that the beneficiary has a bank or post office account. However, as discussed earlier, only 54 per cent of the Indian population has access to banking/financial infrastructure. A major challenge for cash transfer schemes to succeed would be to accelerate the establishment of a corresponding banking system to reach the poor.

Similarly, for the poor to utilize the cash for their own benefit, it would be essential that appropriate avenues for expenditure (schools, private grain traders, health care centres, etc.) are available to them. Cash transfers help in creating a demand for the essential services by providing incentives to the poor to avail them. However, they can be successful only if these services are easily available and efficiently delivered. In fact, a useful lesson learnt from the successful cases of cash transfer programmes is that they were always preceded by investment in development of the social

Table 6.1: Comparisons of BPL population estimates across different studies

Poverty report	BPL population (per cent)
Arjun Sengupta Committee Report (Conditions of Work and Promotion of Livelihoods in Unorganized Sector)	77
NC Saxena Committee Report (Report of the Expert Group on the Methodology for the BPL Census 2009)	50
Tendulkar Committee Report (Report of the Expert Group to Review the Methodology for Estimation of Poverty)	37
World Bank Multi-Dimensional Poverty Index	59

Source: NCEUS (2007); MoRD (2007); Planning Commission (2009); Oxford Poverty and Human Development initiative (2010).

infrastructure. For instance, the success of Bihar's Mukhyamantri Balika Cycle Yojana (MBCY) was not just due to cash transfers;[4] it was preceded by the appointment of 300,000 teachers, establishment of 100,000 classrooms and a substantial increase in expenditure on elementary education (Swarup 2010). Similarly, the success of Brazil's Bolsa Familia[5] and Mexico's Oportunidades[6] was vastly due to the earlier investments in, and existence of, the essential services, such as banking infrastructure, schools, health care facilities and so on (Himanshu 2011). In India, as of now, the social infrastructure, which would allow the poor to benefit from cash transfers, is minimal.

4. *Region specific socioeconomic aspects of cash transfers*: Lastly, one of the critiques

of cash transfer proposal is that in many ways, it does not address the problems of access, which are largely embedded in the socioeconomic conditions of specific regions and population segments (Alagh 2011). For instance, cash transfers for fertilizer subsidies do not address the issue of inaccuracy of land records, and that they would exclude the tenants and sharecroppers, whose livelihoods depend on land which they cultivate but do not own. Moreover, the use of fertilizers depends much on local factors, such as soil fertility, weather conditions, availability of water and so on. These regional variations are not captured by the mechanism of cash subsidies.

Likewise, cash for grains does not factor in the inflation in food prices, which has increasingly become a recurrent phenomenon during the last few years. In fact, some studies (Cunha et al. 2010) show that cash transfers have an inflationary effect since they increase the demand of normal goods and services. Moreover, this inflationary effect is more prominent in remote villages where there are few shops, and therefore low competition among sellers.

Large-scale procurement for PDS also acted as a mechanism for stabilizing grain prices and keeping inflation in control. In the absence of such checks on market prices, the cash transfers can inadvertently incentivize hoarding, black-marketing and, consequently, inflation. In order to prevent this, and make the cash subsidies a viable mechanism for poverty reduction, they would need to be complemented by an equally focused effort on improving the governance mechanisms.

[4] Mukhyamantri Balika Cycle Yojana (MBCY) was launched in 2006 in Bihar to encourage the girl child from dropping out of education. Any girl who enrols for Class IX is given ₹2,000 to buy a bicycle, and ₹700 for uniform. Till 2010, Bihar government had spent ₹174.36 crore on bicycles for 871,000 schoolgirls. The programme has had positive impact on girls' education. The dropout rates went down from 17.6 per cent to 6 per cent during 2006–09, and the enrollment of girls tripled from 160,000 to 490,000 during 2006–10.

[5] Bolsa Familia was launched in Brazil in 2003 as a regular monthly grant to poor households, provided they could meet three conditions: 85 per cent attendance for 6–15-year-old children, regular health check-ups and immunization for children and for pregnant women. Considered to be the world's largest CCT programme, it had a remarkable impact, with poverty rates falling down from 22 per cent to 7 per cent, school attendance and enrollment increasing by 4.4 per cent and 11.7 per cent respectively, and 26 per cent increase in the health indices of children.

[6] Oportunidades was launched in Mexico in 2002, and offered a monthly allowance to poor families provided they met certain conditions related to school enrolment and attendance, participating in health-related meetings, and regular health check-ups, especially for women and children. By 2010, the programme had shown significant improvements in the health and educational status of the poor. The average household consumption and nutrition had increase by 13 per cent, and visits to health care centres during pregnancy had gone up by 8 per cent . School enrolment rate had shot up by 70–78 per cent, while the labour-force participation of boys had decreased by 15–25 per cent.

References

Ahluwalia, M.S. 2011. Prospects and policy challenges in the twelfth plan. *Economic & Political Weekly* 21 May, XLVI (21): 88–105.

Alagh, Y.K. 2011. What cash transfers can't solve. *The Financial Express*, 31 March. Available at http://www.financialexpress.com/news/column-what-cash-transfers-cant-solve/769403/0#

Business Standard. 2010. Corruption and irregularities in implementation of NREGA: Study. *Business Standard*, 23 May. Available at http://www.business-standard.com/india/news/corruptionirregularities-in-implementationnrega-study/95288/on

Census of India. 2011. Provisional population totals: Census 2011. Available at http://censusindia.gov.in/2011-prov-results/indiaatglance.html

Cunha, J.M., G. Giorgi, and Jayachandram Seema. 2010. The price effects of cash versus in-kind transfers. Paper presented at CEPR Development Economics Workshop, 8–9 October, in Barelona. Available at http://www.cepr.org/meets/wkcn/7/784/papers/Jayachandranfinal.pdf

D'Monte, S. 2011. Rethinking fossil fuel subsidies. Infochange News and Features, March. Available at http://infochangeindia.org/environment/ecologic/rethinking-fossil-fuel-subsidies.html

Dass, R. 2011. Unique identity project in India: A divine dream or a miscalculated heroism? Working Paper 2011-03-04, Indian Institute of Management, Ahmedabad.

Dreze, J. 2010. Unique facility, or recipe for trouble. *The Hindu*, 25 November. Available at http://www.hindu.com/2010/11/25/stories/2010112552171100.htm

Eluvangal, S. 2010. Center plans to slay NREGA corruption with Aadhaar. *Daily News & Analysis*, 10 August. Available at http://www.dnaindia.com/money/report_centre-plans-to-slay-nrega-corruption-with-aadhar_1426373

Hanlon, J., A. Barrientos, and D. Hulme. 2010. *Just give money to the poor: The development revolution from the global south.* Sterling VA: Kumarian Press.

Himanshu. 2011. Putting cash transfer in its place. *Livemint*, 1 March. Available at http://www.livemint.com/2011/03/15210253/Putting-cash-transfer-in-its-p.html

IFMR Blog. 2011. UIDAI and financial inclusion—Unlimited possibilities. 25 April. Available at http://www.ifmr.co.in/blog/2011/04/25/uidai-and-financial-inclusion-%E2%80%93-unlimited-possibilities/

India Infoline. 2010. Visa develops electronic payment solution using UIDAI platform. *India Infoline*, 16 November. Available at http://www.indiainfoline.com/Markets/News/Visa-develops-electronic-payment-solution-using-UIDAI-platform/4992896216

Kanekal, N., and L. Mathew. 2011. Apex court questions BPL logic. *Livemint*, 30 March. Available at http://www.livemint.com/2011/03/30003647/Apex-court-questions-BPL-logic.html

Kapur, D., D. Mukhopadhyay, and A. Subramanian. 2008. More on direct cash transfers. *Economic & Political Weekly*, 12 April.

Khera, Reetika. 2011. The UID project and welfare schemes. *Economic & Political Weekly*, 26 February, XLVI (9).

Kocher, S. 2009. *Speeding financial inclusion.* New Delhi: Skotch Development Foundation.

Mehrotra, S. 2010. *Introducing conditional cash transfers in India: A proposal for five CCTs.* New Delhi: Planning Commission.

MoRD. 2007. *Report of the Expert Group on the Methodology for the BPL Census 2009.* Report submitted to Ministry of Rural Development, New Delhi, 2009. Available at http://rural.nic.in/latest/rpt_bpl_census2009.pdf

Moss, D. 2011. India's ID scheme—Drowning in false positives, March. Available at http://dematerialisedid.com/BCSL/Drown.html

Mybangalore.com. 2011. Digitizing villages is the way to take India forward. Mybangalore.com, 1 June. Available at http://www.mybangalore.com/article/0611/digitizing-villages-is-the-way-to-take-india-forward.html

NCEUS. 2007. *Conditions of work and promotion of livelihoods in unorganized sector.* New Delhi: National Commission for Enterprises in the Unorganized Sector.

Oxford Poverty and Human Development initiative. 2010. *Multidimensional poverty index.* Oxford: Oxford Poverty and Human Development initiative. Available at http://www.ophi.org.uk/policy/multidimensional-poverty-index/

Parikh, Kirit S. 2010. *Report of Expert Group on a Viable and Sustainable System for Pricing Petroleum Products.* Report submitted to Ministry of Petroleum & Gas, Government of India, New Delhi.

Planning Commission. 2005. *Performance evaluation of targeted public distribution system.* New Delhi: Planning Commission.

———. 2009. *Report of the expert group to review the methodology for estimation of poverty.* New Delhi: Planning Commission.

———. 2011. *Issues for the approach to the twelfth plan—Presentation by planning commission on 21 April 2011.* New Delhi: Planning Commission.

Politzer, Malia. 2010. Resolving the identity crisis. *LiveMint*, 10 January. Available at http://www.livemint.com/2011/01/10235903/Resolving-the-identity-crisis.html

———. 2011. Locked out of the banking system. *LiveMint*, 11 January. Available at http://www.livemint.com/2011/01/11210212/Locked-out-of-the-banking-syst.html

Rajshekhar, M. 2011. A question of rights. *The Economic Times*, 5 April, p. 17.

Ranjan, N. 2010. Mahatma Gandhi national rural employment guarantee scheme: Convergence with agriculture programs. Presentation at Livelihood India Conference, 17–18 November, New Delhi.

Saxena, N.C., and H. Mander. 2008. *A Special Report on the Most Vulnerable Social Groups and Their Access to Food*. Report submitted to The Commissioners of Supreme Court, New Delhi.

Sharma, V.P., and H. Thaker. 2009. Fertilizer subsidies in India—who are the beneficiaries? Working Paper No. 2009-07-01, IIM Ahmedabad.

Shrivastava, H. 2011. Planning as if people mattered. GovernanceNow, 11 July. Available at http://governancenow.com/views/think-tanks/planning-if-people-mattered.

Swarup, V. 2010. Bihar's virtuous cycle. *LiveMint*, 8 August. Available at http://www.livemint.com/2010/08/08221239/Bihar8217s-virtuous-cycle.html

TeamLease. 2009. *India labour report*. Bangalore: TeamLease.

The Hindu. 2010. Aadhaar number to act as a valid document to open bank account. *The Hindu*, 21 December. Available at http://www.thehindu.com/news/national/article967952.ece?css=print

Tiwari, S. 2011. Move to make Aadhaar basis for all KYC needs. *Business Standard*, 27 April. Available at http://www.business-standard.com/india/news/move-to-make-aadhar-basis-for-all-kyc-needs/433653/

UIDAI. 2010. *Aadhaar handbook for registrars*. New Delhi: UIDAI and Planning Commission.

UNDP. 2009. Conditional cash transfer schemes for alleviating human poverty: Relevance to India. Paper presented to United Nations Development Programme, New Delhi, India.

About the Editors and Contributors

The Editors

Sankar Datta is Dean, The Livelihood School, Hyderabad and Director, Indian Grameen Services, Hyderabad. He worked with Madhya Pradesh State Co-operative Oilseeds Grower's Federation (OILFED), PRADAN and IIM-Ahmadabad, before joining the faculty of Institute of Rural Management Anand (IRMA) for five years. Dr Datta has been involved in extending professional services for rural development activities, specially focusing on livelihood promotion, working with micro-enterprises for over two decades.

Orlanda Ruthven has researched and consulted in the field of employment and labour standards since 2003, most recently for the Orissa-based skills provider, Gram Tarang, and the London-based ethical trading consultancy, Impactt.

Vipin Sharma is CEO, ACCESS Development Services, New Dlehi. He is responsible for institutionalization and expansion of the organization as a pan-India resource organization to support livelihoods and microfinance outreach. He earlier worked in CARE-India as Programme Director, Microfinance, heading CASHE (Credit and Savings for Household Enterprises), CARE's largest microfinance programme worldwide. Prior to that, he was Executive Director, Rural Non-Farm Development Agency (RUDA), Government of Rajasthan.

The Contributors

Radhika Desai is a scholar in political sociology and women's studies, and has been active in the development sector for the past two decades. Her work is distinctive in its focus on promoting interconnections between knowledge and practice, and for mainstreaming social inclusion into thematic domains. Her areas of work proficiency include livelihoods, decentralized governance, gender, social impact and social performance management in microfinance.

Suryamani Roul is Senior Vice President, ACCESS Development Services. He has earlier been Project Director, Sustainable Tribal Empowerment Project, CARE-India, Andhra Pradesh. He was also Project Manager, CREDIT Project under CARE-India's Small Economic Activities Development (SEAD) Programme that was supported by DFID's JFS support with WFP and Rotary Foundation in undivided Bihar (Ranchi).

Madhukar Shukla is Professor, OB & Strategic Management, XLRI School of Business and Human Resources, Jamshedpur, India. A member of the Advisory Council of University Network for Social Entrepreneurship (founded by Ashoka: Innovators for the Public and Skoll Centre for Social Entrepreneurship, Oxford University, UK), he was also the Conference Coordinator for the National Conference on Social Entrepreneurship in 2009, 2010 and 2011.

Ashok Kumar Sircar is Professor, Development Studies and Action, Ajim Premji University, Bangalore, India. Professor Sircar is a PhD and had spent 17 years in the corporate sector, in the fields of R&D and management.

Technical Partner—The Livelihood School, Hyderabad, India, has been set up by BASIX and it aims to impact the livelihoods of millions of poor and other disadvantaged sections of the society, especially of *Bharat* (India), by building knowledge about processes, methods and principles of livelihood promotion and disseminating the same to enhance the capacities of its practitioners. The School has received recognition from the Government of India as Scientific and Industrial Research Organization (SIRO), which makes it a recognised institute in social science research in the country.

Since its inception in 2007, The Livelihood School has offered educational programmes to over 350 livelihoods, reaching over 15,000 participants, including elected representatives of Panchayati Raj institutions, officers of various government programmes and professionals from NGOs and multilateral agencies engaged in promoting and supporting livelihoods. It develops training modules, resource materials and case study protocols related to livelihood promotion across agriculture and non-farm livelihood sectors. It is a knowledge partner for various programmes on livelihood promotion with ACCESS, Azim Premji University and Centre for Economic and Social Studies (CESS), Hyderabad. The School is also associated with the Ford Foundation for assessing the human resource needs of the National Rural Livelihoods Mission (NRLM).